Investing

in

BRIC

COUNTRIES

Investing
in
BRIC
COUNTRIES

Evaluating Risk and Governance in Brazil, Russia, India & China

Edited by

SVETLANA BORODINA
OLEG SHVYRKOV
with JEAN-CLAUDE BOUIS

New York Chicago San Francisco Lisbon London
Madrid Mexico City Milan New Delhi San Juan
Seoul Singapore Sydney Toronto

The *McGraw-Hill* Companies

1 2 3 4 5 6 7 8 9 0   WFR/WFR   1 5 4 3 2 1 0

ISBN: 978-0-07-166406-6
MHID: 0-07-166406-8

This publication is designed to provide accurate and authoritative information in regard to the subject matter covered. It is sold with the understanding that the publisher is not engaged in rendering legal, accounting, or other professional service. If legal advice or other expert assistance is required, the services of a competent professional person should be sought.

—From a Declaration of Principles Jointly Adopted by a Committee of the American Bar Association and a Committee of Publishers and Associations

McGraw-Hill books are available at special quantity discounts to use as premiums and sales promotions, or for use in corporate training programs. To contact a representative, please visit the Contact Us pages at www.mhprofessional.com.

This book is printed on acid-free paper.

About the Editor and Contributors

Main Editor

Jean-Claude Bouis has been an editor for Standard & Poor's since 1998 after 25 years at the Associated Press and the *New York Times*.

Contributors

Svetlana Borodina is director of corporate governance at Standard & Poor's Equity Research, based in Moscow.

Oleg Shvyrkov is associate director of corporate governance at Standard & Poor's Equity Research in Moscow.

Eduardo G. Chehab is director of Standard & Poor's corporate governance services in São Paulo.

Preeti S. Manerkar is a senior research analyst at CRISIL Research, part of the Mumbai-based affiliate of Standard & Poor's.

Peter Montagnon is chairman of the board of the International Corporate Governance Network.

Sergey Stepanov is assistant professor of Corporate Finance at the New Economic School, Moscow.

Warren Wang is partner and CEO of Institutional Investor Services, a research and consultancy firm based in Beijing.

Contents

Foreword: Good Governance Does Make a Difference

by Peter Montagnon

Good corporate governance involves two essential things. Boards of companies should be equipped to make robust strategic decisions and manage risk, and they should be accountable to the shareholders that own them. In this way they will be better able to generate value over the long term for investors, secure the jobs of their employees, and be reliable partners of their customers and suppliers, thus contributing to the general wealth.

There is a great deal of academic research about whether and how governance does actually add value, but seen from this perspective it is surely little more than common sense. Should company boards actually be expected to make weak decisions and ignore risk management? Of course not. We all know that is the way to failure, not success.

The issue is more about what boards actually need to do to deliver on these basic principles. Sometimes an approach to governance can seem very prescriptive, almost as if it were an alternative form of regulation. Governance that is imposed from outside in this way is less likely to succeed, because the boards that undertake it will not have understood what it is trying to achieve. Rather, good governance is something that directors should aspire to, because they know it will help their company.

Shareholders, too, have a role to play, because accountability to shareholders can help boards deliver. If there is no accountability, management will be free to do as it pleases, and this may mean operating in their own narrow interests rather than those of the company as a whole.

This is true in all markets. Failures of governance can be very costly. Look at the subprime banking crisis, the collapse of Enron, and other corporate scandals early in this decade, or the Asian financial crisis of 1997. All of these had a common feature in that corporate governance failed. Companies were making poor decisions, using flawed business models, failing to understand the implication of off-balance-sheet business, or pursuing highly risky borrowing policies that involved massive exchange risk. Many companies collapsed at huge cost to shareholders and employees, shaming and humiliating the management that ran them.

Sometimes it is difficult to know what difference good governance makes on a day-to-day basis. In developed markets where standards are similar, there is not always a discernible difference in the cost of capital. In emerging markets, where standards may vary, the contrast is clearer. Companies that can demonstrate that they adhere to high standards tend to outperform in stock market terms those that do not by a wide margin. The benefit is a lower cost of capital, which adds to competitiveness. This book offers the reader many ways to measure governance standards by outlining the methodology developed over the years by Standard & Poor's Governance Services. The book can also stimulate thought to help guide investors in a wide variety of governance questions, for example: Given a choice, would governance be enhanced best by improving shareholders' ability to remove underperforming directors, or by expanding shareholders' control over executive pay packages?

But the most valuable idea behind this book is to stress the importance of good governance to companies in the BRIC countries. It is clear that many companies in these economies are already aware of the benefits, as demonstrated by the success of Brazil's special listing arrangements for companies meeting high basic governance standards.

Yet it is also hard to deliver good governance in young markets that have developed very rapidly. In China, many listed companies are still majority-owned by the state, and this creates important issues with regard to the rights of minority shareholders. Such issues also frequently arise in companies where there is a dominant family owner or blockholder. And, of course, corporate law is in its infancy in many of these markets.

Developing good governance will require an effort, but, especially in times of economic and financial uncertainty, capital flows will favor those willing to make it work. Oleg Shvyrkov, Svetlana Borodina, and Jean-Claude Bouis have served us a timely reminder that good governance makes a difference.

Peter Montagnon is chairman of the board of the International Corporate Governance Network, a not-for-profit body founded in 1995 that has evolved into a global membership organization of 450 leaders in corporate governance from 45 countries.

Preface: Why Governance Is Key to the Future of BRIC Countries

by Svetlana Borodina and Oleg Shvyrkov

"Money management is as resilient as the medical profession," one fund manager said recently. There will always be people looking for doctors, and there will always be investors looking for ways to grow their fortunes. How to balance fear and greed, the two ruling forces of the investment world, or in more professional terms, risk and return—this is what all market participants want to get right. While quantitative financial analysis has become a fairly standard but complex area of research, there is a huge portion of risk associated with the qualitative side of any business, such as conflicting interests of shareholders or motivations of top management.

Corporate governance is a very broad area, governing not just things related to shareholder rights and annual shareholder meetings. Independent directors on the board, related-party transactions, executive remuneration, managing risk, strategic planning, and measuring performance against strategy—these are all pieces of the same jigsaw puzzle. How to build a sustainable business resistant to any market weather, fine-tune it to be a going concern under generations of CEOs and COOs—these are the ultimate goals of any good corporate governance system.

Two decades ago, Brazil, Eastern Europe, China, Russia, and India opened up to foreign capital, creating new opportunities for investors. Yet many burned their fingers underestimating the risks. The economic crisis in Mexico in 1994, the Asian crisis in 1997, and then the debt default in Russia of 1998 uncovered governance flaws on a scale unseen in the West. Ramifications of the crises included slowing the rise of civil societies within these economies in transition, interrupting the generation of capital and the creation of wealth, crimping standards of living for millions of people, forcing them into unemployment and poverty, and delaying the development of beneficial infrastructures such as water purification and health care networks, to name a few. About this time, the Governance Services group was created within Standard & Poor's (S&P), aimed at helping investors and analysts understand nonfinancial risks specific to countries and individual companies around the globe.

Twenty years after liberalization, Brazil, Russia, India, and China are known as the BRIC pack and continue to be strong investment prospects. China still boasts the fastest GDP growth, India's expanding population is bound to propel domestic consumer demand, while investors in Russia and Brazil bet on oil and gas reserves and an upward trajectory in commodity prices. Even though tightened regulations helped curb blatant abuse of minority investors, governance practices remain generally weak. Sadly, many companies in the BRIC countries fail to unlock their potential value because of the intrusive role of controlling families or governments.

However, no two companies are the same. Some companies in the BRIC countries aspire to the highest international governance standards and some don't. Others have the same governance issues as their Western peers, and some have inherited country-specific risks. Investors need to do thorough due diligence before taking a bet. This book explains S&P's Governance Services' approach to analyzing nonfinancial risks in emerging economies. Our methodology (the GAMMA—Governance, Accountability, Management Metrics, and

Analysis—scores) builds on 10 years of experience in analyzing governance globally. We hope that in sharing our ideas and lessons learned, we will help investors avoid murky stocks and reward deserving companies with new growth opportunities.

Our book builds on the earlier S&P publication, *Governance and Risk* (edited by George Dallas), and reproduces some elements of that text that are still crucial today. We are in great debt to Amra Balic, Nick Bradley, George Dallas, Laurence Hazell, Julia Kochetygova, Dan Konigsburg, and other pioneers of governance research at S&P, to whom we owe a great deal of our analytical know-how.

Svetlana Borodina
Oleg Shvyrkov

PART ONE

INTRODUCING THE BRICs AND THEIR GOVERNANCE STATUS

Chapter 1

A Guiding Light for Investors in Brazil

Eduardo G. Chehab

Introduction and Executive Summary

How Brazilian Corporate Governance Bloomed

Corporate governance is a set of practices designed to optimize a company's performance, protect stakeholders (investors, employees, and creditors), and facilitate access to capital. The analysis of corporate governance practices as it is applied to securities markets encompasses transparency of ownership and control, equal treatment of shareholders, disclosure of information, board effectiveness, and risk management controls, among other topics.

For investors, this analysis is an important aid in making investment decisions. These practices determine the kind of role investors may play in a company, enabling them to influence its performance. Good corporate governance practices increase a company's value and reduce the cost of capital, increasing the viability of securities markets as sources of funding. Companies with a governance system that protects all investors tend to have higher valuations because investors recognize that everyone will receive the due and appropriate return on his or her investments.

In the last few years significant reforms have been made in Brazilian corporate governance, including the introduction of the New Market (*Novo Mercado*) concept and changes in company and securities law that stem from a conviction that capital markets should play a much larger role in the country's economic development than they did in the past. Proponents of capital markets in Brazil believe that one of the keys to a healthy and successful market is the introduction and support of strong corporate governance measures.

Historically, Brazil's capital markets played only a minor role in providing companies' financing needs, which were met from companies' retained earnings and funding provided by financial institutions and state-owned entities. However, the country's enormous social demands and scarce financial resources have limited the state's ability to maintain its role as a capital provider. A gradual change in funding availability started with the opening of the Brazilian markets in the 1990s. Companies faced intense international competition and required more capital to upgrade and meet competitive threats. Those capital demands could be met only by developing and expanding local capital markets and improving the domestic economy. In support of those goals, new laws addressed governance problems and focused primarily on greater transparency and disclosure requirements as well as protection of the rights of minority shareholders.

The Brazilian stock market has developed strongly since 2006. Almost U.S.$40 billion was raised through equity issuances, along with U.S.$78 billion through issuances of debentures in the period 2006–2008. At the same time, investor concerns about corporate governance also increased, mainly in regard to the rights of minority shareholders and corporate enterprise risk management. In November 2008, to help address those concerns in Brazil, Standard & Poor's (S&P) launched the GAMMA (Governance, Accountability, Management Metrics, and Analysis) score, an important tool for selecting companies with higher corporate governance levels and guiding companies in improving their governance policies.

Market Infrastructure

Summary of Economic History: Brazil Emerges as a Resourceful Dynamo

When Portuguese explorers arrived in Brazil in 1500, the native tribes, totaling about 2.5 million people, had lived virtually unchanged since the Stone Age. From Portugal's colonization of Brazil (1500–1822) until the late 1930s, the market elements of the Brazilian economy relied on the production of primary products for export, such as sugar, precious minerals, and coffee. The post–World War II period up to 1962 featured intense import substitution, especially of consumer goods. A period of rapid industrial expansion and modernization occurred between 1968 and 1973. Import substitution of basic inputs and capital goods and the expansion of manufactured goods exports highlighted the 1974–1980 period.

However, the following years, mainly the period 1981–1994, were marked by considerable difficulties because of the world oil crisis, a moratorium on payments of the external debt in 1982 and 1987, and the consequent low increase in gross domestic product (GDP) (average of only 1.4% per year). Those difficulties were fueled by several unsuccessful economic stabilization programs that were aimed at reducing high inflation rates and the impeachment of a president, Fernando Collor de Mello, in 1992 for corruption.

Finally, in 1994, the Real Plan was implemented, and the annual inflation rate dropped from more than 5,000% to 20% in 1996 and eventually in the range of 5%.

The successful Real Plan was based on three pillars:

- Monetary reform
- Further opening of the economy
- Privatization of several state-owned companies in the steel, power, banking, mining, and telecommunication segments, raising around U.S.$100 billion

After another period of ups and downs, the economy began to grow more rapidly starting in 2003, strongly influenced by the worldwide trade boom. GDP grew 5.7% in 2004, 3.2% in 2005, 3.8% in 2006, and 5.4% in 2007. In 2008, the economy grew another 5%. In the beginning of the current global economic crisis, Brazil surprised observers with its resistance to an extreme fallout. Nevertheless, the stunning drop in world demand has affected the domestic economy. The GDP growth forecast for 2009 ranges around 0%.

Currently, with abundant natural resources and a population of 190 million, Brazil is one of the 10 largest markets in the world, with a GDP of U.S.$1.35 billion (R$2.7 trillion, considering an average exchange rate of U.S.$/R$ of 2.00 for 2009). Exports reached almost U.S.$198 billion in 2008, an increase of 23.2% over 2007. The major exported products were aircraft, iron ore, soybeans, footwear, coffee, vehicles, automotive parts, and machinery. Imports amounted to U.S.$173 billion, 43.6% higher than in 2007, influenced by the local currency appreciation up to September and increased domestic demand. The major goods imported were machinery, electrical and transport equipment, chemical products, oil, automotive parts, and electronics. For 2009, a drop of 25% in exports and 30% in imports was expected due to the world economic crisis.

Nominal per capita GDP remained around U.S.$6,500 in 2008. The industrial sector accounts for 60% of the Latin American economy's industrial production. Foreign direct investment has experienced remarkable growth, averaging U.S.$30 billion per year in recent years (reaching a peak of U.S.$45 billion in 2008), compared with only U.S.$2 billion per year during the last decade.

This growth is attributed to a stable economy with lower inflation rates and higher technological development that attracts more investors. The agribusiness sector also has been remarkably dynamic. For two decades, agribusiness has kept Brazil among the most highly productive countries in areas related to the rural sector. The agricultural sector and the mining sector also supported trade surpluses that allowed for huge currency gains (rebound) and external debt pay-down.

The Brazilian Financial Markets: Institutionalizing the Effectiveness and Regulation of Capital Markets

We consider Brazil's capital market one of the most strongly regulated in the world. The basic features of the Brazilian financial system were set by a series of institutional reforms that started in 1964–1965 with the creation of the National Monetary Council (CMN, the Brazilian acronym for the Conselho Monetário Nacional) and the Brazilian Central Bank (BCB) and were completed in 1976 with the creation of the national Securities and Exchange Commission (CVM, or Comissão de Valores Mobiliários). The role of these entities is described below.

National Monetary Council

The finance and planning ministries and the president of the Central Bank are the main members of the National Monetary Council. The CMN is the main rule-making, or normative, agency of the financial system and regulates the constitution and functioning and supervision of financial institutions. It has no executive function. The CMN is also responsible for establishing the inflation target to be pursued by the Central Bank. The inflation targets are established two years in advance and may be revised in the year before which the target takes effect. For instance, in June 2008 the CMN confirmed the inflation target for 2008 and defined the target for 2009, both at 4.5% with a range of ±2.0%.

Central Bank of Brazil

The Central Bank was created in 1965 and is a federal agency, officially part of the national financial system. Although the CMN is the principal normative body, the Central Bank carries out executive functions for the financial system. It is responsible for ensuring compliance with the CMN's directives and decisions regarding monetary policy and the exchange rate system and for monitoring and enforcing the activities of financial institutions. The main goal of the Central Bank is to ensure the stability of the purchasing power of the currency and the soundness of the national financial system; those goals currently are being pursued by means of an inflation-targeting policy.

Both the president and the directors of the Central Bank are appointed by Brazil's president and must be approved by the full Senate. Since the implementation of the Real Plan, the president and directors of the Central Bank have operated with strong autonomy, especially in the management of monetary policy. However, there is no law guaranteeing formal autonomy, and the directors do not have fixed mandates.

Some important functions of the Central Bank are

- Managing monetary policy to meet the inflation target
- Managing international reserves, including both decisions to buy and sell dollars in the market and decisions on investment policies
- Organizing, regulating, and supervising the national financial system

The Central Bank regulates the national financial system, grants authorization, and provides regulation for the functioning of financial institutions. The supervisory activity may be performed directly or indirectly. Direct supervision is done by technical teams in the Central Bank's regional offices. Indirect supervision consists of monitoring, through a computer system, financial institutions and conglomerates regardless of the demand for such supervision.

In the middle of the 1980s the creation of Sisbacen, an information system, established electronic communication between financial institutions and the Central Bank. All transactions made by financial institutions are registered within Sisbacen, facilitating the Central Bank's supervision of the whole financial system.

Securities and Exchange Commission

The CVM, a federal agency linked to the Ministry of Finance, was created in 1976. It is administratively independent and is empowered to discipline, govern, and supervise the activities of all market participants. The CVM's main objective is to regulate and strengthen the capital markets in Brazil. Its regulatory activities encompass all matters related to the securities market, such as the following:

- Registration of listed companies, offers, and asset distribution (e.g., stocks and debentures)
- Accreditation of independent auditors and mutual fund managers
- Establishment of rules concerning the institution, functioning, and operational procedures of stock exchanges and securities trading and intermediation
- Suspension of the issuance, distribution, or trading of a specific asset or the decreeing of withdrawal rights from stock markets

Brazilian law empowers the CVM to investigate, judge, and punish any irregularity in the securities markets. Its supervisory activities involve monitoring the information disclosure process, the behavior of all securities traded, and the registry and follow-up for foreign and domestic investors. After the huge losses in derivatives booked in the end of 2008 by companies known for careful management, the CVM became stricter in mandating listed companies to expand the disclosure of hedging deals, including sensitive analysis, with expected and worst-case scenarios.

BM&F Bovespa

Founded in 1890, the São Paulo Stock Exchange (Bovespa, or Bolsa de Valores de São Paulo) trades assets, contracts, and financial securities such as stocks, options, stock futures, stock forwards, debentures, and ABSs (asset-backed securities). It is composed of a stock market segment and an OTC (over-the-counter) segment. The fixed-income securities are traded on the Bovespa Fix and the SomaFix, markets intended for the trading of debentures and ABS shares. The Brazilian Mercantile & Futures Exchange (BM&F, or Bolsa de Mercadorias & Futuros), founded in 1986, is responsible for the intermediation and registration of trades made on the trading floor or via electronic system and also for clearing and settlement services, both physical and financial. The BM&F creates an environment for the trading of commodities' and indexes' future contracts in the forward futures segment. It has three clearinghouses—for derivatives (cash, forward, futures, options, and swap agreements), foreign exchange, and securities—that are in charge of the settlement of all trades, with a risk management structure in place to eliminate the major risks.

In 2008, Bovespa and BM&F merged their activities. They created a company called BM&FBovespa S.A. and became the largest exchange in Latin America and the third largest worldwide in terms of market value.

Other Relevant Entities

National Association of Investment Banks

ANBID is an association that was created in 1967 to represent the financial institutes operating in the Brazilian capital markets. It acts to strengthen the capital markets as a vehicle for the self-regulation of activities upon the adoption of standards that are normally more rigid than those required by the applicable legislation. ANBID is also the leading source of information for the country's capital markets. Therefore, ANBID works on the promotion of actions and practices for improving capital markets' efficiency, information, transparency, and security, by doing the following:

- Supporting the CVM as a supervisor
- Providing incentives for the adoption of better practices among associates and respect for investors' rights

- Improving services and operational practices
- Enhancing law, regulatory aspects, and the taxation of capital markets

In 1999, in addition to the representative and informational functions, the company started its autoregulatory activities. Today ANBID has over 70 associate members.

National Association of Financial Market Institutions

Established in 1971, Andima is a non-profit-oriented entity that brings together numerous financial institutions, from multiple, commercial and investment banks to stockbrokers and securities distributors. Its main objective is to provide technical and operating support to those institutions, encompassing daily monitoring of market behavior and legislation supervision, publication of statistical data and prices for the market, development of systems to improve financial transactions, and economic analyses and reports to supply relevant information on the national financial system. Andima gave rise to the following important systems, providing financial transactions with greater security, transparency, and agility:

- The Special Settlement and Custody System (Selic), an electronic trading system for publicly traded securities
- The Center for Custody and Financial Settlement of Securities (Cetip), which is an entity, regulated by the Central Bank along with the CVM, that specializes in trading private securities
- The National Debenture System (SND), developed by Andima and operationalized by Cetip, where debentures are kept in custody
- The System of Protection against Financial Risks (SPR), which enables the registration of swaps without a guarantee

and also accepts the registration of swap transactions with delimiters (cap, floor, collar, and third curve delimiter), swaps with barriers (knock in, knock out, and knock in–knock out), and swaptions

Andima offers the public indicative rates for all market maturities of domestic federal public securities. It also releases statistics on the stock, profitability, and turnover volume of bank deposit certificates (CDBs). These prices have been used as parameters for market scoring the bonds that constitute the portfolios of financial institutions and third-party asset managers.

The Domestic Bond Market

Resuming Strong Growth in Issuance Volume

The market for private fixed-income bonds has grown at a very strong pace in recent years, benefiting not only from Brazil's greater macroeconomic stability but also from changes in legislation that have enabled the development of new credit methods, such as larger utilization of receivables as backed securities.

The private sector issues various types of securities in the domestic market, especially CDBs and bank deposit receipts (RDBs), private securities debt (debentures), bank credit notes (CCBs), real estate receivables certificates (CRIs), and credit receivables funds (FIDCs). Among those securities, the most significant are CDBs/RDBs and debentures. The stock of corporate debt bonds in the domestic market has grown at a very rapid pace, driven by the strong growth in the volume of issuances, mainly in the last three years. Trading in the secondary market is carried out on the trading floor or on an OTC market by institutions authorized by the Central Bank and the CVM. The secondary market of debentures in Brazil still has very low liquidity compared with the liquidity of assets such as shares and public bonds and is concentrated almost entirely in the SND.

Ownership Structure of Public Companies

Overcoming Brazil's Governance Weaknesses

The ownership structure of Brazilian companies, in particular the concentration of control in the hands of a few shareholders, has been associated with many of the country's governance weaknesses. Those weaknesses range from poor functioning of boards to disregard for minority shareholders' rights and low liquidity of the stock markets. In fact, more than 60% of publicly held companies have a single shareholder controlling over 50% of the voting shares. With corporate control concentrated in the hands of few shareholders, if not a single shareholder, there is very limited scope for hostile takeovers. Thus, the managerial discipline imposed by such mechanisms is not a relevant feature of the market for corporate control in Brazil.

The original Corporate Law, enacted in 1976, authorized the listed companies to have a minimum of one-third of ordinary shares, with voting rights, and two-thirds of preferred shares (nonvoting shares). In 2001, with the acceleration of the opening up of the Brazilian economy, some modifications were made in this law, including a change in the mix of shares. The number of preferred shares was limited to 50% of a company's total shares. Despite this change, until recently it was very common to have the founder and major shareholder of a company as the owner of 100% of the ordinary shares and the free float composed exclusively of preferred shares. However, several significant improvements have been made in terms of shareholding structure in the last few years, as detailed below.

Development of the Stock Market

Boosting the Volume of Foreign Capital Inflow

The Brazilian stock market experienced an outstanding evolution in the last five years. To attract the interest of large foreign investors, the Brazilian Stock Exchange (Bovespa) created three new kinds of segments according to the minimum demand in terms of corporate governance (see Table 1-1).

The Tag-Along Right

The sale or transfer of shares representing a company's control commits the buyer to make a tender offer for all common shares not in the con-

Table 1-1 Brazilian Stock Exchange Segments

Segments of Bovespa	Traditional Segment	Level 1	Level 2	New Market
Number of listed companies	280	44	18	101
Kind of shares	Both ordinary and preferred shares	Both ordinary and preferred shares	Both ordinary and preferred shares (with additional advantages)	Only ordinary shares
Percentage minimum of free float	No rule	Minimum 25% of the total shares	Minimum 25% of the total shares	Minimum 25% of the total shares
Composition of board of directors	Minimum 3 members	Minimum 3 members	Minimum 5 members, of which 20% are independents	Minimum 5 members, of which 20% are independents
Tag-along	80% for ordinary shares	80% for ordinary shares	100% for ordinary and 80% for preferred shares	100% for ordinary shareholders
Disclosure of consolidated and cash flow statements	Mandatory	Mandatory	Mandatory	Mandatory
Financial statements in U.S. GAAP or IFRS	Optional	Optional	Mandatory	Mandatory
Public presentation to analysts and investors	Optional	At least once a year	At least once a year	At least once a year

trolling group for at least 80% of the price paid for each control share (the tag-along right), thus limiting that premium to 20%. Such rights are, however, not extended to preference nonvoting shares except in companies listed on Bovespa's Level 2, for which the exchange's listing rules determine tag-along rights for nonvoting preference shares of 80% and for ordinary (voting) shares of 100%. In the case of companies listed on the Bovespa's New Market, which requires all listed companies to issue ordinary shares only, tag-along rights are set at 100%, assuring equal treatment of all shareholders after a change in control. Brazil's Company Law helps align the interests of controlling and minority shareholders and eliminate economic distortions that arise from attempts by controlling shareholders to maximize the control premium through a depreciation of the remaining shares. Not surprisingly, the grant of tag-along rights to ordinary shares was reflected in appreciation of ordinary share prices relative to those of preference shares, with the price movement most evident for companies at a high risk of a change in control.

Dividend Payment Processes

The Brazilian Company Law determines the payment of a compulsory dividend of no less than 25% of the annual net profit, and fiscal incentives provide further motivation for that form of distribution, as dividend payments are tax-exempt whereas capital gains are taxed at 15%.

The creation of the new segments and the strong improvement of Brazil's economy in the last five years led Standard & Poor's Ratings Services to raise the country's long-term foreign currency sovereign credit rating to investment grade (BBB–/Stable/A–3) in April 2008. This helped boost the volume of foreign capital inflow in the last three years. Taking advantage of the high capital inflow, several companies launched initial public offerings (IPOs) and/or issued debentures and additional equities, as shown in Table 1-2.

Equity issuances were halted in October 2008 as a result of the worldwide economic crisis, and the volume of debentures placements diminished considerably.

Table 1-2   Issuance Volume by Year, 2004–2008 (in U.S. $Million)

	2004	2005	2006	2007	2008
Equity issuances	1.528	1.794	6.533	17.176	17.171
Debentures issuances	3.287	17.072	31.908	24.121	20.007

Board of Directors Structure

Further Safeguarding of Shareholder Rights

As was stated previously, the capital structure of listed companies can consist of ordinary and preferred shares, depending on the segment in which a company is listed in Bovespa. Ordinary shareholders representing at least 15% of the voting shares for at least three months have the right to appoint and dismiss one member to the board of directors. Also, a preferred shareholder who holds the equivalent of 10% of total capital can appoint a member to the board. This board member has the prerogative of vetoing the hiring of the independent auditor but not the firing of the auditor. Brazilian boards of directors are composed of at least three members who must be approved by shareholders. The mandate terms cannot be longer than three years, and for companies listed on Bovespa's Level 2 or New Market, the term is one year.

Boards are responsible for the general strategy of a company and for overseeing its implementation by senior executives as well as approving company finances and appointing and dismissing the independent auditors.

In general, boards have been composed of company insiders, and board processes are mostly informal. Frequently, the roles of the chair and the chief executive officer (CEO) are combined and generally represent the company's controlling shareholder. As a result, majority ownership and executive control can be one and the same, with board structures often maintained to meet legal requirements as opposed to providing an independent system of checks and balances. However, the evolution and expansion of the capital markets are resulting in more formalized board procedures and directors' duties to attract investors. Brazilian best practices standards advocate boards with a majority of independent directors, but this applies only to companies listed in the Level 2 and New Market segments. The stricter requirements of corporate governance have been attracting mainly foreign investors. As a result, some companies listed in the Traditional and Level 1 segments are planning to migrate to the other two, where the shares have higher valuation because of the increased corporate governance requirements.

The Legal Environment

How Brazil Is Modernizing Its Financial Laws

Based on Roman codes, Brazil's legal system is classified as a civil law code. Three main laws guide the structure and functioning of the securities markets and address governance issues: the Securities Law, the Company Law, and the Bankruptcy Law. These laws often are complemented by resolutions or instructions issued by the regulatory agencies, the CVM, and the Central Bank as well as by the Bovespa stock exchange. The Securities Law sets forth the rules governing the securities market and its main regulatory body, the Securities and Exchange Commission. It is under this law that the markets are regulated. The Company Law provides the basic rules that determine the operation and governance of both public and private companies. Since 2001, Company Law has been changing gradually, first with the purpose of improving several governance issues and in the last couple of years with the goal of becoming more similar to the International Financial Reporting Standards (IFRS) rules.

The New Bankruptcy Law

Culminating a decade-long effort to modernize Brazil's bankruptcy laws, the New Bankruptcy Law of February 9, 2005, came into effect in June 2005. This law, which applies to most corporations and certain other business entities, provides enhanced protection and flex- ibility for debtors in financial distress that want to reorganize while continuing to operate their businesses. At the same time, creditors, particularly secured creditors, are likely to see their debt recovery prospects improved when businesses are liquidated, giving them a more significant role in the negotiation of restructuring plans and in reorganization proceedings than was the case under the previous bank- ruptcy law, which had been in effect since 1945. The new regime also provides special treatment for certain secured transactions involving the transfer of credit rights or receivables as collateral by means of fidu- ciary assignment to a creditor, which ultimately may give rise to the development of new hybrid securitizations in the domestic market.

The New Bankruptcy Law introduced several significant changes that give debtors greater flexibility in restructuring their debt and reor- ganizing their businesses.

Out-of-Court Restructuring

The advantage of this type of procedure for a debtor is that it can nego- tiate a reorganization plan with many of its largest creditors outside of a formal court proceeding and have that plan approved by the court to apply to all of the debtor's creditors that are subject to the plan, including nonconsenting creditors, provided that the plan is viable and is approved by the requisite number of creditors.

Judicial Reorganization

Unlike in the preventive *concordata* proceeding under the previous law, where a bankruptcy stay affected only unsecured creditors, a debtor now can receive a stay from the court against legal actions by almost all creditors, secured and unsecured, once the bankruptcy petition has been accepted by the court. This provides significant protection for debtors and is similar to the automatic bankruptcy stay in Chapter 11 reorganizations in the United States. In both cases, a company has up to 60 days to present a reorganization plan that demonstrates its long-term financial viability. The plan must outline detailed information and positive steps to turn around the company's operational and financial performance. The financial projections and valuation of assets must be examined by a legally certified professional or company. The new law gives companies up to 180 days to emerge from bankruptcy. It also allows the creation of a credit committee that is expected to take an active role in the reorganization process. In case of liquidation, the priority order for claims is as follows: (1) labor liabilities, (2) secured creditors, (3) tax liabilities, and (4) unsecured creditors (including bondholders in this particular case).

Informational Infrastructure: Increasing the Transparency of Financial Data

Accounting Practices: Embracing IFRS Rules for Public Companies

The convergence of Brazilian generally accepted accounting principles (GAAP) with international accounting practices has been accelerated in the last few years as a consequence of globalized markets and the increasing presence of foreign capital in Brazil. International bodies such as the International Accounting Standards Committee (IASC), the International Organization of Securities Commissions (IOSCO), and Securities and Exchange Commission (SEC) have supported the process of converging accounting practices, mainly toward IFRS, to standardize the format and disclosure of financial statements to conform with global rules. In December 2007, Brazil enacted Law 11.368, which modified several items of the original Corporate Law to accelerate the convergence toward IFRS scheduled for 2010.

The main topics addressed were the following:

- The mandatory inclusion of the statement of cash flow and the statement of value added

- A requirement for the company to analyze periodically the recoverability of the amounts booked at permanent, intangible, and deferred assets
- The adjustment to market value of financial instruments
- A requirement for financial leasing transactions to be recorded in balance sheets

Transparency and Disclosure: Enhancing Rules for Disclosure, Reporting, and Independence of Auditors

Quality of Disclosure

Companies are required to prepare annual financial statements that include a balance sheet, a statement of retained earnings, an income statement, a cash flow statement, and notes to the financial statements. For comparative purposes, statements must show corresponding amounts for the preceding fiscal year. Publicly held corporations registered with the CVM must meet these filing requirements and also disclose their management and auditor reports as well as a comprehensive set of quarterly and periodic information through the CVM's and Bovespa's Web sites, allowing online access to company regulatory disclosure for investors. Most of the listed companies with more than 25% of shares traded in stock exchanges have Web sites in Portuguese and English on which investors can find a comprehensive set of documents. These documents include not only financial statements but also details on corporate governance, the historical experience of all members of the management team and board of directors, bylaws, policies, dividends history, an events calendar, and frequently asked questions (FAQs). Almost all listed companies in Brazil maintain an active investor relations department.

Timing of Financial Reporting

In following the CVM's rules, listed companies have to publish annual audited financial statements up to March 31 of the following year. The quarterly statements must be released up to 45 days after the end of the respective quarter. In the case of delay, the company has to pay daily penalties.

Auditor Independence

Independent auditors must audit the annual financial statements of publicly held corporations. Those auditors must be both registered and accredited by the CVM to do audited work in Brazil. An independent auditor's responsibilities include attending a client's annual shareholders' meetings and providing information about the company's audit financial statements to shareholders. Independent auditors are liable for any damages incurred by third parties that rely on their audited statements. In May 1999, Brazil enacted a mandatory audit firm rotation requirement with a five-year maximum term and a minimum time lag of three years before the predecessor auditor of record can return. The CVM indicated that the primary reason for this mandatory rotation was to strengthen audit supervision after accounting fraud at two local banks (Banco Economico and Banco Nacional). Brazil does not have a partner rotation requirement, as the CVM believes that the requirement of rotating audit firms is stronger than would be changing partners within firms. However, as a component of its mandatory audit firm rotation requirement, Brazil prohibits an individual auditor who changes audit firms to audit the same corporations he or she previously audited. In September 2008, the Central Bank allowed financial institutions to maintain their audit firm for an undetermined number of years with the condition that every five years the partner responsible for the audit service in a financial institution be replaced along with all the team leaders in charge of the audit services in that financial institution. So far, the CVM has suspended temporarily the rotation obligation only for companies that would have to change the audit firm in 2008/2009 to avoid impairing the conversion of the Company Law to IFRS.

Chapter 2

Corporate Governance Is Advancing in Russia

Oleg Shvyrkov

Introduction and Executive Summary

Governance Needs Are Driven by Attraction to Global Capital Markets

Governance standards are improving gradually in Russia as that nation's companies increasingly participate in international capital markets. Fourteen Russian companies performed international equity placements in 2006 and another 14 participated in 2007, raising $16.3 billion and $18.7 billion, respectively. The overall number of Russian companies with international listings reached 60. Although IPO (initial public offering) activity was interrupted by the global financial meltdown in 2008, the vast investment needs of Russian businesses probably will keep them attracted to the global capital markets and motivated to raise governance standards in the medium term and long term.

The negative financial trends of 2008 put the governance mechanisms of many companies to the test. There are increasing pressures on companies and banks to engage in related-party lending to support affiliated entities in distress; this is potentially against the interests of external investors. Also, to many large investors, the liquidity squeeze increases the appeal of exploiting legal loopholes to circumvent their obligations to minority investors, such as avoiding mandatory buyout procedures in takeovers. The fact that several large investors have been able to do this without facing legal penalties highlights the remaining weaknesses in the legal and regulatory infrastructure.

Another concern relates to the fact that many Russian companies are satisfied with attaining moderate governance standards in the absence of specific national regulations and in view of the relatively mild governance requirements that most international exchanges present to foreign issuers. This usually involves bringing transparency up to the minimum standards of international exchanges, setting up an investor relations function, and appointing a limited number of independent directors to the board. Although there are notable positive exceptions, most companies do not attempt to establish effective checks and balances at the board level or perform a strong independent internal audit. Further progress often is hampered by lax domestic regulation of governance practices, weak national accounting standards, and a weak market infrastructure. The limited role of financial markets and significant government participation in the equity of large companies remain major roadblocks to improvement.

The resulting risks to investors come in the form of a loss in value or a failure to create value when significant shareholders use their influence to pursue external agendas. Conflicts of interest are particularly pronounced in government-controlled companies, which often are pushed to serve strategic and social goals, usually by engaging in unprofitable transactions, and thus bear a quasi-fiscal burden beyond the obligations provided by law and regulation. Despite the generally liberal regulatory reforms in several industries, such conflicts of interest remain pronounced in fixed-line telephony, oil and gas, transport, and some other sectors. There are significant differences in terms of the extent to which individual companies are exposed to such risks, even within a single industry.

Domestic regulation of governance practices is fairly mild and applies in earnest only to 26 Russian companies that are first-tier-listed on domestic stock exchanges. Regulation of disclosure practices is particularly weak. Whereas regulators in other large emerging economies are pushing for adoption of International Financial Reporting Standards (IFRS), Russia lags significantly in this respect. For example, China adopted new IFRS-based accounting principles in 2007. Russian accounting standards have a number of significant flaws and differ enormously from IFRS or any modern national standard. Proliferation of IFRS or U.S. generally accepted accounting principles (GAAP) reporting is limited mostly to a group of large companies and banks and is due mostly to pressure from financial markets rather than efforts by regulators.

Market Infrastructure

Economy and Investment: Equity Financing Is Vital to Further Progress

The rapid expansion of the Russian economy has increased the investment needs of local industries as well as the dependence of businesses on international capital markets. In particular, there is an increasing need for equity financing. Although the negative market trends temporarily eroded the appeal of equity placements and caused the postponement of a number of IPOs in 2008 and 2009, many Russian companies are likely to float shares internationally as global markets rebound. Several factors are at work here. A protracted period of underinvestment that lasted for nearly two decades ensures demand for vast amounts of investment funds across the economy. This demand cannot be met by debt financing alone, and many firms have already reached the limits of comfortable debt levels. At the same time, ownership structures are heavily concentrated, meaning that many companies are able to perform additional share issues without having to require the blockholders to yield or compromise control.

The Russian economy has experienced a spectacular rally since 1999, with an average annual growth rate of 7%, spurred by high hydrocarbon prices. However, further economic progress hinges on the ability of businesses across industries to finance their rising investment needs. Most industries experienced a long period of underinvestment in the 1990s, when the investment rate stood at 15% or less of gross domestic product (GDP). The investment rate remained at a moderate level of 21% between 2000 and 2006 and was expected to reach 26% of GDP in 2008. Rapid growth in real wages has created additional pressure to raise factor productivity performance through capital expenditures. In 2007, wages went up 34.6% but labor productivity rose only 5.8%.

Despite the development of domestic financial institutions, the sheer volume of capital needed to finance investment has induced many Russian companies to tap the international capital markets. Funds included in the Moscow Interbank Currency Exchange (MICEX) main index reached daily average trading volumes of $2.5 billion in the first six months of 2008. This was above the levels shown by any exchange in Central and Eastern Europe but significantly below the daily trading volumes of the New York Stock Exchange (NYSE) of $53.5 billion and the London Stock Exchange (LSE) of $19 billion. In 2007, eight Russian companies performed domestic equity placements, jointly raising $1.6 billion. At the same time, 14 Russian companies performed international placements, all of them on the LSE, raising $18.7 billion, up from $16.3 billion in 2006 and $4.6 billion in 2005. Rosneft OJSC and VTB OJSC raised $10.7 billion and $8 billion, respectively. These mammoth placements highlight the investment appetites of the larger Russian companies, which probably will continue to tap into international capital markets in the future. The economic reform policies, particularly in infrastructure, specifically aim to attract capital for investment and promote competition. RAO UES, the state-controlled utility holding company, spun off 20 generating companies (6 wholesale and 14 territorial generation companies) that jointly raised around $17 billion through domestic and international equity placements between 2006 and 2008. RAO UES was liquidated in July 2008, marking the completion of utilities reform. Similarly, Russian Railways JSC has adopted an ambitious reform plan that previews raising capital through share placements by several subsidiaries and eventually by the core entity.

Prevailing Ownership Structures

Ownership Concentration in Russia Remains Very High

Dispersed shareholding is the exception rather than the norm. The participation of the state in the equity of public companies is significant and continues to grow, extending well beyond the commanding heights of the economy. In the case of the largest companies and banks, the state plays a dominant role.

There are around 300 public companies in Russia, but most of them are traded infrequently and only about 90 have moderate to high liquidity of shares. S&P's research on the 90 largest public companies shows that their ownership structures are highly concentrated, with 56 of those 90 companies being majority-owned and another 24 having one or more blocking shareholders (i.e., holding over 25% of votes). Only 10 companies have widely dispersed shareholders. However, even in those cases, hidden groups of holdings and shareholder agreements are likely to exist, allowing for more influence than may be evident.

Indeed, ownership concentration is typically high in jurisdictions that provide a wide measure of direct shareholder rights. To achieve stable control in such environments, investors need to consolidate a majority, or at least a near majority, position in voting stock. This also means that it is impossible for external investors to consolidate a stake sufficient to challenge or take over control. The disciplining pressures on management associated with these mechanisms in Anglo-Saxon markets are virtually nonexistent.

Ownership transparency has improved considerably in the last five years, as most private significant owners have disclosed their ultimate ownership positions. According to our 2008 Transparency & Disclosure Survey, conducted jointly with the New Economic School (NES), 45 of 56 controlled companies (80%) disclose their beneficial controlling shareholders and ownership of 60 out of 80 blocking stakes (75%) is transparent. This compares positively to our 2004 results, which showed that 64% of companies disclosed beneficial ownership by significant shareholders. However, even today some block holdings and smaller consolidated stakes (such as 5% or 10%) that are held indirectly remain opaque in the absence of a legal requirement for shareholders to report consolidated stakes.

The government is an increasingly important shareholder, with particularly strong equity positions in large companies that it considers to be of strategic importance. According to the same research by S&P and NES, 20 of the 90 largest public companies were majority owned by the state directly or through intermediaries. In another nine companies the government had a significant noncontrolling beneficial equity position. Moreover, since government-related companies tend to be among the largest, their market value represented 57% of the aggregate market capitalization of the 90 companies. A number of state-owned enterprises (SOEs) performed additional share placements in recent years, yet with the exception of some former RAO UES subsidiaries, they did not yield control to private investors. Effectively, these IPOs led to an increase in government participation in the economy, as they allowed the SOEs to expand. Some of the largest SOEs, most notably the energy giant Gazprom OJSC and the largest state-owned banks, continue to expand through acquisitions, sometimes in loosely related or entirely unrelated businesses. Companies controlled by private financial groups are usually more open to introducing international governance standards and particularly more likely to embrace open and transparent decision-making routines than are state-controlled enterprises. This tendency exists despite the short history of private business in Russia and the fact that many privately owned companies still are struggling to break away from former practices of entrepreneurial management. Separating ownership from management and introducing professional management structures and effective governance mechanisms are difficult yet increasingly popular choices for many founders.

Governance at SOEs

State Involvement in the Economy Likely to Continue

Governance issues associated with state control, such as lack of motivation to create value, rigidity, and corruption, have been recognized by the government. However, the proposed solutions do not appear convincing and do not include plans to limit government participation in the economy. The privatization program for 2008–2010 is fairly modest, as it does not include any large enterprises. For example, Svyazinvest, the government-controlled telecommunications holding company, has been slated for privatization since 1997, yet its prospects remain unclear. Clearly, the healthy state of government finances in recent years has reduced incentives to sell off assets, and the desire of the state bureaucracy for greater economic clout has created internal resistance to privatization.

Confusion of Regulatory and Ownership Functions

Blending the Government Roles of Shareholder and Regulator

In several industries, most notably oil and gas, banking, telecoms, and airlines, the government tends to act through corporate structures to achieve social and strategic goals rather than delegate that mission to regulatory bodies. This is a clear contradiction of the basic principle of governance of SOEs, promoted by the Organization for Economic Cooperation and Development (OECD), that the government's roles of shareholder and regulator should not be confused. These practices expose external investors in SOEs to the risk that the government will use its influence to promote its own social and strategic agendas at the expense of shareholder value. In some cases, they also run the risk of vested private interests supporting the influence of the government on public companies.

Bureaucratic Decision-Making Procedures

State Actions on SOEs Are Time-Consuming and Cumbersome

In recent years, the government's approach to exercising control at SOEs has consisted of maximizing its board presence and requiring its representatives to vote under instructions. Those instructions typically reflect a consensus position of certain government branches, which usually include the government asset management agency (FAUGI); the Ministry of Economic Development, an industry-specific authority; and in some cases the prime minister's and president's offices. These agencies usually are represented on the boards of SOEs by their senior officials. In cases involving the most important enterprises, which are included on the "strategic list," an additional sign-off from the prime minister is required.

This arrangement apparently was intended to solidify government control and reduce the risk of corruption by making the proposed transactions subject to approval by several government branches. Indeed, it is fairly unlikely that all the agencies involved are united in a shared vested interest. The cost of this arrangement comes in the form of the time these agencies take to reach a consensus and their focus on preservation of assets and social security rather than value creation. Very few government officials have actual business experience, and this negatively affects the skill mix available to the boards of SOEs. Involving external directors in actual decision making also becomes difficult, as decisions effectively are made outside the boardroom.

Government-Appointed Independent Directors a Mixed Success

Contradictions Abound in Board Appointments

The recent initiative to improve the effectiveness of boards of directors by introducing independent directors is fairly liberal in spirit yet is contradictory because of unclear implementation policies. In July 2008, President Dmitry Medvedev announced that most state representatives on the boards of SOEs would be replaced by independent directors and semi-independent "professional attorneys in fact," with the latter being required to follow voting instructions only on certain major issues.

A number of new appointments to the boards of several large state-owned companies followed, including Russian Railways OJSC, Sberbank OJSC, and Transneft OJSC, among several others. Some of the appointments were obvious successes, such as the appointment of Oleg Vyugin, a highly regarded finance professional, to the board of Transneft. However, many other appointments raised questions about the professional background of directors and their ability to act independently of the government. For example, several newly appointed directors are executives of SOEs or managers of government-funded academic institutions. Other directors are executives of private companies that provide services to SOEs.

The exact criteria for director independence and expertise remain unclear, as do the procedures for selection of candidates and evaluation of board performance. This casts doubt on the ability of the government to make successful external board appointments consistently. Skeptics argue that the changes that have been initiated actually may make the SOEs less accountable and the government's influence on them less transparent, with a rise in corruption and a decline in governance standards.

State Corporations: Additional Risks at Indirectly Controlled SOEs

Disclosure and Auditing Are Challenges

Another concern relates to indirectly controlled companies, particularly in light of the recent rise of *state corporations*, a legal term for not-for-profit enterprises wholly owned by the government. State corporations have no public disclosure requirements, are exempt from bankruptcy procedures and audits by the Audit Chamber (the parliament's arm), and provide wide powers to executives. These entities, created mainly in 2007 and 2008, took over the government's equity interests in a number of public companies in industries as diverse as machinery and defense production (Rosoboronexport, Rostechnologii), airlines (Rostechnologii), and banking (Vnesheconombank).

There are risks that public companies controlled by state corporations will face risks similar to or potentially greater than those observed at subsidiaries of state holding companies. Indirectly controlled SOEs often are exposed to risks caused by governance flaws at controlling companies in addition to the general risks of government ownership. State corporations, with their lax oversight mechanisms, limited disclosure requirements, and unclear performance criteria, may become less desirable to shareholders than the state proper or public SOEs.

Shareholder Activism and the Role of Mass Media

Activists Drive Good Governance

International institutional investors with a Russian presence and the growing community of domestic institutional investors are the main drivers of shareholder activism. Their joint efforts have ensured some minority representation on the boards of most public companies and have given minority investors an important role in disciplining the controlling shareholders. Individuals and ADR/GDR (American Depositary Receipt/Global Depositary Receipt) holders are typically passive investors in Russia.

Many public Russian companies are effectively old Soviet enterprises that were mass privatized in the early 1990s or amalgamations of those enterprises. Consequently, a certain proportion of capital typically is scattered across a large number of current and former employees. This category of shareholders is generally passive and has a tendency to support the management at board elections. ADR/GDR holders represent yet another passive category as a result of both technical constraints (such as limited time for analysis and submission of proxies) and limited local expertise. Most Russian companies receive very few proxies from their ADR/GDR investors, if any.

Shareholder abuses at public companies have led over the years to the emergence of shareholder rights watchdog associations. Those associations play an important role in disciplining the government and the private owners, yet their powers remain limited. The National Association for Securities Market Participants (NAUFOR) established a coordination center for investor protection in 1999 that subsequently developed into the Investor Protection Association (IPA). The IPA defends investor interests through lawsuits and board nominations by consolidating investor votes. The IPA was able to win 26 seats on the boards of 21 companies in 2008 (20 and 18, respectively, in 2007, and 19 and 17 in 2006). The association maintains an informative Web site that alerts investors to potential abuse (www.corpgov.ru). Publicity created by IPA and other minority activists can have a disciplinary effect on the management and majority owners of public companies and help curb significant abuse. This is only a moderately effective tool, however, that cannot compensate fully for the absence of checks and balances at the board level. Also, experience shows that there may be limits to the amount of shareholder activism some powerful players in

Russia will accept. William Browder, head of Hermitage Capital Management, formerly the largest single-portfolio investor in Russia, with over $4 billion in Russian funds in 2005, had his entry visa withdrawn by Russian authorities in 2005. The fund's Russian offices subsequently were raided by the police on charges of tax evasion. Browder, who was forced to divest the fund's Russian assets, was known as a critic of several large Russian companies, not the least of which was the gas giant OJSC Gazprom.

The influence of shareholder rights activists is fostered by the business media, including the *Vedomosti*, *Kommersant*, and *RBC Daily* newspapers, which often act as vocal critics of shareholder abuses and management failures. However, public awareness of governance issues is constrained by the fact that unlike the business media, newspapers of general appeal and the main television channels provide very limited coverage of governance issues (and relatively little economic and business analysis in general). Most of the popular media outlets are controlled by the state. Journalists at state-owned newspapers and television channels are believed to be constrained in their freedom to criticize SOEs and government policies.

Legal Infrastructure

Russian legislation is based on the Franco-German legal tradition and provides a wide measure of direct shareholder rights by international comparison. These rights include the low holding thresholds required to nominate a candidate to a board of directors, one-year directors' terms, and cumulative voting procedures in board elections. Limitations on voting rights, antitakeover defenses, and dual CEO–board chair positions are not allowed. Changes in Russian corporate law introduced in the late 1990s and early 2000s removed many of the loopholes that allowed abuses of minority shareholder rights to take place in the early and middle 1990s.

One important positive outcome has been the presence of minority representatives on the boards of most public companies. This arrangement increases the minority investors' awareness of strategic decisions and associated risks and allows activists to initiate a public debate on controversial initiatives. Although falling short of ensuring proper checks and balances at the board level, this opportunity for minority investors to be informed and heard is an important disciplining factor for majority owners.

Nevertheless, important loopholes remain in the area of shareholder rights. Laws do not provide for effective regulation of ownership disclosure. They adopt an atomistic view of companies and lack the notion of consolidated groups. Russian law and regulations allow companies to pay out dividends as late as 12 months after the reporting year and do not provide for a single-day payout. In addition, the judiciary has a chronic lack of resources, expertise, and independence that inhibits the effective enforcement of corporate legislation. This institutional weakness complicates the resolution of corporate disputes.

These weaknesses present tangible risks to minority investors, as recent events at several power generation companies have shown, including those at TGC–1, TGC–2, TGC–4, TGC–14, WGC–2, and WGC–6. At these companies, large investors exploited a variety of technical grounds to avoid launching or completing mandatory buyouts after assuming a majority or near-majority stake. Amendments closing certain remaining loopholes are being discussed in the State Duma's committees, including shareholders' obligation to disclose beneficial ownership. The scope and effectiveness of eventual amendments remain to be seen, however.

Russian law distinguishes between open and closed joint stock companies (OAO and ZAO). Only OAOs are allowed to float shares, yet ZAOs may raise public debt. The laws most relevant to shareholder rights include the Civil Code, the Code of Arbitration Procedure (which provides a basic legal framework), and federal laws with more specific foci, such as the Joint-Stock Company Law (JSC Law), the Law on Limited Liability Companies (OOO), the Law on the Securities Market, the Law on Banks and Banking Activities, and the Bankruptcy Law.

The Major Legal Provisions Protecting Shareholder Rights

Classes of Stock

There is a one share–one vote principle that applies to all common stock. However, companies are allowed to issue preferred stock with fixed or variable dividends for up to 25% of charter capital. Dividends on preferred stock usually are defined as a minimum share of net income under Russian Accounting Standards (RAS), with 10% being by far the most common proportion. Preferred shareholders have voting rights only on the most significant corporate decisions, such as reorganization, liquidation, and amendments to the charter that affect the status of preferred shares. However, preferred shareholders acquire voting rights on a par with those of common shareholders if due dividends on preferred shares are not made until this commitment has been fulfilled. Preferred shares usually trade at a discount to common stock despite the fact that dividends on common stock are usually three times smaller. This suggests that there are substantial benefits of control that accrue only to common stock. For example, mandatory bids in takeover situations do not extend to preferred stock.

Preemptive Rights

The JSC law grants preemptive rights to shareholders for new share issues placed via open subscription (OAOs) and in the case of share placement via closed subscription by OAOs and ZAOs. In the latter case, preemptive rights apply only to shareholders who voted against the additional share issue or did not participate in voting. Shareholders of ZAOs also have preemptive rights in the case of all stock sales by other shareholders.

The Registrar and Its Independence

The JSC law prescribes that the share register be kept by an outside professional registrar in companies that have more than 50 shareholders. This does not mandate, however, that the registrar be unaffiliated with the issuer or its significant shareholder. In fact, there is some sort of affiliation between a controlling shareholder and the registrar at most public companies. When that affiliation is present, the controlling shareholder may enjoy informational privileges during board elections, potentially facilitating board appointments when competition for board seats is intense. More significant abuses are uncommon at public companies, yet they are not entirely absent.

Dividend Payout Procedures

Under the JSC Law, companies must use a 60-day dividend payout period unless a different term is set in the charter. Most companies extend this period, typically to six months. Furthermore, since dividends are approved at annual general meetings (AGMs) as late as the end of June, actual payouts may happen almost 12 months after the end of the reporting year. There is no regulation preventing companies from paying out to a significant shareholder before the rest. Additionally, dividends nominally are paid out of net income as defined under RAS, which may cause year-to-year volatility because of the numerous inadequacies of domestic accounting rules.

Board Composition

A board of directors must include a minimum of five members. All directors are elected for a one-year term. Directors' mandates can be terminated at any point or extended by no more than a year through voting at a general shareholder meeting. The law limits the percentage of members of a management board that can be on a board of directors (no more than 25% of seats), but it does not specify how many executives outside the management board can be on the board. The CEO cannot serve as board chair. There are no requirements regarding board committees.

The Authority of Shareholder Meetings and the Board of Directors

The range of issues exclusively reserved for the approval of shareholders and directors is specified in the JSC Law. The list of issues under the authority of the shareholder meeting is explicit and cannot diverge from the JSC Law, whereas the authority of a board of directors and the executive bodies can be made more specific in a company's charter. Thus, the shareholder meeting decides all major company matters, including reorganization, liquidation, increases and decreases of charter capital, elections of boards of directors, large transactions involving amounts exceeding 50% of a company's assets, and related-party transactions exceeding 2% of assets (where only the disinterested shareholders vote). The appointment of the CEO and the management board can be undertaken by a shareholder meeting or by a board, according to the corporate charter. The authority of the board includes approvals of transactions that exceed 25% of the company's assets. Charters, however, may stipulate lower thresholds, and some companies go below 1%.

Material transactions involving 25 to 50% of a company's assets require unanimous consent by the board. If unanimous consent is not reached, the issue may be referred to a shareholders' meeting in which a simple majority vote is required. Decisions on material transactions involving amounts equal to or greater than 50% of assets are made exclusively at shareholders' meetings and require supermajority approval by a three-quarters voting share.

Decisions by the board to approve related-party transactions are made by disinterested directors, and the rest are required to abstain. This definition accounts only for direct affiliations, however, such as being a board member of the counterparty in question, whereas more complex individual conflicts of interest are not addressed by the law. If the number of disinterested directors is less than a quorum, the decision will be made during a shareholders' meeting.

Placement of Items on the Shareholders' Meeting Agenda

Shareholders owning (individually or jointly) at least 2% of voting shares can put forward proposals for the agenda of the AGM and can nominate candidates for the board of directors.

Voting Rights and Procedures

Shareholders may vote in person, in absentia, or by proxy. Companies with more than 100 shareholders must hold votes by ballot. Ballots are to be sent out together with notification of an upcoming meeting. There is a one share–one vote principle for common shares except for the mandatory cumulative voting for board members. The JSC law requires that large transactions, liquidations, amendments to charters, and changes in the number of shares authorized for new issues be approved by a supermajority of 75% of the votes represented at the meeting.

Procedures for Calling Shareholder Meetings

Annual shareholder meetings must be held within six months after the end of the reporting year, which is two months later than common practice in most jurisdictions. Most annual meetings are held in the second half of June. Companies must announce annual meetings at least 20 days in advance, 30 days in advance if reorganization is going to be discussed, and 50 days in advance of an extraordinary shareholder meeting if the election of a board of directors is involved. Notification must be via registered mail or a mass media publication. There are also detailed stipulations regarding the right to attend, registration, and voting procedures.

Procedures for Protesting Corporate Decisions

Shareholders who voted against a certain resolution or did not take part in a general shareholder meeting can challenge a decision in court within six months. This direct provision is one of the shareholders' most significant defenses, and this right is granted to all shareholders regardless of share size. However, a court may not challenge a shareholder meeting decision if appealing the vote would not influence the voting results, if the infringement was insignificant, or if the decision of the shareholder meeting did not result in significant losses for the shareholders.

Mandatory Buyouts

Russian law does not allow antitakeover provisions (poison pills, classified boards, or freeze-out provisions). However, the procedures for reviewing takeover bids to ensure a fair price are not addressed by the law either. The JSC Law stipulates a mandatory share buyout offer only once a shareholder exceeds a threshold of 30% of voting stock. Similar obligations apply when 50% and 75% thresholds are exceeded. The buyout price should exceed the higher of the six-month weighted average exchange price and the highest price paid by the bidder over the six months preceding the bid. The effectiveness of this regulation is reduced by the formalist definition of affiliated entities, which is not based on ultimate common control. This approach makes it possible for bidders to acquire de facto control through several affiliated entities without triggering a buyout requirement. Another negative effect is that the mandatory buyouts do not extend to nonvoting preferred shares.

Tansparency of Ownership and Affiliated-Party Transactions

Legal requirements regarding transparency of ownership are relatively ineffective, mainly because significant shareholders who hold equity stakes indirectly are not required to report their equity positions, as is common in most jurisdictions. At the extreme, this leads to situations in which companies are unaware of blockholders who hold equity indirectly and have no means to obtain this information.

The concepts of beneficial ownership and common control are not recognized under Russian law; changes are being discussed by legislators. Russian law requires that public companies disclose immediate shareholders who own more than 5% of share capital and second-tier shareholders who own over 20% in the immediate owners (when known). Shareholding by directors and members of the management board also are supposed to be disclosed in quarterly statutory filings, yet this also includes only the directly held shares that appear in the registrar.

Squeeze-Out Provisions

Squeeze-out provisions were introduced in the JSC Law in 2006 and came into force in earnest in 2007. These amendments allowed holders of over 95% of common stock to squeeze out the remaining 5%, subject to specific time constraints and specific stock valuation procedures. The procedures for valuation are generally sound, yet they leave scope for manipulation that is based on varying external conditions and artificial stock trades between related entities. Thus, stock valuations may be affected by prices used in artificial share trades between nominally unaffiliated entities under common control. Also, in launching a squeeze-out, the dominant shareholder in practice may choose between using a valid appraisal that is based on recent data from previous months and requesting a new appraisal if external conditions favor this.

Regulations on Insider Trading

The Law on the Securities Market prohibits the use of insider information in transactions with a company's shares. Corresponding regulations provide that directors and managers of equity interests be disclosed in a company's statutory filings. However, changes in interest are not reported separately and can be tracked only in quarterly statutory filings. Along with other reporting requirements, such regulations are skirted easily through the use of nominee accounts or dummy companies.

Regulatory Framework

Despite the progress in the last decade, Russia trails the developed economies as well as most of the BRIC pack in terms of the effectiveness of its regulatory infrastructure. Russia's most direct form of governance regulation affects only 26 of more than 300 public companies. This compares negatively with India, where regulation affects all 5,000-plus public companies, and Brazil, where about 100 top-listed companies of about 440 are directly affected by governance regulation.

The leading regulatory role with regard to governance practices resides with the Federal Service for Securities Markets (FSFM), which succeeded the Federal Commission for Securities Markets (FCSM) in 2004 under the administrative reforms of President Vladimir Putin. FSFM has the core regulatory function in the sphere of securities markets, with the exception of insurance, banking, and audit activities regulation. Most of the changes in the laws that curbed the widespread blatant minority abuses of the 1990s are due to FCSM's initiatives.

In 1998, FCSM established quarterly filing requirements for issuers and developed the format of the quarterly report, which is now the main mandatory disclosure document for public companies. In 2001, the regulator initiated the mandatory registration of depositary receipt issuances by Russian companies, which prevented companies' management from using discretionary proxy voting (e.g., using the votes of ADR holders who had not provided proxy-voting instructions). Finally, FCSM supervised the development of the Code of Corporate Governance (the code), which was issued in 2002. Based on international best governance practices, the code includes recommendations across a variety of areas, including independent directors (no less than one-fourth of the board and no fewer than three individuals), board committees and their composition (audit, compensation, and nominating committees should include only independent directors), shareholder meetings, the independence of share registrars, internal controls, and public disclosure. FCSM recommended the code to all public companies, yet compliance has been largely voluntary.

Other codes and guidelines issued in Russia, such as the White Paper on Corporate Governance in Russia issued by the OECD and the Corporate Governance Manual for companies issued by the International Financial Corporation (IFC) have no legal or regulatory standing. Stock exchanges require that all companies listed on their top markets comply with certain provisions of the code and report on their compliance quarterly. The Russian trading system (RTS) and the Moscow Interbank Currency Exchange require compliance with a range of code provisions (including the minimum requirement of three independent directors) for companies listed on the top-tier A1 and A2 quotation lists. There are weaker requirements, for example, only one independent director, for companies listed on lower markets and for issuers of debt only. Although the code does not require preparation of financial statements in accordance with IFRS, A1 and A2 listings on the exchange do. However, in December 2008, there were only 26 Russian companies listed in the top markets to which these rules applied. With growing domestic investment potential, more companies could be motivated to upgrade their listing status on domestic exchanges and become bound by the code's provisions, yet progress has been slow to date. In fact, foreign regulations associated with listings on the U.S. and U.K. exchanges have so far had a greater impact on governance practices of public Russian companies than have the domestic regulatory initiatives. Depositary receipts on shares of five Russian companies are listed currently on the NYSE, one company is listed on the Nasdaq, and 54 have floated depositary receipts on the LSE [including those on the Alternative Investment Market (AIM).

In practice, the influence of the code on Russian corporate governance has been limited because of its voluntary nature and its only partial application to listed firms. Other regulatory weaknesses in the Russian context have to do with the questionable effectiveness of demands for board independence. The criteria for determining independence are in practice highly formal and do not take into account real-life conflicts of interest. To take the most common example, boards of directors at government-controlled firms often include directors who are executives at other state-controlled companies. These executives depend heavily on the government for almost all their activities, yet they technically meet the code's requirements for independence. The same flaw exists in the rules for the independence of share registrars, who in most cases are indirectly affiliated with the controlling shareholder, and in the rules for the independence of internal auditors. Those weaknesses cast doubt on the effectiveness of regulatory oversight in other areas, such as the rules addressing insider trading.

The Bank of Russia mandates parallel governance requirements for banks, and listed banks must meet the requirements of both regulators. Thus, the Bank of Russia imposes additional requirements on the financial disclosure and risk management practices of banks. The disclosure requirements of the Bank of Russia are generally considered burdensome, as they typically exceed 140 filings per month, and most of those filings, including those on beneficial ownership, are kept confidential. Also, there is no requirement to issue IFRS accounts, although the bank imposes quasi-IFRS reporting standards.

Informational Infrastructure

The transparency of Russian public companies is generally on the rise, yet domestic regulation cannot be credited for this progress. Legal and regulatory shortfalls and obsolete national accounting standards have led to significant variability in disclosure performance by Russian companies. Although there are positive exceptions, improvements in transparency generally are associated with cross-border placements of public debt or equity. A significant share of the Russian economy is not involved in international financing transactions and therefore remains in relative obscurity.

According to the series of annual Transparency & Disclosure Surveys of Russian companies conducted by Standard & Poor's since 2002 (see Appendix A, page 245), the average transparency of public companies generally is improving. Our Transparency & Disclosure Index, based on the average disclosure performance of the largest public Russian companies, rose from 34% in 2002 to 56% in 2008, and its coverage increased from 42 to 90 companies, mainly as a result of the previously mentioned IPO activity. This progress is far from universal, however, and generally is due to market stimuli or international listing requirements. The range of disclosure levels by individual companies remains wide, and even among large public companies, a significant share (26.7%) provide low to very low levels of disclosure by international comparison (less than 50% of the disclosure items in our checklist). Significant variability in disclosure levels between individual companies reflects the fact that some companies seek to match the disclosure standards of leading international peers whereas others simply meet the minimum mandated requirements, which remain fairly weak.

Domestic Disclosure Requirements

The weakness of domestic disclosure regulation results partly from the drawbacks of the Russian Accounting Standards and their enforcement, which reduce the value of these accounts to investors. Thus, the nominally required consolidation of subsidiaries seldom is performed in practice, since tax authorities do not recognize consolidated taxpayers and require only stand-alone financials. Indeed, RAS rules primarily apply as a basis for corporate taxation, which creates incentives for management to reduce results systematically rather than accurately reflect corporate performance. RAS also materially differ from IFRS across a number of accounting principles, including business combinations, revenue recognition, valuation of fixed assets, inventory, pension liabilities, and reserves. The accounting of related-party transactions is based on the narrow definition of related parties under the antitrust law and does not mandate the disclosure of beneficial ownership. Furthermore, interim reports do not present cash flow statements, and profit and loss statements in the interim reports are presented in an abbreviated format.

FSFM requires all issuers of public debt to make quarterly filings with a specific structure. These reports must provide information on a company's governance structure, including board composition and board remuneration; affiliates, including equity positions of 5% or more; business descriptions, including key business lines, risks, major corporate actions, branches, and the number of employees; and shareholder and equity information with identification of authorized capital, outstanding shares, registrar, depositary, and auditors. Financial information includes RAS accounts accompanied by a description of liabilities (with notification of contingent ones), breakdowns of sales and costs by type of operation, breakdowns of accounts payable and receivable, and lists of related-party transactions as defined under Russian law. Companies must present such reports within 45 days after the end of the quarter. In addition, public companies are required to inform the FSFM of any major developments and changes in a company's structure within five days after the event and to disclose information about essential facts in the form of media releases within one day of a change or development.

Filings to the FSFM are in a sense not fully public, as they can be very difficult to locate when not available from the filers' Web sites. The main informational FSFM resource is www.disclosure.fcsm.ru, which contains quarterly reports and information about the major corporate actions of all issuers of public equity or debt. The Web site, however, is updated irregularly and usually does not contain recent filings.

Despite the multiple drawbacks of national accounting standards and their enforcement, India, Brazil, and China are moving toward IFRS much faster than Russia is. In 2007, China moved to accounting standards that are quite close to IFRS. Brazil and India use their own domestic standards, but those standards in general reflect the true economic activity of firms much better than Russian standards do. Russia's plans for adopting IFRS are vague. Brazil and India are preparing to move to IFRS in 2010 and 2011, respectively. A project initiated by Technical Aid to the Commonwealth of Independent States (TACIS), the technical aid program of the European Union, proposes to bring Russian accounting standards slowly closer to IFRS and at the same time require IFRS for an ever-widening circle of companies, based on assets and amount of public float.

Pressures from Financial Markets Drive Progress

Even in the absence of requirements, most large companies have been producing IFRS or U.S. GAAP statements to improve their access to capital. According to our 2008 Transparency & Disclosure Survey, 82% of large public companies released their audited IFRS or U.S. GAAP accounts for 2007 by mid-August 2008. This compares with 52% of such companies in 2004 and 36% in 2002. Even among companies not involved in the international markets, IFRS accounting is gaining ground, since banks often require IFRS reports as a condition for opening credit lines and especially for providing syndicated loans. Although most banks are not listed, IFRS reporting is common among the larger banks and banks involved in international operations. However, at smaller companies and banks, IFRS accounts are not prepared or not disclosed.

Most large companies employ major international audit firms, and this strengthens the audit process, although the independence rules mandated in developed countries are not always followed. Because of a chronic shortage of qualified in-house finance staff and in the absence of law or regulation requiring otherwise, many companies hire their external auditors to consult on the preparation of IFRS/U.S. GAAP accounts, and this can present a conflict of interest for the auditors. Most companies do not disclose the volume of consulting services, and this can raise questions about an auditor's independence. This situation is exacerbated when the auditor has multiple contracts with subsidiary companies at a larger holding company.

Independent audit committees remain a rarity, creating risks of breaching the integrity of the audit process. Government-controlled companies are particularly reluctant to yield control over the audit process to independent board members. This weakens auditor selection and supervision procedures and does not allow the internal audit to be independent from management and significant shareholders. Because of an explosion in demand for audit specialists, competent internal audit staff is in short supply in the marketplace; this has complicated the development of strong internal procedures at companies that intend to create them.

Chapter 3

Corporate Governance Is Growing Modestly in India

Preeti S. Manerkar

Introduction and Executive Summary

Corporate Scandal and Global Recession Spark Reforms

Corporate governance and economic development are intrinsically linked, particularly as the world economy struggles for equilibrium while volatile markets and trade dynamics lead to job and investment stresses. Before the global recession, the scale and distribution of wealth had increased dramatically in India. Liberalization of the economy in 1991 and the move toward globalization sparked the growth of a strong investor culture. At the same time, concerns over scandals have led to wide-ranging changes in legislation and regulations, resulting in a positive transformation of the corporate sector and the governance landscape. Despite these advances, there are substantial areas that are far from reaching the international best practices level.

Perhaps the single most important development in the field of governance and investor protection in India has been the creation of the Securities and Exchange Board of India (SEBI) in 1992 and its gradual and growing empowerment. Established with a mandate to regulate and monitor stock trading as well as to protect investors and improve transparency in the securities market, SEBI has played a crucial role in shaping the basic minimum ground rules of corporate conduct in that country.

The launch of the National Stock Exchange (NSE) in 1994 provided further impetus to capital market transparency as well as significant competition for the Bombay Stock Exchange (BSE) by introducing an electronic trading platform in 1995 to overcome the agency conflicts often associated with the broker-owned BSE. Internet-based trading also made an appearance in India. Healthy competition between the two exchanges produced higher transaction volume and led to improvements in the technology for processing both trading and settlements. That opened the securities market to the nation's geographically dispersed population, fueling increased participation by institutional and retail investors.

However, serious concerns about corporate governance in India were triggered by three major scandals spanning more than 17 years. Each was considered the biggest corporate scandal of its time and involved businesspeople accused of artificially manipulating vast amounts of shares and bank loans or inflating earnings and assets: Harshad Mehta, Ketan Parekh, and Ramalinga Raju. Raju was a cofounder of Satyam Computer Services (the company was subsequently renamed Mahindra Satyam), a leading Indian outsourcing firm that served more than a third of the Fortune 500 companies.

India's biggest stock fraud at the time, linked to Harshad Mehta, surfaced in 1992. It concluded around 2001 when a SEBI action charged him with colluding with the management of BPL, Sterlite, and Videocon to ramp up the prices of their shares. The next big scandal during the dot-com explosion of 2000–2001 involved Ketan Parekh. Parekh targeted the shares of 10 companies for his dealings (now known infamously as the K–10 scrips) and colluded with promoters. However, he ran head-on into the so-called Bear Cartel traders (Shankar Sharma, Anand Rathi, and Nirmal Bang), who dumped sell orders on the K–10 stocks and crushed the inflated prices. Parekh's chief lenders, the Global Trust Bank and the Madhavpura Mercantile Co-operative Bank, failed. SEBI found prima facie evidence of price rigging in the scrips of Global Trust Bank, Zee Telefilms, HFCL, Lupin Laboratories, Aftek Infosys, and Padmini Polymer. That pushed SEBI to impose a ban on short selling.

The latest shock to the markets came in January 2009 and involved Satyam and its cofounder. Raju resigned as chairman after admitting that 50.4 billion rupees (INR), or U.S.$1.04 billion, of the INR53.6 billion in cash and bank loans the company listed as assets for its second quarter were nonexistent. In a letter to the directors that was distributed by the Bombay Stock Exchange, he said that the revenue for the quarter was 20% lower than the INR27 billion reported and that the company's operating margin was a fraction of what it had declared.

There were also smaller-scale incidents with businesses allotting deeply discounted shares to their promoters and fly-by-night companies that disappeared with investors' money. However, this latest scandal became the focus of all the country's regulatory agencies, including the Reserve Bank of India, SEBI, and the Institute of Chartered Accountants of India. They considered one possible regulatory outcome: requiring the founders of companies to disclose shares pledged in return for loans.

These concerns about corporate governance and a push for more open competition and globalization gave rise to an overhaul of the regulatory system. In 2001–2002, some accounting standards were modified to require more disclosure of related-party transactions, segment income (revenue, profit, and capital employed), deferred tax liabilities or assets, and consolidation of accounts. These reforms caused extensive changes in the Indian capital market and its governance landscape. Against this backdrop, corporate governance is now at the top of the government's agenda, and we have observed significant progress on the governance front. For example, shareholders, institutional investors, lenders, and other stakeholders in Indian corporations now demand more information about the capability and integrity of boards and managers.

Despite the recent volatility amid what some economists consider the world's worst financial crisis since the 1930s, the last couple of years produced a dramatic increase in the scale and distribution of wealth in India. Buoyant financial markets, the process of globalization, and greater accessibility to investment tools strengthened investor culture in India and some of its Asia Pacific neighbors. The rapid growth and spectacular returns from local equity and property markets in recent years attracted new investors, some of them quite inexperienced. Failure to diversify assets became a common characteristic, but analysts expect investor education to bring about improvements. Further, because investor well-being and protection are at the core of the SEBI ideology, its balancing act of imposing restrictions and then relaxing them has been well received by corporate leaders and investors.

Reeling from the global stock market sell-off and plunging stocks of even fundamentally strong blue chip companies, SEBI recently relaxed the Takeover Code, its 1997 Substantial Acquisition of Shares and Takeovers Regulations. That extended the so-called creeping acquisition limit from 55% to 75% in listed companies to facilitate promoter consolidation and increase investor confidence in such companies.

SEBI's efforts are likely to be received favorably by promoters and be seen as an opportunity to consolidate and/or increase their shareholding in the target companies without triggering the complex and more expensive public announcement requirements. Although SEBI intends to promote consolidation of promoter shareholding, it has tried to ensure that retail investors can participate in that consolidation by subjecting the creeping acquisition (under the automatic route) to only open market purchases in the normal market segment and excluding consolidation via negotiated deals or preferential allotment.

SEBI's move is aimed at helping prevent irrational movements of stock prices and reinforcing promoters' faith and confidence in the battered shares of their companies. In the current circumstances, the market appears to be driven more by symbolic and psychological reasons than by fundamentals, further consolidation by promoters would be expected to help the sliding market and companies shore up investors' confidence and sentiment. On the flip side, there could be apprehensions that promoters will get unrestricted leverage to gain a special majority (75% shareholding) over the target by acquiring less than 5% of shares of the target each financial year without providing an exit opportunity through an open offer to all the shareholders. Lack of liquidity in the market may hinder SEBI's efforts to garner the requisite investor interest.

Overall, publicly traded Indian companies must, by law, follow fairly strict standards of governance and disclosure. The standards are far stronger than those in all other Asian nations. Regulators and companies have adopted some of the best international practices, including good quarterly reporting standards, which have improved the availability of timely information.

However, to reach consistent global best practices levels, India's capital markets need to build on these advances and improve governance standards in many areas through voluntary compliance and self-regulation. Potential areas of improvement include the role of dominant shareholders, the composition and functioning of boards of directors, increased shareholder activism, controls on self-dealing, and regard for minority shareholder rights.

Market Infrastructure

India's Market Infrastructure Has Become More Market-Oriented

The large role of the state and the legacy of the historically closed economy still can be felt. Corporate ownership generally is concentrated in the hands of promoters or family-owned conglomerates, which obtain a great deal of power.

Domestic investors are not generally active in pressing for greater shareholder rights, and there is relatively limited ownership by foreign institutional investors (FIIs). In general, minority shareholders and financial markets have limited influence on the governance practices of public companies. The reason for this is partly the absence of active minority shareholders and partly a result of the large shareholding concentrations by families and other closely knit groups that in great measure prevent market-driven changes in control.

General Stages of Economic Development

The State Loosens Some Controls, but Privatization Still Lags

India followed a socialist-based approach for most of its first four decades of independence, with strict government control over private sector participation, foreign trade, and foreign direct investment. Its economy and financial markets underwent radical changes in the early 1990s, largely in response to the country's economic crisis in the late 1980s. India gradually opened its markets by reducing government controls on foreign trade and investment. Still, the privatization of publicly owned enterprises and the opening of certain sectors to private and foreign interests have proceeded slowly amid strong political debate. However, we consider that India's weak integration with external economies and the comparatively late onset of reforms helped keep the economy largely isolated from the 1997 Asian financial crisis.

Even now, we view the relatively calibrated pace of reforms, including going slow on full capital account convertibility, as a reason why the Indian economy was somewhat sheltered at the start of the global economic downturn. However, in March 2009, an economic outlook analysis by CRISIL, the Mumbai-based affiliate of Standard & Poor's (S&P), stated that although domestic demand should shore up the economy, there was only a remote chance that India would emerge unscathed. The country's economy had not come to a standstill, but its growth clearly was slowing as the dramatic changes in the macroeconomic environment took their toll. We expect that domestic demand (though slowing) and India's high savings will continue to play a key role in financing the country's growth.

India is the world's second most populous nation, with its population of 1.1 billion trailing only that of China. Its fast population growth has been a double-edged sword that is likely to challenge already strained infrastructure and struggling health and education systems yet also create a dynamically youthful demographic profile. Its dependency ratio of children and the elderly to income earners was predicted to drop from the current 60 to 48 by 2025, providing a rapidly growing labor force and a rapidly expanding consumer base. Most of the workforce still earns its livelihood directly or indirectly through agriculture and manufacturing. However, in the last 20 years, high-tech services have surged as the large number of young workers, educated and fluent in English, has provided a "back office" base for global outsourcing of customer services and technical support.

The Internet has created another export: highly skilled workers in software and financial services and software engineering. Other sectors, such as manufacturing, pharmaceuticals, biotechnology, nanotechnology, telecommunication, tourism, and retailing, are showing strong potential with higher growth rates. At the same time, the nation faces demands for the reduction of economic and social inequality in a newly liberated populace freed from historical castes and discrimination. Poverty remains a serious problem, although it has declined significantly since independence.

Ownership Structure

Dominant Shareholders Pose Governance Problems

Essentially, there are three large ownership categories in India. The first consists of the public sector units (PSUs), in which the government is the dominant and/or majority shareholder and the general public holds a minority stake, often as little as 20%. The second consists of the multinational companies (MNCs), in which the foreign parent is the dominant (in most cases majority) shareholder. The third consists of the Indian business groups, in which the promoters (together with their friends and relatives) are the dominant share-holders with large minority stakes, the government-owned financial institutions hold a comparable stake, and the balance is held by the general public. Most Indian companies today are a hybrid of family-owned and publicly listed companies in which ownership and management usually are not segregated. This gives rise to informality in governance policies and inadequate controls. Most corporations fall short of having an established succession plan.

As in other emerging markets, there is considerable work ahead to improve corporate governance practices, particularly regarding the constitution and functioning of boards of directors, self-dealing, regard for minority shareholder rights, and transparency and disclosure.

For example, among 50 of India's largest public companies on its Nifty Index, only 2 have a dispersed ownership structure, according to 2007 research by CRISIL. Deutsche Bank research shows that 54% of large Indian companies are controlled by a single family, 16% are majority-owned by foreign investors, and 20% are controlled by the state. In most cases, this control is maintained with as little as 12 to 20% of the voting shares, which in theory should make it possible to have a market for corporate control. In reality, however, there has not been a single hostile takeover since that practice was legalized in 1997.

The governance problems posed by the dominant shareholders in these three categories of companies are slightly different, and governance troubles connected to the predominant form of family owner-ship historically have run the gamut of issues from unprofessional management to direct abuse of minority shareholder rights via related-party transactions on nonmarket terms.

In Indian business groups, the concept of dominant shareholders is more amorphous for two reasons. First, the promoters' shareholding is spread across several friends and relatives as well as corporate entities; this often makes it difficult to establish the total effective holding of a group. The actual ownership within these companies is far from completely transparent, with widespread pyramiding, cross-holding, and the use of nonpublic trusts and private companies for owning shares in group companies. Second, the aggregate holding of all these entities taken together is typically well below a majority stake. In many cases, the promoter may not even be the largest single shareholder. What makes the promoters the dominant shareholders is the fact that a large proportion of the shareholding is with state-owned financial institutions that historically have played a passive role, and so the promoters are effectively dominant shareholders and are able to get legislative approval for their actions. This remains a governance challenge.

Financial Markets

Economic Growth Slows, but Strong Banking Sector Still Meets Credit Needs

In less than two decades India has transformed itself from a slowly developing agrarian country into one of the world's most dynamic economies. Its gross domestic product (GDP) has grown an average of more than 8% annually over the last three years, making it the second fastest growing major economy in the world. In reviewing the global financial crisis, however, CRISIL estimated that India's economic growth would slow down to 6.0% in 2009 from 7.4% in 2008. Industrial growth was expected to remain subdued. Services expansion also was expected to moderate but still continue to be the main growth engine. The agriculture sector was expected to show marginal growth. The outflow of FII funds and the dollar demand from Indian oil companies in the open market was predicted to increase depreciation pressure on the rupee.

Banking Industry

India has a well-functioning banking sector that has been meeting the credit needs of corporations and retail individuals. Currently, banking in India is generally mature in terms of supply, product range, and reach, though rural areas still present a significant challenge for private and foreign banks. Since liberalization, the government has established significant banking protections relating to nationalization of banks and other reforms that have opened the banking and insurance sectors to private and foreign players. The Indian financial system and Indian banks in particular were left comparatively untroubled by the crisis, primarily because of their limited exposure to U.S.-mortgage-backed securities. Further, the banking sector has benefited from government support and strong capitalization. These factors mitigated the profitability pressures caused by higher funding costs and mark-to-market requirements on investment portfolios and asset quality pressures resulting from a slowing economy.

Reserve Bank of India (RBI) statistics indicate that the country had 82 commercial banks (SCBs), excluding the Regional Rural Banks (RRBs), in 2006–2007. There were 28 public sector banks (in which the government holds a stake), including the largest SCB, the State Bank of India, and together they hold 73.4% of the total banking business. In addition, 25 private banks (which have no government stake and may be publicly listed and traded on stock exchanges) account for 20.7% of total business; 29 foreign banks have the smallest share at 5.9% of total business. The 82 banks have a combined network of over 59,000 branches.

Prudential Norms

There has been a marked shift from hands-on government control to market forces as the dominant instrument of corporate governance in Indian banks. Competition has been encouraged by the issuance of licenses to new private banks and by the granting of more power and flexibility to bank managers both in directing credit and in setting prices. The RBI has moved to a model of governance by prudential norms rather than direct interference, even allowing debate about the appropriateness of specific regulations among banks.

Regulation of Banks

The market orientation of governance in banking has been accompanied by stronger disclosure norms and greater attention to periodic RBI surveillance. Since 1994, the Board for Financial Supervision (BFS) has inspected and monitored banks by using the CAMELS (Capital adequacy, Asset quality, Management, Earnings, Liquidity, and Systems and controls) approach. Audit committees in banks have been stipulated since 1995. Greater independence of public sector banks has also been a key feature of the reforms. Nominee directors from the government and the RBI are being phased out gradually, with an emphasis on boards being elected rather than appointed from above. Corporate governance in cooperative banks and non-banking financial companies (NBFCs) perhaps needs the greatest attention from regulators. Rural cooperative banks frequently are run by politically powerful families as their personal fiefdoms, with little professional involvement and considerable channeling of credit to family businesses.

DRTs and the SARFAESI Act

The institution of Debt Recovery Tribunals (DRTs) in the early1990s and the passage of the Securitization and Reconstruction of Financial Assets and Enforcement of Security Interest (SARFAESI) Act in 2002 were aimed at speeding up the judicial process for handling financial disputes and crimes. The SARFAESI Act paved the way for establishing Asset Reconstruction Companies (ARCs) that can take nonperforming assets (NPAs) off the balance sheets of banks and recover them. The act also allows banks and financial institutions to seize directly the assets of a borrower who defaults and fails to respond within 60 days of a notice. The SARFAESI Act by itself, however, does not provide a final solution to debt recovery problems. With the borrower's right to appeal to the

DRT, the DRAT (Debt Recovery Appellate Tribunal), and in some cases even a high court, a case can take three to four years to conclude, during which time the seized assets are frozen and cannot be sold. Regardless, several banks have had notable success in recovering loans and the recovery rate of bad debts registered a sharp rise in 2005–2006 and afterward.

Development of Equity Markets

As in the other large and successful emerging markets, the stock market has been a major source of wealth creation in India. The two main stock exchanges, the NSE (established in 1994) and the BSE (Asia's oldest stock exchange, formed in 1875), have among the highest number of trades in the world. The NSE is a limited liability company owned by public sector financial institutions and now accounts for about two-thirds of stock trading in India as well as nearly all derivatives trading.

Equity investment through the IPO or the secondary market route is growing rapidly. The capitalization of the domestic stock market has increased by approximately 30% in the last two years and reached INR51.4 trillion (U.S.$1.332 trillion) in March 2008. At the same time, there has been a dramatic increase in the amount of money raised through IPOs. In the last two years, there have been 173 IPOs in India that have raised some INR2.1 trillion (U.S.$51.8 billion). The result has been superlative returns from equity investment. The continuing turmoil in global financial markets was somewhat muted in the Indian market. Indian equity indexes have mirrored global sentiments, but few financial institutions have been required to make provisions for potential losses caused by credit exposure to foreign financial institutions; fewer still have reported major losses. Since local capital markets are developing and domestic investors are more eager to participate, investor education must remain a priority to ensure that newcomers can build appropriate investments and portfolios.

The relatively young SEBI has a rigorous regulatory regime to ensure fairness, transparency, and good practices. Most important, the governance landscape has been changing rapidly in the last decade, particularly with the enactment of Sarbanes-Oxley-type measures and legal changes to improve the enforceability of creditors' rights. In 2005, SEBI discovered a multiple dematerialization (demat) account scam in the IPO of Infrastructure Development Finance Company (IDFC), raising alarming questions about the oversight of demat accounts, which are used by millions of investors. The SEBI probe showed that about 8.29% of the retail portion of the IDFC IPO, amounting to 11.7 million shares, was received by fictitious applicants who operated multiple demat accounts. Roopalben Panchal, along with associates and other entities, cornered large chunks of IDFC shares by opening about 47,000 fictitious accounts, which were opened with Karvy, the depositary participant. The swindle raised issues concerning oversight of demat accounts to prevent their misuse and the role of depositary participants such as Karvy and the merchant bankers. The regulator examined the role of Bharat Overseas Bank, HDFC Bank, Indian Overseas Bank, ING Vysya Bank, and Vijaya Bank in opening the bank accounts of those entities and apparently funding their IPO applications in the case of IDFC. IDFC's IPO hit the market in July 2005, and the retail portion of the issue was oversubscribed by 5.27 times and the noninstitutional portion was oversubscribed by 56.53 times. SEBI barred more than 40 players from buying or selling shares in the market and directed them not to apply for any forthcoming IPOs.

The recent know your customer (KYC) guidelines are aimed at curbing the operations of name lenders, or nongenuine persons who have common addresses. These standards have become the international benchmark for framing anti-money-laundering efforts and combating financing of terrorism policies by the regulatory authorities. Compliance with these standards is compulsory for banks, financial institutions, and NBFCs in India and has become necessary for international financial relationships. KYC guidelines advise following a certain customer identification procedure [Permanent Account

Number (PAN) Card] for the opening of accounts and monitoring transactions of a suspicious nature for the purpose of reporting them to the appropriate authority.

In August 2008, SEBI unveiled operational reforms designed to reduce risks for both investors and issuers. It changed the pricing norms for qualified institutional placements (QIPs) and preferential allotments and collapsed the timeline for rights issues from 109 days to 43 days. SEBI also amended Clause 41 of the Listing Agreement to give companies more time—from one month to two—to declare consolidated results. In addition, it has telescoped the timeline for mutual funds to declare annual results from six months to four.

An analysis shows that in some cases SEBI's regulations need stronger enforcement penalties. For example, SEBI's decision in October 2008 to remove restrictions on issues of participatory notes (P-notes) by FIIs is expected to have only a cosmetic impact on the flow of foreign funds. In October 2007, the regulator banned FIIs from issuing P-notes with underlying derivatives and imposed a 40% limit on P-notes assets. However, few FIIs even approached the limits. Those FIIs which exceeded the 40% limit found waivers and kept their higher levels. That meant that the five to seven FIIs that accounted for the bulk of that market remained untouched. Also, no changes have been made in the norms of registration and regulation required of foreign funds or to the KYC norms to be maintained by them with respect to their subaccounts.

Listing on Global Exchanges

Perhaps a dozen Indian companies currently are listed on the premier stock exchanges, the New York Stock Exchange (NYSE) and Nasdaq. Only one Indian company, Infosys Technologies Limited, has secured a spot on Nasdaq's Global Select Market. Although the pipeline of Indian companies waiting to be listed on these global exchanges remains strong, many more are far from meeting such standards.

Private Equity Market

The global credit crunch may bring better business for private equity interests. Many firms recently have deferred share issues, suffering after years of ambitious expansion plans that had been bolstered by plentiful cash and an environment of low interest rates. Therefore, Indian firms are likely to tap private equity (PE) as markets and economies deteriorate further, limiting firms' ability to raise funds for expansion. The progressive liberalization of the foreign investment environment has provided a major boost to PE and venture capital investments in Indian companies. With the advent of more sophisticated players in the PE and venture capital arena, the deal terms, including standards of governance, are growing more complicated and sophisticated.

Domestic Debt Market

The Indian debt market consists of two segments—government securities (G-Secs) and corporate debt—with corporate debt amounting to about 14% of the total debt market. This is reflective of both the relatively high recurrent fiscal deficit and the underdeveloped status of the corporate debt market. Reforms in the G-Secs market were undertaken as a part of the overall structural reform process that was initiated in 1991–1992. The early reform initiatives were intended to create an enabling policy environment; the second phase of reforms was directed toward institutional development to enhance market activity, settlement, and safety; and the third phase is aimed at enhancing liquidity and efficiency. In addition, several recent initiatives have been taken to widen the investor base from the traditional framework in which commercial banks and insurance companies have been the largest holders of G-Secs, generally as statutory investments.

Further, the entry of mutual funds and NBFCs has broadened the investor base. FIIs are allowed to invest in the Indian debt market subject to quantitative limits that are reviewed on an ongoing basis and amount on average to several U.S.$ billions.

Other Institutional and Cultural Factors: Mature Nongovernmental Organizations and Shareholder Activists Can Make a Difference

Role of Nongovernmental Organizations

Nongovernmental organizations (NGOs) have joined the public and private sectors as partners in the development process. More than a million NGOs operate in India, covering all the development sectors, but their impact in terms of final outcomes has been marginal. Only a handful of NGOs, and only in a few sectors, have had a significant influence on the development process. Civil society groups also need to play a greater role in bringing about a change in the corporate governance scenario, including bolstering the NGO movement.

Lack of Shareholder Activism

Shareholder activism has had little impact in India. The markets are young, and there are few active long-term investors such as pension funds that take a five- to seven-year view of companies. Most investors are focused on short-term gains. Even private equity investors are relative newcomers. In addition, there is a history of limited institutional ownership, with promoters and the government holding majority stakes in most cases, followed by retail investors and then by institutions. Another reason for shareholder indifference could stem from the multiple layers of regulatory bodies. Wavering faith in the system itself, the high costs involved, practical problems such as a widespread shareholder base, and the manipulative practices of many promoters make it difficult for shareholder activists to survive.

We believe the situation is changing gradually, however, and we are seeing shareholders taking a more active role. India has an Investor Education and Protection Fund (IEPF) that was established under Section 205C of the Companies Act of 1956 and the Companies

(Amendment) Act of 1999 to promote investors' awareness and protect the interests of investors for trades executed on the NSE. The IEPF is maintained by the NSE to process investor claims that may arise from failure to settle obligations for traders on NSE transactions. The IEPF also is used to settle claims of investors whose trading member has been declared a defaulter or expelled. The maximum amount of the claim payable from the IEPF to the investor is INR1 million (U.S.$21,390).

Legal Infrastructure

Background of Legal System and Legal Tradition

India's legal infrastructure regarding corporate governance provides some of the best investor protection in the world. It is closer to the common law traditions of the United Kingdom than to the continental civil law that served as a model for the other three BRIC countries. However, the legislative process can be exceptionally slow.

India's Department of Justice reports that over 3 million cases, both criminal and civil, were pending in the nation's 21 high courts and that a backlog eight times larger (26.3 million cases) was pending in subordinate courts nationwide as of May 2007. Indian law permits three types of companies—companies limited by shares, companies limited by guarantees, and companies with unlimited liability—but only limited share companies can be traded publicly. Many government organizations that operate in the infrastructure sector, such as the railways, postal systems, electric utilities, public works departments (PWDs), and ports, are all economically significant but are run as quasi-governmental departments.

The legal infrastructure defines minority shareholders' rights rather narrowly, largely referring to the way shareholders elect boards of directors at listed companies (the law recognizes only majority voting for directors) and describing board tenure. Directors may serve for up to five years before reelection. Board membership may be permitted for representatives of nominee shareholders, who may not have fiduciary responsibilities to the ultimate owners. On the positive side, Indian law restricts the board membership of those in management at listed firms to just one-third of all seats and requires boards to maintain audit committees with a majority of outside directors. It also sharply defines shareholders' financial rights. Corporate law prescribes a three-year prison sentence for executives found guilty of nonpayment of dividends if more than one month has passed since the dividend announcement.

Principal Legal Provisions

The Companies Act

The most important legislation governing corporate India is the Companies Act, which regulates most aspects of a public limited company, including incorporation, formation of the board of directors, and a company's share capital. The act was introduced to Parliament in 1956 and substantially updated in 1997, 2000, 2004, and 2006 through a series of amendments. The latest bill, in 2008, sought a comprehensive revision of the Companies Act. The biggest change is expected in the relaxation of the requirement for independent directors, reducing the strength of independent members of the board to 33% from the earlier requirement of 50%. Meanwhile, as a result of increased incidents of insider trading, the bill is harsh about the operations style of company officials. It has proposed that if any official at the level of chief executive officer (CEO), chief financial officer (CFO), or company secretary takes part in insider trading, that official will be criminally liable. The financial penalties levied on such officials will be treated separately from the company. The bill also has proposed streamlining the merger and acquisition process by having a single forum for the approval of such transactions.

One of the most important proposals in the bill involves the vested power given to the government to make amendments to the

Companies Act in the future through notification rather than by act of Parliament. In terms of legal overlaps in a company's operations, it is clearly proposed that the Company Law be applicable to all companies but that any sectoral binding such as the SEBI Act is applicable to all listed companies in the matter of the issuance and trading of shares, dividends, and the like, and it has an overriding power over the Company Act in that regard. In addition, the Company Bill includes proposals for more checks on not-for-profit firms, and mandatory consolidation of subsidiary companies with holding companies, among other provisions.

Laws Related to Corporate Governance Practice

The initiative has been developed by an industry association, the Confederation of Indian Industry (CII). One of the first endeavors was the CII Code for Desirable Corporate Governance, which was drawn up in a committee chaired by Rahul Bajaj, a prominent Indian businessman. The committee was formed in 1996 and submitted its code in April 1998.

After the CII's initiative, SEBI named two committees to examine its plans, the first led by Kumar Mangalam Birla, chairman of the Aditya Birla Group, and the second by N. R. Narayana Murthy, a chief architect of Indian information technology (IT) outsourcing successes and the current nonexecutive chairman and chief mentor of Infosys. The first committee submitted its report, the Birla Code, in early 2000.

In 2004, the code was updated under the chairmanship of Murthy, and the new version of the clause came into effect in 2006, with the revisions to the independence of the chair and the proportion of independent directors. These committees have brought far-reaching changes in governance and have provided the basis for Clause 49 of the Listing Agreement, with mandatory rules for all listed companies in India. The Birla Committee recommendations, patterned in part on the United Kingdom's 1992 Cadbury Report, led India to adopt the key planks of an "international best practice" code. Similar to the United Kingdom and the United States, the Indian regulations focus on the role of the board as the bridge between owners and management. The committee recommendations leading to Clause 49 suggest that in India the influence of concentrated and controlling shareholders is much greater. Thus, the presence of a majority of independent directors on the board as suggested by the amended Clause 49 is intended to moderate that influence.

Concurrent with these initiatives by SEBI, the Department of Company Affairs (DCA) and the Ministry of Finance (MoF) of the Government of India (GoI) also began contemplating improvements in governance standards. Those efforts included the establishment of a study group to implement the Birla Code in 2000, the Naresh Chandra Committee on Corporate Audit and Governance in 2002, and the Expert Committee on Corporate Law (J. J. Irani Committee) in late 2004. All those efforts were aimed at reforming the existing Companies Act of 1956, the backbone of corporate law in India, to incorporate specific governance provisions regarding independent directors and audit committees.

Regulatory Framework

The Securities and Exchange Board of India

SEBI regulates the securities market. It was created by the government in 1988 and given its statutory form by Parliament through the SEBI Act in 1992 to replace a fragmented regulatory framework that made regulatory supervision and enforcement difficult and ineffective. SEBI's framework provides for investor safeguards through disclosure requirements and accounting standards, arbitration procedures, and the establishment of a small investors' protection fund. It also promulgates rules against insider trading and other market abuses. SEBI is responsive to the needs of the three groups that constitute the market: issuers of securities, investors, and market intermediaries.

The SEBI has three umbrella functions:

1. Drafting regulations in its legislative capacity
2. Conducting investigation and enforcement actions in its executive function
3. Passing rulings and orders in its judicial capacity

It wields considerable power but lacks an appeals process to establish accountability. There is a Securities Appellate Tribunal with three members, and a second appeal goes directly to the Supreme Court. SEBI has had success regulating the capital markets by pushing systemic reforms aggressively. It has been active in setting up regulations to meet legislative measures for insider trading, takeovers, mergers and acquisitions, and disclosure of information. Most recently, SEBI has introduced a formal requirement to disclose compliance with a governance code of best practice.

Ministry of Finance

The MoF reports directly to Parliament and has broad powers within the government, including taxation, financial legislation and reforms, and oversight of financial institutions, capital and financial markets, center and state finances, and the Union Budget. The MoF does not interfere directly in the business and financial markets, but it has an intense, if indirect, influence on the RBI and SEBI because the minister's portfolio is central to the nation's overall economic health.

Department of Company Affairs

The DCA operating under the MoF is primarily responsible for the task of proper governing and diligent functioning of the corporate sector through administration of the Companies Act. It also provides an appeal mechanism for grievances by investors, creditors, and others.

Registrar of Companies

The Registrar of Companies (RoC) has the primary duty of register-ing companies floated in the respective states and the union territo-ries and ensuring compliance with statutory requirements under the Companies Act. It is also responsible for collecting and making avail-able information on those companies, including annual accounts, annual reports, and interim reports. The agency has transferred nearly 50 million pages of legacy records such as permanent documents of companies, annual returns, and balance sheets for the two preceding years into an electronic registry so that stakeholders can access the information online for a fee.

Company Law Board

The central government established an independent Company Law Board (CLB) on May 31, 1991, as a quasi-judicial body that exercises some of the judicial and quasi-judicial powers that earlier were exer-cised by the High Court or the central government. The board is not subject to the control of the central government and has the power to regulate its own procedures and act at its own discretion. The board has its Principal Bench at New Delhi, an Additional Principal Bench for southern states at Chennai, and four Regional Benches at Delhi, Mumbai, Kolkata, and Chennai.

Reserve Bank of India

The RBI, established in 1935, is the central bank of India and is entrusted with monetary stability, currency management, and super-vision of the financial and payments systems. Its functions and focus have evolved in response to the nation's changing economic environ-ment. It acts as the banker to the state and national governments, the lender of last resort, and the controller of the country's money supply and foreign exchange. The RBI supervises the operations of all banks and NBFCs in the country. It is responsible for monetary policy, sets benchmark interest rates, manages treasury operations (both borrowings and redemption) for the government, and acts as custodian and controller of foreign exchange reserves.

Banking Ombudsman

This unit tries to resolve customer complaints through conciliation or mediation and even grants an award if the complaint is not resolved through that settlement. The ombudsman, however, has the right to reject complaints if they are frivolous, vexatious, in bad faith, without any sufficient cause, and so on. Under the scheme, the RBI has appointed 15 ombudsmen, mostly in state capitals. The RBI has made crucial amendments to the ombudsman system that now enable aggrieved customers not only to appeal any ombudsman's decision but also to appeal if their complaints are rejected. An appeal can be made to the deputy governor's office of the RBI.

Self-Regulating Organizations

India has a host of self-regulating organizations that complement the efforts of the entities mentioned above.

The Institute of Chartered Accountants of India

The Institute of Chartered Accountants of India (ICAI) is the principal body of accountants and audit professionals in the nation. It monitors its profession, maintains professional standards, and runs a certification program for chartered accountants (CA). In India, a CA implements and certifies most matters under the Companies Act and other legislation, including excise laws, customs laws, and the Income Tax Act. Moreover, all companies are required to have their annual accounts audited by a qualified CA of the ICAI. The CA also is required to submit an audit report to company shareholders on the veracity and fairness of the annual accounts. The ICAI is also the body responsible for issuing and monitoring implementation of various accounting standards, auditing standards, and guidance notes.

The Institute of Company Secretaries of India

The Institute of Company Secretaries of India (ICSI) is the principal body of company secretaries in the nation. The ICSI monitors and maintains professional standards and runs a certification program, for company secretaries (CS). In India, every company with paid-up capital greater than INR5 million is required to employ a full-time CS, who is responsible for ensuring compliance with various legislative and regulatory requirements and certifying compliance with governance requirements in accordance with the relevant stock exchange listing agreement.

The Fixed Income Money Market and Derivatives Association of India

The Fixed Income Money Market and Derivatives Association of India (FIMMDA) is a self-regulatory organization whose mandate is to encourage the orderly development of the debt and derivative markets.

The Association of Mutual Funds in India

The Association of Mutual Funds in India (AMFI) is dedicated to developing the Indian mutual fund industry along professional and ethical lines and to enhancing and maintaining standards that protect and promote the interests of mutual funds and their unit holders. It has been instrumental in successfully introducing international accounting standards and best practices to the mutual fund industry.

The Institute of Cost and Work Accountants of India

The Institute of Cost and Work Accountants of India (ICWAI) audits and certifies the cost accounts of certain companies, primarily in the agricultural and commodity sectors.

Key Listing Rules

The Stock Exchange Listing Agreement forms the basis on which the shares of a company are listed on any public stock exchange. The listing agreement contains a number of provisions requiring a company to keep the stock exchange informed about all material events at that company, both positive and negative. In general, the regulation of corporate governance practice in India harmoniously contributes to legal norms and produces stronger demands than do those of other BRIC countries, particularly when it comes to the composition of management and the board. These demands apply to all the 5,000-plus publicly listed companies in India.

Board Structure

Clause 49 introduced an array of relatively strong requirements for the composition of India's boards of directors: Independent directors should represent no less than one-third of the entire board when an outsider (nonexecutive) chairs the board and no less than one-half when the chair is an executive at the company. Clause 49 prescribes the formation of an audit committee and a shareholder grievance committee at all firms with independent directors representing two-thirds of the membership of the audit committee, and at least one committee member should be an expert in the area of finance and audit. Clause 49 also contains an array of disclosure requirements, including those for disclosure of nonexecutive director compensation. In parallel with the stock exchanges and Clause 49, the Indian Ministry of

Finance released its own recommendations for the audit process, known as the Naresh Chandra Committee Report (its contents have been incorporated into Clause 49), which has similarities to the Sarbanes-Oxley Act that the U.S. Congress passed in 2002.

Shareholders' Rights

Although the Companies Act has always provided an excellent framework and clear instructions for maintaining and updating share registers, in reality minority shareholders often have suffered from irregularities in share transfers and registrations. Sometimes nonvoting preferential shares have been used by promoters to channel funds to the detriment of minority shareholders. There have been cases in which the rights of minority shareholders were compromised by management's private deals in the relatively infrequent event of corporate takeovers. Company boards often have been largely ineffective in their monitoring role, and in several instances their independence has been perceived as highly questionable.

Disclosure Requirements

Indian corporate law regulates public companies with respect to public offerings, management, borrowing, and interactions with shareholders and creditors. Public companies must register with the Indian Registrar of Companies and distribute to security holders quarterly results, half-yearly results with a limited review by auditors, and audited results for the full financial year together with detailed cash flow statements that comply with the minimum disclosure requirements and regulations that govern their manner of presentation. Each company's listing agreement regulates governance and requires that listed companies submit unaudited or audited quarterly and year-to-date financial results to their stock exchange within one month from the end of each quarter and immediately notify their stock exchange of any information that would affect the stock price. When unaudited results are furnished, they must be followed with a Limited Review Report. This is designed to enable investors to know the performance of listed companies as early as possible. The revised clause also has simplified provisions for the explanation of variations between items of unaudited and audited quarterly, year-to-date, and annual results. The revised clause requires that the explanation for variations be furnished in respect to net profit or loss after tax and for exceptional and extraordinary items. The percentage of variation for this purpose has been revised from the earlier 20% or more to 10% or INR1 million (U.S.$21,390), whichever is higher.

In regard to the publication of financial results, SEBI recently cleared changes to Clause 41 of the Listing Agreement to enable companies that have a number of subsidiaries and want to declare consolidated financial results to do so within two months of the end of the quarter. Those declaring stand-alone results still will be required to do so within a month. Currently, both stand-alone and consolidated results have to be declared within a month. Listing agreements also require companies to appoint a compliance officer (normally the company secretary) who is responsible for ensuring that the company follows all the various rules and regulations to which it is subject. The compliance officer is also responsible for addressing investor complaints.

Other Recent Developments

IPO Grading

According to SEBI guidelines, all issuers in the primary market who file a draft red herring prospectus, draft prospectus, or offer documents on or after May 1, 2007, must get an IPO grading from any credit rating agency registered with SEBI. The grading exercise involves an assessment of business and financial prospects, management quality, and governance. An assessment of corporate governance is arrived at through detailed management meetings with the CFO; functional, plant, and strategic business unit (SBU) heads as applicable; independent directors; and the CEO, preferably in that order.

Independent Directors: Role and Independence

Despite years of scrutinizing the role of independent directors, analysts have found a great gap in the professionalism and training needed to enable independent directors to remain apart from corporate managers and obtain internal information that would allow them to question related-party and group exposures. The need for training is becoming more crucial as new laws require more compliance with environment standards, quality of products and services, and global competition, all calling for specialized knowledge and skill at the board level.

Accounting Practices and Standards

The shift in India's economic environment in recent years has brought intense emphasis on accounting standards that would ensure transparent corporate financial reporting. In particular, massive global capital transfers have generated considerable interest in the U.S. generally accepted accounting principles (GAAP) standards. Initiatives by the International Organization of Securities Commissions (IOSCO) establishing International Accounting Standards (IASs) and International Financial Reporting Standards (IFRSs) issued by the International Accounting Standards Board (IASB) have become the uniform language of business to protect the interests of global investors; this process has brought more focus on India's IASs/IFRSs. The ICAI took on the leadership role by establishing the Accounting Standards Board more than 25 years ago to meet international and national expectations. The accounting standards prescribe appropriate accounting treatment of complex business transactions but also foster greater transparency and market discipline. Accounting standards also help the regulatory agencies determine benchmark accuracy.

Accounting standards in India are influenced by the requirements of the Companies Act and to some extent by the listing agreements. India's corporate accounting principles are moving toward international standards, and disclosure is improving; however, certain gaps do exist.

Accounting Standard 18

Accounting Standard (AS) 18 makes reporting of related-party transactions by Indian companies mandatory. Related parties include holding and subsidiary companies, key management personnel and their direct relatives, "parties with control" (including joint ventures and fellow subsidiaries), and parties such as promoters and employee trusts. Transactions that must be disclosed include the purchase or sale of goods and assets, borrowing, lending and leasing, hiring and agency arrangements, guarantee agreements, transfer of research and development, and management contracts. Adoption of this standard is a significant improvement for corporate transparency, particularly group affiliates.

Accounting Standards 30 and 31

AS 30 deals with "Financial Instruments: Recognition and Measurements," and AS 31 addresses "Financial Instruments." Presentations are based on the corresponding International Accounting Standards: IAS 39, "Financial Instruments: Recognition and Measurement," and IAS 32, "Financial Instruments: Presentation," respectively, with no material differences.

The AS was to come into effect for accounting periods commencing on or after April 1, 2009, and will be optional for two accounting years. It will become mandatory beginning April 1, 2011.

Differences between Local Standards and IFRS and Timelines for Switching to IFRS

Indian accounting standards still differ from IFRS but in many ways have converged with U.S. GAAP. The process of aligning Indian standards with IFRS began in earnest in 2000, when the regulator, the Accounting Standards Board of India, together with ICAI, introduced 12 new accounting standards, bringing Indian standards closer to IFRS. However, the remaining differences are still material and in many circumstances require new legislation. For example, the Indian Company Law narrowly defines control of a firm as control over a majority of outstanding shares or a majority of votes on the board of directors. The definition of firm control in AS 27 proposes a wider definition that includes those who lack a majority of shares or votes but still have the power to control. In October 2007, the ICAI released a concept paper recommending a full switch to IFRS for Indian firms, and the market consensus is that full conversion will happen by April 2011. At that point, IFRS will be mandatory for all "public interest entities," that is, publicly traded companies and large nontraded firms, including financial companies. All other companies will report according to IFRS standards for small and medium-size enterprises.

Transparency and Disclosure

Financial Reporting and Quality of Disclosure

India's listed companies get strong marks for following the legal mandate establishing fairly strict standards of governance and disclosure, particularly compared with their neighbors. Comparisons show that the standards are far stronger than those in all other Asian countries and in general are stronger than those in most OECD countries. Indian corporate sector regulators and companies have been quick to accept some of the best practices for international governance and disclosure. Indian companies have made significant progress with good quarterly reporting standards that have improved the distribution of timely date. Information technology has made possible easy dissemination of information about listed companies and market intermediaries. Equity research and analysis and credit rating have improved the quality of information. SEBI has an Electronic Data Information Filing and Retrieval System (EDIFAR) to facilitate electronic filing of public domain information by companies. The trend of presentations to analysts is also positive. Also, we observe that the governance practices are strong in companies with listings in overseas markets and those with high credit quality. Still, more training is crucial for directors, including independent directors, audit committee members, and senior executives of companies. The challenge is to design and sustain a system that embraces the spirit of corporate governance, not merely the letter of the law. There is also a need to improve the quality, timeliness, and ease of access to information for all stakeholders. Further, the disclosures need improvement in terms of facilitating increased shareholder participation at meetings.

Auditor Independence

Most large public Indian companies use an internationally recognized auditing firm to audit their IFRS/U.S. GAAP accounts. Many also conduct a parallel audit according to IFRS or U.S. GAAP standards or provide reconciliation. Other Indian companies use local accounting firms, which, to a greater degree than their international counterparts, can increase the risks associated with dependence on a large client. Elements of the Naresh Chandra Committee Report, which have been incorporated into Clause 49, also regulate the independence of the auditing process. Though financial disclosure norms in India traditionally have been superior to those in most Asian countries, noncompliance with disclosure norms was rampant and even the failure of auditors' reports to conform to the law attracted only nominal fines and little punitive action.

Chapter 4

Moving toward Accountability in China

Warren Wang

Introduction and Executive Summary

How Far Will China's Transparency Campaign Go?

Capital markets in China are embracing tougher corporate governance regulations 19 years after that nation's stock exchanges opened. However, the standards of transparency for businesses and the responsibilities of boards, investors, and stakeholders, along with their obligations in regard to risk management, have been overshadowed by the superheated successes that have made China the world's third largest economy after the United States and Japan when measured in exchange-rate terms. National scandals throughout the last decade, including Yinguangxia, the stock scandal that became known as China's Enron; Sanjiu Medical; and ZOJE Sewing Machine, have shown the urgent need to establish and implement those standards as well as exposing many weaknesses in the country's legal, regulatory, and accounting systems. The central government named 2005 the Year of Corporate Governance, making it a top priority among government bodies, regulators, intermediaries, corporations, and investors.

Legislators, regulators, and professional institutions have new laws, rules, regulations, and standards to provide a solid foundation for good corporate governance and stability to draw investors.

A consensus for developing corporate governance codes and guidelines that meet international standards has been building in the last decade. The goal is to change corporate culture through improvements in capital markets, particularly at the company level. Despite some progress, many issues underscore the fundamental weaknesses of China's corporate governance infrastructure: the continued concentration of state ownership, complex private ownership structures, lax enforcement of shareholder rights, little transparency and disclosure in financial accounting, lack of attention to board independence and effectiveness, and the absence of shareholder activism. All require attention to achieve meaningful improvements.

As China continues its transformation from a centrally planned economy to a market economy, the government's role in corporate ownership is similarly in transition. Through its Grasp the Large, Release the Small policy, the government gradually has given up control of nonstrategic state-owned enterprises (SOEs) while maintaining tight control over media, telecommunications, and some financial services.

Meanwhile, it is strengthening its role as a regulator by establishing commissions such as the China Securities Regulatory Commission (CSRC), China Insurance Regulatory Commission (CIRC), and China Banking Regulatory Commission (CBRC) in the financial services sector. CSRC in particular has become a driving force for corporate governance reform across the country.

Underlying these challenges is the rapid but uneven development of the domestic capital markets. Retail investors remain a significant presence on the two major stock exchanges but as a group have not demonstrated strong interest in corporate reforms. Institutional investors are growing in importance, but without a legal structure in place, they seldom challenge companies on such matters. Qualified Foreign Institutional Investors (QFIIs) are still few in number and have little impact on the market. It is likely that standards adopted by pension funds such as the China National Social Security Fund, the country's largest pension fund, will have a positive influence on institutional investors to develop their own improved governance.

Key rules and regulations safeguarding the governance of financial and capital markets are embedded in the People's Republic of China's (PRC) Company Law, Securities Law, and Code of Corporate Governance. Recognizing its importance to the success of its capital markets, China has made significant progress in building a solid information infrastructure. On February 15, 2006, the Ministry of Finance issued new accounting standards: Accounting Standards for Business Enterprises (ASBE). The ministry and the International Accounting Standards Board both regard the new standards as substantially in compliance with International Financial Reporting Standards (IFRS). In 2007, the Regulation on Information Disclosure of Listed Companies issued by the CSRC set strict rules regarding disclosure requirements for public companies. Public companies are required to adopt a two-tier board system, but there are no clear requirements regarding board members' responsibilities and accountability, and board independence remains a key challenge.

Market Infrastructure

Despite the privatizations of recent decades, the Chinese government's control of the economy remains high, with more than 75% of 600 large-cap public companies under its control. Private ownership typically takes the form of highly concentrated equity stakes, generally limiting the ability of average shareholders—even large institutional investors—to accumulate enough shares to influence corporate control. Weak shareholder activism further compounds the problem.

General Stages of Development: Transforming a Planned Economy to a Market Economy

From its establishment in 1949, the Communist Party of China (CPC) controlled the economy. A new generation of government under the leadership of Deng Xiaoping introduced a market economy as a complement to the planned economy. During the 1980s, domestic economic reform was launched nationwide and China opened its doors to the outside world in a decade-long experiment with a market economy.

The initial effective changes began in 1991 as China established its first stock exchange in Shanghai. A second followed in Shenzhen a year later. The driving force now was a "socialist market economy" that emphasized the role of markets rather than central planning. By the end of the twentieth century, the mainland had become an economic phenomenon. China's acceptance as a partner in the World Trade Organization (WTO) in 2001 accelerated the transformation through massive deregulation and privatization. Except for a few industries, such as the media, the economy operates according to market forces rather than administrative policies.

Changing Roles for Government Bodies

As China's economy is changing from planned to market, its governmental bodies also are redefining their economic policies. The government is changing from a direct business operator to a public service provider and regulator, gradually retreating from direct business operations. Certain ministries with responsibility for enterprise management have been abolished, and new oversight groups such as the CSRC, CBRC, and CIRC are growing in influence within the government. Nevertheless, the government controls SOEs in strategic industries such as banking, resources, telecommunications, and media. As of July 2008, the latest available figures show that the central government controlled 149 SOEs and provincial governments controlled hundreds of local ones. For small and midsize SOEs, mostly at local levels, those governments now have the discretion to sell or maintain them as assets, based on local needs and economic conditions.

Ownership Structure

Open-Door Policy Transforms State Ownership

The government is the largest single owner of businesses in China. From the early 1950s to the late 1970s, SOEs were the only corporate structures allowed. In the 1980s, however, a market economy was introduced and small private workshops and entrepreneurs began to emerge, first in the rural areas and later in the cities. As China launched its open-door policy, foreign enterprises began pouring in. By 2005, nonstate ownership accounted for 65% of gross domestic product (GDP), up from 44% in 1978.

Grasp the Large, Release the Small Policy Guides Privatization

The establishment of China's first stock exchanges in the early 1990s marked the beginning of true ownership diversification. SOEs can float a portion of their shares in the public markets to be purchased by private individuals, institutions, or even foreign shareholders, although the government retains majority control. Privatization soared in the late 1990s when the Communist Party decided to retain full control only in industries considered critical to the nation's economy and national security and transfer nonstrategic factories and enterprises to private hands. Local governments, which administer about 90% of the state firms, gained more authority to dispose of those businesses. The policy is known as Grasp the Large, Release the Small. According to official reports, the number of state enterprises declined by 61% from 262,000 in 1997 to 159,000 in 2002. With the new millennium, officials began speeding the initial public offering (IPO) process for large strategic enterprises, further diversifying ownership among private individuals and foreign investors.

Financial Markets

Macroeconomic Conditions Call for Stimulus Measures

China has maintained a strong growth trend despite the recent global economic upheaval. According to its National Bureau of Statistics, for five consecutive years up until 2007 China had a double-digits GDP growth rate, which slowed down in 2008 to 9%. At the end of 2008 Chinese GDP amounted to 30,067.0 billion yuan, or approximately U.S.$4.4 trillion, foreign exchange reserves reached U.S.$1,946.0 billion, an increase of U.S.$417.8 billion or 46% as compared with that at the end of the pervious year. The national currency exchange rate continues to appreciate, having reached RMB6.8 to U.S.$1.

Even during the growth surge, fundamental weaknesses have become apparent in the national economy, chiefly from inflation, which is expected to keep rising considerably. The rate of investment in GDP is high, and the prices of consumer goods are rising significantly along with asset prices. However, global food shortages sent prices skyrocketing in China, lifting the consumer price index to 5.9 percent and the prices for food alone went up by 14.3 percent year-on-year.

Corporate Governance Is Crucial to Banking Industry Reforms

Banks are the primary funding source for companies, with bank financing accounting for more than 90% of all capital raised in China in the past decade. The "big four" state-owned commercial banks— the China Construction Bank (CCB); the Industrial and Commercial Bank of China (ICBC), which is the largest; the Bank of China

(BOC); and the Agricultural Bank of China (ABC)—have dominated both the lending and bank deposit markets. In a banking reform in the early 2000s, the central government recapitalized three of them, stripped out nonperforming loans, brought in foreign strategic investors, and introduced a new governance system. Since that time, CCB, ICBC, and BOC have been listed on the stock exchanges and turned into state-held joint-stock commercial banks. After some scandals and jail terms for officials in 2003, the government reorganized the three banks before listing them on the stock exchanges and committing them to improve corporate governance, strengthen internal controls, and speed up management reform to prevent a recurrence of nonperforming loans.

Joint-stock banks owned by local governments and private entities have achieved significant growth in the last few years, with total assets increasing to 16.2% in 2006 from 13.8% in 2003. These banks represent a serious threat to the big four, particularly in retail banking. China's membership in the WTO in 2001 opened the door to foreign financial institutions, which have put considerable competitive pressure on the domestic banks. However, over the longer term, that competition should be a positive influence in terms of management skills, customer service awareness, product diversification, new technology, and additional funding sources. Analysts expect to see a more open and competitive banking market by the end of this decade.

Development of Equity Markets as a Vital Source of Funds for Corporations

Aside from bank financing, the equity markets represent the main funding source for corporations in China. The Chinese equity market grew to 1,550 domestic listed companies and became number two in the world (after the United States) with market capitalization reaching U.S.$7 trillion in March of 2008, while correcting to U.S.$3.5 trillion by mid 2009. Tradable shares were expected to account for 25% of total market capitalization. There are two stock exchanges—one in Shanghai and the other in Shenzhen—trading four types of equity stocks: Shanghai A shares, Shenzhen A shares, Shanghai B shares, and Shenzhen B shares. All stock issuance is subject to the approval of the CSRC.

Individual investors dominate the Chinese equity market. Among about 93 million general accounts, over 99% represent individual investors. Individual investors hold 85% of tradable shares and institutional investors have the remaining 15%. The number of institutional investors is increasing gradually. By September 2008, 60 mutual fund companies were listed in China; among them, 31 were joint-venture (JV) funds. In addition there are 69 QFIIs.

The Chinese stock markets have been volatile since their inception in 1990 and continue to be one of the most frequently discussed topics among the general public. In 2006–2007, China's stock market was one of the world's best performers, with returns of over 100% each year. However, the correction in 2008 cut the index almost by half in market capitalization.

Domestic Bond Market Lacks an Established Credit Rating System

In contrast to the stock market, the domestic bond market is underdeveloped. Currently, four types of bonds are traded domestically: central bank notes, treasury bonds, policy financial bonds, and corporate bonds, with 52%, 27%, 14%, and 7% market shares, respectively. There are three types of corporate bonds: bonds issued by listed companies, enterprise bonds, and short-term financing bonds. A fourth type—bonds issued by SOEs with a guarantee provided by commercial banks—was canceled in 2008.

The three types of corporate bonds are regulated by three different authorities: CSRC, the National Development and Reform Commission (NDRC), and the People's Bank of China (PBOC), respectively. Notably, most corporate bonds issued in China are guaranteed either by the parent company or by commercial banks. The existence of a guarantee lowers the default risk and reduces the need for an independent credit rating. Although there are over a dozen local credit rating agencies, a number that is increasing constantly, none has been able to establish a recognized domestic benchmarking standard. After 2007, a small number of listed companies started to issue corporate bonds without a guarantee, but without an established credit rating system, the pricing of nonguaranteed corporate bonds is a challenge to institutional investors.

Other Institutional and Cultural Factors

Growing Role of State and Nongovernmental Organizations

Social and industrial associations in China also play important roles in providing guidelines, policies, and, most important, business connections. There are three classes. The first class consists of associations that are directly under the leadership of the State Council and/or the ministries and normally may act as quasi-governmental bodies, regulating and monitoring their members. They also may act as enforcers in improving the corporate governance standards of their members. Research institutes are another type of nongovernmental organization (NGO) that wields considerable influence, such as the Chinese Academy of Social Sciences and research centers under the PBOC. The third type—nongovernment-related organizations—is growing in importance as the representative of the markets.

Shareholder Activism Is Rare

As in other emerging markets, shareholder activism is rarely seen in the PRC. Shares owned by institutional investors make up 40% of floating shares, compared with an average of more than 50% owned by controlling shareholders, making it difficult for institutions to have a real impact on the listed companies.

The absence of regulation also explains the lack of shareholder activism. Unlike in the United States, where fund companies are able to exert great pressure on the companies in their portfolios, in China institutional investors have no regulatory support. Institutional investors are reluctant to push for shareholder rights for fear of being shut out of communications companies.

Rule of Person Takes Precedence over Rule of Law

Transformation from the traditional rule of person to the more systematic rule of law will require a major educational and cultural transformation. Although China has moved to separate government from business over the last 20 years, strong personal ties and interlocked relationships still make the two inseparable. Relationships are still one of the most important factors in China, routinely taking precedence over decisions based on laws or regulations.

Legal Infrastructure

After its entry into the WTO in December 2001, China fast-tracked the promulgation of commercial and securities laws to comply with global best practices and create a business-friendly environment for both Chinese and foreign investors. However, that effort often is undermined or sporadically enforced because of politics, national and local interests, and a social system that favors personal relationships.

Background of Legal System and Legal Tradition

Legal Development Makes Significant Progress

Mainland China has a 4,000-year history of jurisprudence, but its current legal system, at slightly more than a half century old, is in its infancy relative to the U.K., European, and U.S. judicial systems. The PRC has drawn up four constitutions: in 1954, 1975, 1978, and 1982. The National People's Congress (NPC) has the authority to amend the constitution and promulgate new laws. The Standing Committee of the NPC is empowered to interpret laws and draw up decrees.

The development of a legal system was given the highest priority from 1949 to 1956 but then was overwhelmed during two decades of internal turmoil. In 1978, new leadership under Deng Xiaoping announced the open-door policy that launched the country's modernization program, and officials recognized the need for a legal system commensurate with that ambition. Today China has a formal legal system, having made significant progress in just a generation. An increasingly robust National People's Congress and its Standing Committee have enacted sweeping legislation to address most needs.

Tradition Is Not the Only Source of the Legal System's Conflicts and Inconsistency

China's modern-day legal system is a hybrid, chiefly modeled on those in Europe, that is based on fiduciary duty, governmental regulations, and legislation. However, substantial elements have been borrowed from the former Soviet Union and others were inherited from traditional Chinese law, in particular from the Confucian philosophy, which prizes relationships. These elements and philosophies help create a gap between form and reality, between how participants discuss the system and how they act. Again, personal and cultural commitments have produced selective enforcement, if any.

Criminal laws traditionally have been given more emphasis than commercial laws. Therefore, criminal law, civil procedures law, administrative law, and people's court administrative law were among the earliest forms of law to be issued, in 1978. The July 1, 1979, passage of the Law of the People's Republic of China on Joint Ventures Using Chinese and Foreign Investment marked a new era in China's legislation on foreign investment and corporate laws.

It was not until the late 1980s and early 1990s that the majority of rules and regulations dealing with civil and commercial law were passed. Legal developments relating to foreign trade, technology transfer, and investment led this progress. Before the 1990s, the PRC's desire for foreign direct investment drove the creation of a legal framework. Joining the WTO spurred China to make substantive institutional reforms to close the commercial law gap with developed countries. The implementation of those commercial laws is still an issue, particularly in instances of conflict between foreign enterprises and Chinese companies. For example, the French food company Danone is going to appeal a decision by a Chinese court that it no longer has rights to the popular Wahaha beverages brand, which Danone claims had been transferred to it in 1999.

Conflicts regarding joint ventures or foreign enterprises normally first go through China's international commercial arbitration commission, which is now the world's busiest. Some 200 cities have established arbitration commissions to handle domestic and foreign-related disputes.

There are major inconsistencies in China's legal system. Many of these issues were not discussed publicly during the first 30 years of PRC history. State law versus human rights, the independence of the legal system, and whether the CPC can overrule the law are just some of these issues. Legislation is frequently inadequate, and national and local norms often conflict.

Principal Legal Provisions

Company Law Has Some Unique Aspects

The PRC Company Law was passed at the Eighth National People's Congress in December 1993 (effective July 1, 1994) and revised in December 1999, August 2004, and October 2005 (effective January 1, 2006). The law is designed to regulate corporate structures and activities and protect the commercial interests of companies, their shareholders, and their creditors. Two types of companies are described under the law: limited liability companies and joint-stock companies. It also articulates the responsibilities, rights, and liabilities of shareholders, the board of directors, managers, and the board of supervisors. Among the unique aspects are the requirements for minimum registered capital, fixed office space, and legal representatives.

All limited liability companies are required to have a board of directors (BoD). For "large" companies, there has to be a separate board of supervisors (BoS), which is designed to represent the interests of employees, and one-third of its members must be company employees. For a large number of public companies, BoS members also include minority shareholders whose stakes are not large enough to nominate directors to the BoD. The law also gives shareholders the right to appoint and remove directors and supervisors and determine remuneration. A series of listing rules and regulations addressing capital market activities have been enacted to supplement the law (see the details in the section on the regulatory environment).

The latest amended company law, effective January 1, 2006, is designed to deliver commercial and governance improvements. It simplifies company establishment requirements, expands the statutory rights of minority shareholders, strengthens the corporate governance requirements for listed companies, improves protections for creditors, and increases employees' right to participate in company activities.

Securities Law Promotes Growth of the Socialist Market Economy

The PRC Securities Law, passed and effective on December 29, 1998, and amended in October 2005, effective January 1, 2006, regulates the issuance and transfer of securities, protects the rights and interests of investors, safeguards economic order and the public interest, and promotes the growth of the socialist market economy. It defines the regulatory organization under the State Council as the central regulator for the PRC's capital markets.

The amendments that took effect in 2006 represent a significant reform that emphasizes the protection of investors. These amendments establish the sponsor system for public offerings and require an issuer to make advance disclosure of its application documents after filing for an IPO with CSRC; establish a fund to protect investors and allow compensation in cases in which investors have losses as a result of fraudulent activities; guarantee the safety of investors' money by depositing it in separate commercial bank accounts in each investor's name to prevent embezzlement; and increase penalties on illegal acts so that those who commit accounting fraud and inside-trading violators may face criminal charges.

Laws and Code of Corporate Governance Safeguard Shareholder Rights

The Company Law, Securities Law, and Code of Corporate Governance have specific stipulations on the rights of listed companies' shareholders. Shareholders with 10% or more of outstanding shares or more than one-third of the BoD or BoS may propose a general shareholder meeting. Shareholders with more than 3% of outstanding shares (either individually or combined) can bring proposals to the general shareholder meeting. Voting procedures follow the one share–one vote precedent. Shareholders can vote through proxies. Cumulative voting is allowed for the election of directors in the general meeting. For example, a shareholder with one share may vote five shares for a candidate when there are five candidates for one open board position. The BoD is responsible to shareholders and is required to report to the general shareholder meeting annually or on the occasion of a special shareholder meeting. Shareholders with more than 1% of outstanding shares have the right to propose candidates for director. Directors serve for three-year terms, and there is no limit on years of service.

Overview of Other Commercial Laws

The other major commercial laws that guide the PRC include the Bankruptcy Law (1988) to address the bankruptcies of state-owned entities. A revision in 2006 extends the law to private as well as foreign companies and protects the rights of both creditors and employees. The Contract Law (1999) assigns rights to all the parties to a contract; the PRC Security Law (1995) stipulates the creation of security interests such as guarantees, mortgages, pledges, liens, and deposits; and the Labor Law (2008) requires that all labor contracts be written and imposes significant penalties on employers for failure to comply, increases employee participation in the drafting of rules and regulations affecting employees, increases the involvement of unions, requires collective contracts, and clarifies requirements for employee noncompete agreements. The Anti-Monopoly Law (2008) applies to monopolistic behavior within China and outside the country that has "eliminative or restrictive" effects on competition in the domestic market. It prohibits monopoly agreements, resale price fixing, collusion on bids, and abuse of a dominant market position to eliminate or restrict competition and sets out procedures for antimonopoly government authority to carry out enforcement.

Regulatory Framework

The Chinese government is gradually building a professional regulatory system to monitor market activities. The CSRC is the main regulator of capital markets and is growing in importance. The CSRC and the two stock exchanges have listing rules, information disclosure rules, governance codes, and related regulations that are comparable to, although not as comprehensive as, those of developed countries.

NDRC and Ministries Where Policies Are Set

The State Council has final authority over all regulatory bodies. It oversees 27 ministries and some 50 direct subsidiaries, with the National

Development and Reform involved in overall strategic planning. The NDRC formulates and implements strategies for national economic and social development, sets industrial policies and price policies, guides the overall restructuring of the economic system, and manages the national oil reserve. Companies that issue enterprise bonds in the domestic capital market must get formal approval from the NDRC.

The Bank of China Evolves

The BOC has been the regulator for the PRC's financial industry since 1983. After reforms in 2003, the BOC relinquished its regulatory responsibility and became a pure central bank, with responsibility for overseeing monetary policy and safeguarding financial stability by preventing and resolving the consequences of financial risks.

The BOC also acts as an administrator for the regulation of financial markets, administers the circulation of currency, manages official foreign exchange and gold reserves, acts as a fiscal agent, maintains the payment and settlement system, collects and analyzes financial data, and participates in international financial activities.

How Markets Are Regulated by the CBRC, CIRC, and CSRC

The CBRC was established in 2003 to take over regulatory responsibilities from the BOC related to the oversight of banks, credit unions, asset management companies, and trust investment companies. The CBRC is also responsible for drafting and enforcing banking-related laws, rules, and regulations. The CBRC has 13 departments and 30 local offices across the mainland. The CIRC has operated since 1998 to conduct the administration, supervision, and regulation of insurance markets and oversee insurance companies, insurance asset management companies, and insurance intermediary companies. The CIRC is also responsible for drafting and enforcing insurance-related laws, rules, and regulations. The CIRC has 15 departments and 36 local offices nationwide.

Since 1992, the CSRC has overseen all securities business activities, including futures. The CSRC oversees all securities and futures companies; stock, bond, and futures exchanges; listed companies; fund management companies' investment consulting firms; and other intermediaries involved in the securities and futures business. The CSRC, with 16 departments and 36 local offices nationally, is also responsible for drafting and enforcing securities-related laws, rules, and regulations.

Key Listing Rules: Securities Codes and Regulations Emphasize Credibility and Integrity

Two types of shares are listed and trade in the domestic equity markets (see the section on equity markets earlier in this chapter). Shanghai A and Shenzhen A shares are for domestic investors, and Shanghai B and Shenzhen B shares are for foreign investors. All listings must comply with PRC Company Law and the Memorandum by the State Council Regarding Standardizing Limited Company and Joint-Stock Company According to Company Law (2005).

In January 2002, the CSRC released its Code of Corporate Governance for Listed Companies in China. The code emphasizes the importance of credibility and integrity and identifies the relationships between controlling shareholders and listed companies, shareholders and directors, and executives and management.

The code focuses on creating Western-style corporate governance practices, such as the establishment of BoD subcommittees. The code also requires that all annual general meetings (AGMs) comply with PRC Company Law. Requirements for directors and supervisors as well as shareholders' rights and related items are articulated. The code also sets additional specific disclosure requirements for corporate governance for listed companies.

Board Structure

How Much Independence Can Be Expected?

The Company Law requires listed companies to adopt a two-tier board structure. Two-thirds of the board members represent major shareholders, and one-third are independent. The size of the BoD ranges from 5 to 19. The BoD is accountable directly to the shareholders. The second board, the BoS, consists of employees' representatives (no less than one-third), and the remainder represents minority shareholders. Three to five members usually make up the BoS. Directors and top management cannot be appointed as supervisors.

Under this two-tier structure, the BoD, as the core board that works closely with the management (in most cases, board memberships and top management positions are held by the same group of people), operates the company on a day-to-day basis. The BoS is the independent board that provides independent views and monitors the executive management and the BoD. In most cases, the majority of BoS members are employee supervisors with a reporting line to the top management. They usually are appointed by major shareholders. It is difficult for employee supervisors to play a totally independent role because they must consider their career interests.

Are Minority Shareholders' Rights Fully Protected?

Under the existing share registration system, all listed shares are secured and fully transferable. Shareholders have equal rights in terms of profit sharing, participation in shareholder meetings in person or via proxy voting, and monitoring, questioning, and making recommendations to management. However, since companies often have one major controlling shareholder, it is difficult for the minority shareholders to form a large enough pool to reach the minimum thresholds needed to exercise rights such as nominating directors, calling special meetings, and bringing resolutions to the board at shareholder meetings.

The arrangement of tradable versus nontradable shares further limits the rights of minority shareholders. Before the China Shareholding Reform of 2005, close to two-thirds of listed companies' shares were not tradable. That created two markets for listed companies' shares. Tradable shares are bought and sold on the Shanghai and Shenzhen stock exchanges, and nontradable shares normally are traded between interested parties rather than through open-bid markets. In most cases, the price for nontradable shares is significantly lower than that for tradable shares. Such arrangements mean that controlling shareholders, who normally hold nontradable shares, have no interest in increasing shareholder value. Instead, they disadvantage minority shareholders by funneling money from listed companies through related-party transactions and various financial schemes.

Nominally, minority shareholders have the same claim rights on company profits. In reality, they get much less despite having paid more for their shares. The 2005 China Shareholding Reform created a paradigm shift for governance practice by converting nontradable shares into tradable shares. Through that action, holders of tradable shares received free shares from holders of nontradable shares. The reform aligned the interests of controlling shareholders with those of minority shareholders, and maximizing shareholder value has become the goal for both parties.

A company's articles of association have binding force on all shareholders, directors, supervisors, and managers. The articles must be approved at shareholder meetings. The law also allows shareholders to amend the content of the articles. The PRC laws also give shareholders preemptive rights. Those rights can prevent the issuance of shares to new shareholders and thus mitigate the potential for dilution of existing shareholder ownership stakes and voting rights.

Disclosure Requirements Strengthened

In addition to the Company Law, the Code of Corporate Governance requires listed companies to disclose information related to corporate governance such as the composition of the BoD and BoS, evaluations of BoD and BoS members, attendance records of independent directors, and their independent opinions on related-party transactions and executive appointment and removal. The code also requires disclosure of the establishment of functional subcommittees and their operating details, the discrepancies between operating realities and the requirements of the code, and the plan for improving corporate governance.

To improve China-listed companies' information disclosure, in February 2007 the CSRC released Regulation on Information Disclosure of Listed Companies, which applies to four types of capital market participants: listed companies and their BoD, BoS, and management; controlling shareholders; potential buyers of a company; and investment advisory firms and other information disclosure–related intermediaries, such as the media. The rule introduced the fair-disclosure concept, which prohibits listed companies from practicing selective disclosure. The rule also set clear content requirements for specific company operations.

Other Recent Developments Shaping the Governance Landscape

Finance Crime Law and Selective Enforcement

Overregulation and underenforcement routinely characterize Asian governance systems, and China is no exception. Selective enforcement is common across the country, including in the capital markets. Before 2006, punishment for financial crimes was light. Accounting fraud was not even categorized as criminal. As a result, corporate risk takers frequently were willing to challenge the system, hoping that the laws or rules would not be applied to them. If caught, they would be able to pay fines rather than go to prison. Those practices led to a huge number of financial crimes in the early days of China's capital market.

In 2006, China passed Amendment 6 to its Criminal Law to curb the widespread crimes in capital markets and strengthen enforcement. For the first time, those found guilty of accounting fraud or the dissemination of false financial information that injures the interests of shareholders face sentences of up to three years in prison. CSRC joined with the China Public Security Bureau to undertake investigations.

Incentive Systems Are Still Lagging

The Code of Corporate Governance recommends that listed companies set up a performance review system for directors, supervisors, and management and develop an incentive system linked to performance. However, in practice, fewer than 10% of listed companies have disclosed such a review process. Only 5% of listed companies have such an incentive system.

After the 2005 shareholding reform, more and more companies chose to implement stock option plans for senior management, which usually makes up two-thirds of the board. By early 2008, around 50 companies had implemented stock option plans with published performance metrics. For independent directors, the compensation is usually fixed at a certain amount. No listed company in China has ever linked the compensation of independent directors to performance or issued stock options to independent directors.

Independent Directors: Are Good Intentions Enough?

One-third of the board members of all domestic listed companies must be independent. One of the independent directors must be an accounting expert. Independent directors can serve on the boards of no more than five listed companies and can serve on a board for no more than six years. For major transactions and related-party transactions, the guidelines require independent directors' approval before submission to the full BoD. Independent directors also can provide independent views on issues such as important investments, directors' appointment and removal, and directors' and executives' remuneration.

Despite good intentions, China's independent director system still needs to demonstrate its effectiveness in serving as a watchdog for minority shareholders. Unlike Western countries, where a majority of independent directors are businesses executives, in China more than 70% of independent directors are from academic fields and have limited business experience. Over 50% of independent directors have strong local connections. The makeup of independent directors and the nominating process—independent directors usually are nominated by controlling shareholders—constrain the willingness and ability of independent directors to challenge the decisions made by controlling shareholders.

The CSRC regularly conducts short training programs for directors and independent directors. However, these programs provide only general guidance. A lack of qualified persons to fill the 5,000-plus independent director positions remains a major stumbling block. As China continues to open up its capital markets to foreign investors, more foreign directors probably will fill this gap.

Informational Infrastructure

The 2006 promulgation of new accounting standards indicates that China's accounting system is for the most part converging with international accounting standards. Transparency and disclosure is still the weakest area for listed companies in China, compared with the level in developed countries. Companies that are dual listed in China and overseas markets have the best level of disclosure. The comprehensiveness of disclosure is one of the biggest gaps for mainland listed companies, requiring attention from regulators.

Accounting Practices and Standards: Not All Accounting Systems Follow International Rules

Except for some overseas-listed companies, most companies in the PRC are required only to report their financials under local accounting standards. Local standards are based on the PRC Accounting Law and individual accounting standards but are converging gradually with international accounting standards. In February 2006, the Ministry of Finance set forth new rules in its Accounting Standards for Business Enterprises, with one basic standard and 38 specific standards and practical guidelines. The ministry and the International Accounting Standards Board both regard the new standards as substantially in alignment with International Financial Reporting Standards. The Hong Kong Institute of Certified Public Accountants agrees that the new standards substantially converge with Hong Kong Financial Reporting Standards (HKFRSs). The ministry's new standards began to be adopted by enterprises listed in the PRC on January 1, 2007. China's central-level SOEs and large to midscale companies were expected to adopt the new accounting standards by the end of 2009. However, small and medium-size enterprises, which make up 99% of Chinese companies, will not be required to comply with the IFRS.

Searching for Solutions to Local Standard and IASB-IFRS Differences

ASBE are substantially in line with IFRS. However, there continue to be a small number of differences between ASBE and the international standards. The International Accounting Standards Board (IASB) has identified a number of issues for which China, because of its unique circumstances and environment, could be particularly helpful in finding high-quality solutions to further integrating IFRS. These issues, among other things, relate to disclosure of related-party transactions, business combination involving enterprises under common control, and fair value measurement.

Ministry of Finance Weighs in on Accounting Standards

Starting in January 2007, the Ministry of Finance shifted its focus to tracking and analyzing issues stemming from the implementation of the new accounting standard by domestic and overseas-listed companies. At that point, there were 1,408 listed companies in China.

The ministry studied them and considered this a successful transition from old Chinese accounting standards to ASBEs.

Some items may cause changes in shareholder equity. Trading and available-for-sale financial assets will cause shareholder equity to increase. Charge-offs of long-term equity investment resulting from business combinations with enterprises under common control, as well as termination benefits, cause a decrease in shareholder equity.

Transparency and Disclosure
Taking Quality of Disclosure to the Next Level

To improve the quality of information disclosure and be consistent with the new Company Law and Securities Law, in 2007 the CSRC released the Regulations on Information Disclosure of Listed Companies. It regulates not only public companies and their directors, supervisors, and management but also controlling shareholders, the potential buyers of companies, investment advisory companies, and the media, which may play a role in a public company's information disclosure process.

The regulation clearly specifies the content required for disclosure in periodic reports and sets particular rules for the disclosure of incidents in ad hoc reports. To ensure true and complete disclosure, it specifies that the chair of the board, general manager, and board secretary are principally responsible for the authenticity, accuracy, completeness, immediacy, and fairness of the disclosed information. Also, for the first time, the fair-disclosure principle specifically states that the company cannot disclose information to particular investors or media before the general public is advised of it. A public company also is not allowed to use investor presentations or media interviews as substitutes for formal press releases. In the 2008 annual reporting season, many companies voluntarily disclosed lists of their meetings with investors, something that rarely is done even in developed countries.

Ownership Disclosure Becomes Less Opaque

Unlike the case in developed countries, almost every company in China is controlled by a single majority shareholder: the government. Before 2005, it was almost impossible for investors to identify the controlling shareholder from an annual report. This led to numerous stock manipulation scandals. Starting in 2005, the CSRC required all listed companies to disclose the controlling shareholder clearly in diagram form. Companies also are required to explain the backgrounds of shareholders with over 10% ownership.

Timing of Financial Reporting Is Quarterly

All publicly listed companies must file and disclose financial results on a quarterly basis. Continuous disclosure is not required. However, any significant events that may affect stock prices have to be announced to the public immediately. The annual report must be disclosed by April 30.

Who Regulates Information Disclosure for Stock Exchanges?

The CSRC sets the disclosure rules and addresses violations. Guided by the CSRC, the Shanghai and Shenzhen stock exchanges are responsible for monitoring public companies' information disclosure. At the beginning of each calendar year, both exchanges issue information disclosure guidelines for public companies to follow in drafting annual reports. The guidelines usually list additional optional disclosure items beyond CSRC requirements and encourage public companies to follow them.

Executive Pay and Nomination Still Need Attention

Matters involving executive remuneration and nomination have not gained sufficient attention, and the new regulation did not address those issues. Executive nominations generally are decided behind closed doors, since key directors and executive members are appointed by the major shareholder: the government.

The majority of Chinese companies' executive remuneration consists only of salaries and bonuses. Fewer than 15% of public companies issue stock options to management. Starting with the 2006 annual reporting season, a majority of companies have been disclosing compensation details about board and management members, but disclosure of the number and value of those executive stock options was still optional. Starting with the 2007 annual report season, all companies are required to explain the remuneration process and the level of remuneration.

Auditor Independence

High Turnover of CPA Firms for China's Public Companies

The national accounting professional organization, the Chinese Institute of Certified Public Accountants, is operated through the Ministry of Finance and since 1988 has administered and issued the professional designation Certified Public Accountant (CPA) to qualified candidates. The national examination for Chinese CPAs was introduced in 1994. CPA firms are licensed and required to comply with existing rules and standards.

The listing rules require that the external auditors of listed companies have CPA licenses. Most of these appointments are awarded without a public tendering process. Information on how and why a CPA firm is selected remains confidential within the insider circle of top management. This has led to a relatively high turnover of CPA firms for public companies. To assure auditor independence and reduce turnover, the regulation requires that when a public company dismisses a CPA firm, it must inform the auditing firm in a timely manner after a board resolution has been made. When the shareholders vote on the dismissal, the CPA firm is allowed to make a statement. If the shareholders approve the dismissal, the listed company will explain the reasons and provide the CPA firm's statement in the disclosure. Furthermore, there is no requirement for the disclosure of auditor fees versus nonaudit fees in annual reports. Regulators are in the process of setting rules on auditor rotations. When those rules are implemented, it will be a positive step toward enhancing auditor independence.

PART TWO

FUNDAMENTALS OF EMERGING MARKET GOVERNANCE ANALYSIS

Chapter 5

Ownership Influences: The State, Company Founders, Majority Shareholders, and Other Dangers[1]

I n the BRIC economies and in most other emerging economies, significant shareholders often have a profound influence on governance processes. For a variety of legal, cultural, and institutional reasons, dispersed ownership is an exception rather than the norm outside the United States and the United Kingdom. According to recent surveys, over 90% of major public companies in the BRIC countries have one or more dominant blockholders. Although our analytical approach does not view concentrated ownership structures as inherently more risky (or, conversely, less risky) than dispersed ownership, the influence of owners typically becomes a primary consideration in governance analysis in emerging markets.

Some majority owners are responsible and competent and work to increase the value of the company for all shareholders. Indeed, significant shareholders typically have strong incentives to ensure

---

1 This chapter was updated by Oleg Shvyrkov and includes elements from earlier Standard & Poor's methodological documents composed by George Dallas, Dan Konigsburg, and Julia Kochetygova.

management oversight and often also support their affiliate companies with capital, technological and managerial expertise, and contacts in the business community and the government. Over the years, some private industrialists, families, and financial groups in the BRIC countries have earned reputations for being benevolent blockholders that are respectful of minorities' rights.

The influences of significant shareholders can be harmful to the interests of a company's minority shareholders, however. Blockholders can be corrupt or incompetent and may reduce the value of a company by funneling money to related parties, using company resources to support their own interests, or failing to appoint competent management. In Russia and China, governments control a significant number of large public companies and may have a host of conflicting interests, including a desire to use the resources of a company to support the public interest whether or not this is profit making for the company. Family owners, who are common in Brazil and India, are another concern: Issues of succession and management legitimacy often become relevant in those settings, and external investments by shareholders may distort their motivation to increase shareholder value at the focal company.

Key to the analysis of shareholder influence is an understanding of the motivation of the significant owners, such as their exposure to conflicts of interest, and the effectiveness of checks and balances to blockholders' influence. Some significant shareholders deliberately separate ownership from management. This may occur, for example, when company founders recognize that their ventures have grown beyond the entrepreneurial stage and make deliberate efforts to institutionalize governance mechanisms and employ professional management. We observed several cases in which that approach by company founders led to a significant degree of balance at the board level, with independent directors and minority representatives playing an important role in governance. In other cases, such as when the board has limited independence and minority shareholders are powerless, there are few opportunities for checks and balances. The situation can be exacerbated when the owners are personally involved in executive functions or when executives report to blockholders informally.

It must be noted, however, that it is beyond the scope of this methodology to use techniques of forensic accounting to establish evidence of nonmarket transfer pricing.

Scenario 1: Public Companies with Negligible Ownership Concentration

Although uncommon, dispersed ownership structures are certainly not improbable in the emerging economies and probably will become less rare as financial markets develop. When no consolidated ownership stakes exist in the sense that no single shareholder (or distinct group of shareholders) is able to affect board composition autonomously, analysts normally treat ownership influences as an insignificant or minor governance factor with a limited effect on the overall GAMMA (Governance, Accountability, Management Metrics, and Analysis) score.

However, it is important to exercise caution with respect to possible tacit influence. There are well-known cases, most notably in Russia, in which poor regulation of ownership disclosure led to situations in which consolidated stakes emerged without public, or even the company's, knowledge. This may create the potential for greater blockholder influence than otherwise would appear to be the case. Thus, before concluding that no material shareholder influence is present, analysts need to ensure that the ownership information provided by the company (either public or confidential, including information received from shareholders, the share registrar, regulators, and share tracking services) makes tacit ownership concentration unlikely and that no indications of potential blockholder influence have been noted by the media and industry analysts.

In some cases, shareholder influence may be relevant to governance analysis of widely held firms as well and may have a moderate effect on the overall GAMMA score. Indeed, the risk in widely held firms is that no individual shareholder may be in a position to provide meaningful oversight and ensure management accountability. In these situations, institutional investors can play an important role by providing explicit oversight and engagement of management. The lack of a strong blockholder keeping an eye on management therefore can be compensated for partially or substantially by active institutional investors. Those investors may be in a position to punch above their relative shareholding weight in terms of the influence they have. When there is evidence of institutional investors playing a disciplining role, analysts may treat this as a positive governance factor. Also, in many markets today the influence of private equity investors and hedge funds is growing. Although these investor groupings are difficult to characterize, they represent new sectors that influence the corporate governance process and warrant monitoring to the extent that their interests may differ from those of other investors. Table 5-1 analyzes shareholder influence.

Scenario 2: Public Company with a Single Large Private Blockholder

Although blockholder influence warrants considerable scrutiny for potential abuse of minority shareholders, it is only fair to begin the analysis of a blockholder's influence with an agnostic perspective. The effect of blockholders can be positive, negative, or neutral. Each situation has to be assessed on its own merits. The first instinct of the analyst should be to concentrate on potential negative influences: expropriation (through asset purchases or sales, transfer pricing, and related-party transactions) and the entrenchment of incompetent or corrupt managers. At the same time, the analysis should be sensitive to the potential positive effects of blockholder influence. Blockholders often have a strong incentive to increase the valuation of their holdings and tend to be in a superior position to monitor management

Table 5-1   Shareholder Influence

Range of Factor Outcomes	Potential Analytical Assessment
No blockholders exist; there are dispersed shareholders, and institutional investors actively engage with the board and management.	Very strong to strong
There are dispersed shareholders with institutional investors, but there may be evidence of institutional investor passivity.	Strong to moderate
There are dispersed shareholders but no evidence of engagement.	Moderate to weak

(through direct board seats) and ensure proper control over management abuse or incompetence. Ultimately, it depends not only on the commercial abilities of the blockholder but also on the blockholder's overall integrity. This is manifest in an implicit or explicit blockholder commitment to the core principles of fairness, transparency, and accountability in managing the company in accordance with the interests of all shareholders, not just the blockholder's interest.

Most blockholders are likely to represent that they look after the interests of all shareholders, not just their own, but this cannot be taken for granted. Stated policies and principles are a positive start, but they have to be reconciled with a company's specific governance structures and practices. It is important for an analyst to know whether the company has interactions with other companies that may involve transfer pricing on nonmarket terms or whether intercompany linkages give rise to intercompany advances, arrears, or subsidies.

The relative strength of checks and balances in the governance system is an equally important factor in the assessment of blockholder influence. When independent directors and minority shareholder representatives take an active role in decision making, this allows them to monitor and balance a blockholder's influence at the board level. This leads to considerably less scope for value-diluting decisions by a blockholder. Even when such independent constituencies do not have formal veto powers, they can influence a blockholder's decisions by appealing to the general public, legislators, regulators, and shareholder rights organizations.

Some blockholders voluntarily limit their influence on companies and even undertake to support an independent board majority with their votes, as did the founders of Russia's Wimm-Bill-Dann Foods OJSC (GAMMA 7+), for example. Others do not venture to give away the majority of votes on corporate boards yet provide independent directors with considerable veto powers, particularly with respect to investment decisions and related-party transactions (e.g., Kazakhstan's KMG-EP JSC, GAMMA 6). At many companies, however, independent directors receive no support from blockholders. When this is the case, the strength of checks and balances depends on the ability of minority shareholders to secure board seats under the applicable law and the level of shareholder activism. Table 5-2 discusses blockholder influence.

Scenario 3: Public Company with Multiple Large Blockholders

In a conceptual sense, two strong blockholders can constitute an ideal ownership structure, assuming the two blocks operate independently of each other. In this type of structure, two or more independent groups are in a position to monitor management closely to ensure that it is fulfilling its agency role. At the same time, the two blocks are in a position to monitor each other effectively in a checks and balances context. Again, assuming there is no collaboration between the two independent blockholders, this minimizes the scope for abuse by an individual blockholder. In other words, the two keep each other honest. Consequently, the potential distortions of management or blockholder interests are removed, and the company's operations and governance structure is freed to focus on enhancing shareholder value. Hence, a multiple blockholder structure has the potential to mitigate

Table 5-2   Blockholder Influence

Range of Factor Outcomes	Potential Analytical Assessment
There is a blockholder that fulfills all or most of the following criteria: (1) disclosure of separation of influence of blockholder from management, (2) external investments by blockholder present no material conflicts of interest; no related-party transactions or a moderate scope reported on purely commercial terms, (3) significant balancing influence provided by independent directors and/or minority representatives who form a board majority or have a significant minority presence with a wide measure of veto powers, (4) minority shareholder rights are defined in the same terms as blockholder rights, (5) continuous and fair disclosure provides minorities with information comparable to that of blockholder, (6) voting rights and the level of shareholder activity are sufficient to provide meaningful minority representation; (7) where family owned and/or managed, there is evidence of succession planning that does not entrench current family.	Very strong to strong
There is a blockholder that fulfills most of the "very strong" criteria above.	Strong to moderate
There is a blockholder that demonstrates a certain degree of separation of influence from management, related-party transactions are reported on commercial terms, *and* the company must fulfill at least one or two more of the "very strong" criteria listed above.	Moderate to weak
Blockholders exist, but there is evidence of several of the following issues: (1) significant conflicts of interest; related-party or affiliate transactions without evidence of commercial terms, (2) independent directors and minority representatives have very limited ability to influence strategic decisions, (3) minority shareholder rights are defined in the same or weaker terms as blockholder rights, i.e., no special protections, (4) insider management and no disclosure of separation of influence, (5) blockholder has steady access to internal information that is not publicly disclosed, (6) family owned and/or managed and no succession planning to avoid entrenchment.	Weak to very weak

some of the key agency risks by managers and individual blockhold-ers, thus aligning the governance focus with the interests of a com-pany's minority shareholders.

Indeed, no ownership structure is flawless in the real world. The presence of two or more blockholders entails a specific governance risk: that of blockholders engaging in a confrontation, potentially bringing decision making to a halt. A vast volume of academic research provides evidence that a majority of international joint ven-tures actually fail.[2] In most joint enterprises, partners stumble upon an issue where they cannot agree, and an all-out confrontation may follow as disagreements take on an emotional aspect. Therefore, the analyst needs to assess the potential for such disagreements to arise, as indicated, for example, by the presence of distinctive strategic areas in which the interests of blockholders could diverge.

Whether the company's governance structures are resilient in these scenarios is probably even more important than is the potential for a conflict as such. When there is scope for third-party mediation such as that provided by independent directors, a natural method for con-flict resolution may be available. The votes of independent directors or minority representatives may play a deciding role when the posi-tions of blockholders differ. This may or may not ease the personal tensions, but at the very least a stalemate situation can be avoided. When these mechanisms are not present—and particularly when each of the strategic investors has wide veto powers under the company charter or under a shareholder agreement—blockholders may remain locked in a dispute for a long and painful period, with negative con-sequences for shareholder value. Shareholders eventually may have to agree on a buyout so that the business can move forward. Also, the extent to which a conflict affects operational decisions may depend

---

2 Donald Carroll Hambrick, Jiatao Li, Katherine R. Xin, and Anne S. Tsui, Compositional Gaps and Downward Spirals in International Joint Venture Management Groups. *Strategic Management Journal*, Vol. 22, No. 11, pp. 1033–1053, November 2001.

on whether the executives are seconded from blockholders or hired independently. Seconded or transferred managers are more likely to become involved in the confrontation as they may be seen or see themselves as agents of a specific blockholder (see Table 5-3).

Scenario 4: Government-Controlled Public Company

Governments control a significant number of large companies in many emerging economies, particularly in Russia and China. It is important to note that our methodology takes an agnostic perspective on ownership in the sense that it approaches all ownership structures from the same angle of an owner's motivation and the effectiveness of checks and balances. Therefore, as in the case of any other form of block-holding, ownership influence is assessed positively when a government's motivation is generally in line with that of other shareholders, the government maintains a hands-off approach to management, and independent directors and/or minority representatives are empowered to balance influences.

More often than not, however, governments are placed in a conflicted position in their ownership role because of their primary function of implementing public policy. In most cases, governments also have a limited ability to oversee the successful development of commercial enterprises. Recognizing these limitations, several developed countries, such as Australia, Denmark, the Netherlands, Norway, and Sweden, institutionalized specific governance guidelines for state-owned enterprises. In the most general form, such guidelines are presented in the Principles of Corporate Governance for State-Owned Enterprises of the Organization for Economic Cooperation and Development (OECD). The principles recommend, among other things, that the regulatory function of the government be clearly separated and independent of ownership policies. They further recommend that board composition of state-owned companies reflect the companies' need for impartial judgment and specific areas of expertise. This principle favors the appointment of

Table 5-3   Multiple Blockholder Influence

Range of Factor Outcomes	Potential Analytical Assessment
There are multiple blockholders acting independently of each other, and the following criteria are met: (1) none of the blockholders is involved in an executive function or seconds executives to the company, (2) external investments by blockholders present no material conflicts of interest, (3) there is no history of confrontation between blockholders or evidence of a potential conflict, (4) board structure and decision-making procedures provide for a deciding role of independent directors or minority representatives in a situation in which the positions of significant blockholders differ, (5) neither blockholder is entitled to specific veto rights on strategic decisions or executive appointments, (6) continuous and fair disclosure provides minorities with information comparable to that of blockholders, (7) voting rights and the level of shareholder activity are sufficient to provide meaningful minority representation.	Very strong to strong
There are multiple blockholders that fulfill most of the "very strong" criteria above.	Strong to moderate
There are multiple blockholders acting independently of each other, of which at least one is exposed to conflicts of interest. Although relations between blockholders are generally constructive, board structure and decision-making procedures make stalemate situations possible. Some of the executives are seconded from blockholders.	Moderate to weak
There are multiple blockholders acting independently of each other, and several of the following issues are present: (1) a significant proportion of executives is seconded from or formerly was employed by blockholders, (2) at least one of blockholders is exposed to material conflicts of interest, (3) there are precedents of confrontation between blockholders or evidence of a nascent conflict, (4) there is a potential for a stalemate in board decision making in a situation in which the positions of any two blockholders differ, (5) any of the blockholders is entitled directly or as a result of supermajority voting provisions to veto rights on strategic decisions or executive appointments, (6) blockholders have privileged access to company information, and/or (7) voting rights and the level of shareholder activity are not sufficient to provide meaningful minority representation.	Weak to very weak

independent directors with relevant backgrounds rather than the appointment of government officials to corporate boards. In some of those jurisdictions, a cap or even a ban on board seats held by government officials was introduced. Another important aspect highlighted by the principles is the transparency of mutual obligations between the company and the state. If the government expects a company to perform a certain public function and/or is willing to grant certain privileges (such as privileged access to subsoil resources), it is important that the specifics of those commitments be legislated and transparent.

In emerging economies, such governance remedies are rare. Furthermore, many governments do not hesitate to direct that the resources of state-owned companies serve the interests of public policy regardless of whether this creates shareholder value. In fact, the ability to use companies' resources as a public policy tool is often the government's main motivation for maintaining control. The value of government-controlled companies also may be negatively affected by lengthy bureaucratic decision-making procedures. It may be weakened further by corruption in government agencies that may lead to value-destroying transactions conducted in the interests of vested groups or influential individuals in the government.

The evaluation of shareholder influences will be guided primarily by the government's goals and potential conflicts with respect to the focal company, its track record in the controlling function, and the ability of minority shareholders and independent directors to balance government influence. Table 5-4 discusses government influence.

Scenario 5: Private (Nonpublic) Company

GAMMA has the explicit objective of assessing the strength of governance mechanisms in safeguarding the interests of (outsider) equity investors. This makes the application of GAMMA methodology to private companies somewhat counterintuitive. At the same time, a growing number of private companies in emerging economies are seeking

Table 5-4   Government Influence

Range of Factor Outcomes	Potential Analytical Assessment
The government is the ultimate owner of a majority or the largest single equity stake and fulfills most of the following criteria: (1) government has clear policies that separate ownership from other functions, such as industry regulation and social policy, (2) government expects the company to operate on a purely commercial basis, or all companies' commitments and liabilities before the government beyond those provided by law and regulation and privileges granted by the government are legislated and publicly disclosed, (3) all transactions with the government and related entities are reported as related-party transactions conducted on market terms, (4) a significant balancing influence is provided by independent directors and/or minority representatives who form a board majority or have a significant minority presence with a wide measure of veto powers, (5) minority shareholder rights are defined in the same terms as those of the government, (6) continuous and fair disclosure provides minorities with information comparable to that of the government, (7) voting rights and the level of shareholder activity are sufficient to provide meaningful minority representation, (8) executive appointments are performed on the basis of merit and are not limited to current or former officials.	Very strong to strong
Government is the ultimate owner of a majority or the largest single equity stake in the company and fulfills many of the "very strong" criteria.	Strong to moderate
Government is the ultimate owner of a majority or the largest single equity stake and generally follows the corporate procedures in exercising its influence, and the company must fulfill at least one or more of the "very strong" criteria listed above.	Moderate to weak
Government is the ultimate owner of a majority or the largest single equity stake. The government's influence on the company is unbalanced and to a large extent follows public policy goals rather than the objectives of shareholder value creation.	Weak to very weak

access to equity financing. Some of those companies are eager to learn how their governance structures stack up against those of public companies and how effective those structures are in supporting the interests of existing and potential equity investors. In this case, the analysis is similar to that performed at public companies, as suggested by the actual ownership structure (single or multiple blockholders, government-owned). Such analysis then is conducted as if the company were publicly traded. In recent years, Standard & Poor's Governance Services performed a number of these analyses in Russia and Kazakhstan, and several scores were made public (e.g., EuroChem, KEGOC, MDM Bank, TransTeleCom Co.).

Indeed, there may be more to such analysis than an assessment of governance structures in terms of IPO (initial public offering) preparedness. Relatively few private companies are in reality private. They may not issue public equity but may issue public debt, and there are almost always outside constituencies with concerns about fraud and mismanagement (a long list that includes employees, suppliers, customers, banks, coinvestors, and regulators). There are also legal precedents in the United States that indicate that the directors of private companies have fiduciary duties to the firm that are as strict as or stricter than those of public company directors.

There are numerous potential governance issues specific to private companies that may have a negative effect on the interests of such constituencies. In the long run, these issues may harm the large owner's interests as well:

- Key man risk. One person running the whole firm, often in his or her head
- Tunnel vision or lack of perspective as outsiders are kept away from the business
- Confusion between personal and corporate assets; misuse of corporate assets

As in the other ownership situations, an owner's motivation and the strength of checks and balances will guide the analysis of governance structures and practices in terms of their ability to mitigate these risks (see Table 5-5).

Table 5-5 Private Companies

Range of Factor Outcomes	Potential Analytical Assessment
The company is closely held by a limited number of shareholders and fulfills all or most of the following criteria: (1) there is evidence of separation of ownership from management, the board is the true decision-making body, and board procedures mediate the influence of shareholders, (2) external investments by shareholders do not present material conflicts of interest, (3) there is evidence of checks and balances provided by shareholders acting independently of each other or by influential independent board members, (4) the company is subject to public scrutiny (e.g., as a debt issuer or regulated entity), (5) there is a full-fledged internal audit department that reports to the board. The company undergoes independent external audits.	Very strong to strong
The company is closely held by a limited number of shareholders and fulfills several of the "very strong" criteria above. The board is the true decision-making body. Significant shareholders may be involved in executive functions, but there is evidence of a meaningful disciplining role provided by independent directors and minority shareholders.	Strong to moderate
The company is closely held by a limited number of shareholders. Significant shareholders may be involved in the executive functions, yet the management style is not dictatorial and there is a degree of balancing influence from independent directors and/or minority shareholders. Shareholders may have external investments that potentially lead to conflicts of interest, yet there is a clear distinction between corporate and personal assets. The company also must fulfill at least one or two more of the "very strong" criteria listed above.	Moderate to weak
The company is closely held by a limited number of shareholders, and there is very limited potential for checks and balances. Shareholders are subjected to conflicts of interest. There is no clear distinction between personal and corporate assets. There is evidence of executive appointments being relations-based, and there are signs of entrenchment	Weak to very weak

Chapter 6

Shareholder Rights: Do You Really Have Them?[1]

Even companies in the most emerging of emerging markets under-stand these days that enforcement of basic shareholder rights is a priority in attracting Western investment. Shareholder rights have improved remarkably in many of the BRIC countries since the early and middle 1990s through legislation and litigation. Most emerging economies have implemented basic provisions such as ensuring a "one share–one vote" policy, allowing shareholders to nominate and remove directors, providing for rights of first refusal on additional share issuances, and implementing protections against two-tier takeover strategies that result in a new owner buying minorities' shares at a price far less than that offered to the majority owner. In most countries, shareholder rights also cover rules for the annual shareholder meet-ing and prevent important meetings from being called in a remote town in Siberia or Amazonia on one day's notice.

Despite the improvements in recent years, the national statutes and regulatory policies of emerging economies still contain loopholes that may present considerable risks to investors. The significance of these

---

1 This chapter is based on an earlier text by Dan Konigsburg and was updated by Oleg Shvyrkov.

weaknesses and the exact nature of the risks they entail may differ enormously from one country to another. Russian law, for instance, provides a broad measure of voting rights, yet it has shown itself to be powerless in defending the financial rights of shareholders in complex situations such as a change in control or a squeeze-out. Conversely, Indian law provides a relatively narrow scope of direct voting rights (no recognition of cumulative voting in board elections, for example), yet that country has a stronger track record in protecting the financial rights of minority investors. There also can be a big difference in emerging markets between the law or rule on the books and its enforcement. In many cases legal systems and commercial courts are untested or lack precedents for foreign investors seeking recourse. In fact, many shareholder rights in BRIC countries may be illusory in that they offer only the appearance and not the substance of protection.

Partly as a result of regulatory weaknesses, the scope of shareholder rights may differ considerably among individual companies within the same emerging economy. Some companies voluntarily adopt standards of shareholder rights that are higher than those required by law and regulation. In Brazil, for example, companies are allowed to issue nonvoting preference shares with a variable dividend for up to 50% of charter capital. In practice, this arrangement creates a host of governance concerns, since it often is used by founder families to entrench their control while they maintain only a moderate equity interest. However, a growing number of companies (and blockholders) have agreed not to use this form of financing, as they prefer that all equity investors have equal rights. Thus, the Novo Mercado trading floor of the Bovespa exchange now includes over 100 companies that do not have preference shares.

Shareholder Rights: When Do You Need Them, and Will They Be There?

The ability of investors to both exercise control rights and share in the financial benefits of a company's success is at the core of good

corporate governance. Ownership rights can be divided into two categories: control rights and cash flow rights. Cash flow rights include
the right to a dividend and the right to receive proportionate payment for the sale of a share. Control rights are more procedural in
nature and focus on voting rights, including the right to attend
meetings and the right to convene a meeting. Cash flow and control rights may or may not imply fair and equal treatment, however,
and cash flow rights may not be equal among asset classes. It is more
difficult to categorize takeover defenses: Shareholders should have
the right to receive an offer for their shares and the right to be
treated equally with other members of the same share class in the
process. However, takeover defenses also can affect director
accountability. Takeover defense tactics are considered in more
detail later in this chapter.

The scope of control rights determines the potential extent of
minority influence. These rights may remain dormant for extended
periods. At companies in which management and/or blockholders
are reputable and competent independent directors watch over
minority interests, minority engagement often is limited and the
turnout at shareholder meetings is weak or moderate (such as at
Russia's New York Stock Exchange–listed MTS). At companies in
which shareholders are unhappy with management policies and
performance, however, minority investors may mobilize their influence by becoming active in board elections and nominating their
representatives to the board if their control rights empower them to
do that.

The extent to which control rights are given to shareholders
depends on a number of things but can be traced to fundamental
decisions about how much power should be delegated to the board
and how much should remain in shareholders' hands. With the
exception of the United Kingdom, which combines empowered
boards with extensive control rights and strong institutions, markets
that have weaker boards and less effective market regulation often

compensate shareholders by giving them more control rights.[2] In the United States, for example, almost all control rights other than the right to elect directors have been delegated to the board. Corporate law recognizes directors' fiduciary duties to act in the assumed interests of shareholders, and in most cases the threat of legal liability and/or public exposure ensures that this is done. In emerging markets, where the former threats are typically absent or ineffective and there is concern about misappropriation of shareholders' funds, company laws may recognize the need for more shareholder control rights. Russia is an example of a country with weak legal and regulatory institutions and a broad measure of direct control rights. In other countries, there may be less recognition that these controlling institutions are absent or ineffective, and so control rights may have to originate from within companies.

This raises the question of the importance of control rights in different markets, and we may assume that the importance of specific control rights in the context of a company's overall corporate governance will depend to a large degree on external factors that may compensate for such absence. A strong judiciary or a majority-independent board may mean that more of these rights can be delegated to the board.

In each individual case, the analysis of shareholder rights will be informed by a study of the national legal and regulatory infrastructure, examples of which are presented in Chapters 1 to 4. The assessment of this shareholder rights component will reflect the actual scope of control and cash flow rights that accrue to all shareholders by virtue of the legislation and company-specific arrangements reflected in statutory documents.

2 Rafael La Porta, Florencio Lopez-de-Silanes, Andrei Shleifer, and Robert Vishny. "Investor Protection and Corporate Governance." *Journal of Financial Economics.* Vol. 58, 2000, issues 1–2.

Shareholder Meeting Procedures

The right to attend and vote at shareholder meetings is a fundamental component of well-governed companies. At many companies, the annual meeting represents the only opportunity for smaller shareholders to exercise their ownership rights and to meet and discuss their concerns with management. Moreover, fair and equal treatment in the arena of shareholder voting often provides a window into how well companies treat shareholders in other areas. It is relatively easy to assess the strength of shareholder meeting procedures through public sources, though in some cases weaknesses will be made most apparent through attendance at meetings or access to meeting transcripts.

Procedures for advising shareholders about general meetings should provide for equal access to all shareholders and ensure that shareholders are furnished with sufficient and timely information. Questions to ask include how the company advises shareholders (including beneficial shareholders) about shareholder meetings, how much notice is given, what information or papers are circulated before meetings, and what kind of information is included in the notice. Meeting notices should give shareholders a good understanding of why a meeting has been called, how to cast a vote, and the background and rationale for proposed voting items. Companies should provide any supplementary information that would be needed for shareholders to make informed voting decisions (see Table 6-1).

Beyond notices of meetings and disclosure of voting procedures, the procedures themselves should ensure equal and fair participation for all shareholders. If it is unduly expensive or difficult for a large proportion of the shareholders to attend or if the shareholders are required to pay fees to attend meetings, the efficacy and perhaps the legitimacy of meetings may be in question. Fairness and predictability are central concerns here, and if there are minimum share requirements for attendance or if registration procedures are not transparent, convenient, and

Table 6-1 Shareholder Meeting Information

Factor	Range of Factor Outcomes	Potential Analytical Assessment
Meeting Notification	Shareholders are notified individually and by the company Web site, and there is evidence of attempts to ensure that beneficial shareholders receive notice (a professional level of proxy services is provided).	Very strong
	Shareholders are notified individually.	Strong
	Notice is posted in a widely read newspaper or on the company Web site.	Moderate to weak
	Notice is posted only in a locally read newspaper (if the notice is sent out, it is sent only to shareholders).	Weak to very weak
Notice Period	The notice period is at least 21 days.	Very strong to strong
	The notice period is less than 21 days.	Moderate to very weak
	There is no notice period.	Very weak
Notice Information	The information distributed includes (1) date and location, (2) agenda, (3) background information on issues to be decided, (4) details of voting procedures, (5) financial statements, (6) director and auditor reports, and (7) information needed to vote on (a) large transactions and (b) candidates for the board.	Very strong to strong
	The information distributed includes at least (1) and (2) and then one or more of (3), (4), or (5).	Strong to moderate
	The information distributed includes at least (1) and (2).	Weak
	No information.	Very weak

equal for all shareholders, confidence in the company as a whole may be at risk (see Table 6-2).

Even the way proposals are presented to shareholders at meetings can be relevant: Bundled resolutions—that is, combinations of disparate issues in which one issue is favorable to shareholders but

Table 6-2   Meeting Participation

Meeting Accessibility	Meetings are held in the "home city," the company's main region, or a place where the majority of shareholders live. Meetings are held at a venue accessible to most shareholders.	Very strong to strong
	Meetings are held at a venue accessible to most shareholders. Meeting location may be less convenient, but there are no roadblocks to attendance.	Strong to moderate
	Difficulties may be encountered by many shareholders (especially individual minority shareholders) in attending.	Weak to very weak
	Difficulties may be encountered by many shareholders (especially individual minority shareholders) in attending, and they have to pay for attendance.	Very weak

others are not—can present investors with a difficult all-or-nothing choice. At their worst, those resolutions can be used to introduce a negative change that shareholders would not be likely to approve if they were presented on their own. A well-organized shareholder meeting also provides an opportunity for a thorough question and answer (Q&A) session (see Table 6-3).

Another element in the analysis of voting procedures is the way companies handle voting by shareholders who are not able to attend. Companies may entitle shareholders to vote by mail, by telephone, or electronically on the Internet. Many companies facilitate these rights by allowing representatives, or proxies, to attend and vote at shareholder meetings. However, there can be wide variation in the arrangements companies make to ensure that shareholders who are unable to attend meetings can vote through proxies: Deadlines for completing and sending voting forms back to the company or its registrar can be short. Some companies take additional measures to solicit voting instructions from beneficial holders by hiring proxy solicitors to contact custodians; others encourage custodians to provide shareholders with information about their options for the use of their voting rights themselves. Table 6-4 analyzes voting procedures.

Table 6-3   Meeting Discussions

Questions at AGM	Both shareholders and proxies have the right to ask questions in a general meeting of shareholders, and there is usually sufficient time for discussion.	Very strong to moderate
	Shareholders have the ability to ask questions in a shareholder meeting, and there is usually sufficient time for discussion.	Strong to moderate
	Shareholders have the ability to ask questions in a shareholder meeting, but the time allowed has been known to be insufficient in the past.	Moderate to weak
	Shareholders do not have the ability to ask questions.	Very weak

Table 6-4   Voting Procedures

Proxy Rights	Shareholders are entitled to appoint a proxy to attend and vote and/or vote by post and/or vote electronically. Voting standards are clearly articulated and independently verified. If there are ADRs, they cannot be voted without instruction. Proxies are sent out in good time.	Very strong
	Shareholders are entitled to appoint a proxy to attend and vote and/or vote by post and/or vote electronically. Cheap, transparent, and simple voting procedures are in place for all shareholders unable to attend. Proxies are sent out in good time.	Strong to very strong
	Cheap, transparent, and simple voting procedures are in place for all shareholders unable to attend. Proxies are sent out in good time.	Moderate to strong
	Cheap, transparent, and simple voting procedures are in place for all shareholders unable to attend, but voting options granted to proxies are unequal (e.g., director elections are bundled into one resolution on the proxy card) or proxies are not sent out in good time.	Moderate
	Voting procedures are not clear, and there are no provisions for voting in absentia.	Weak to very weak

Companies with bearer shares instead of registered shares must find a way to ensure that those who vote at shareholder meetings are in fact current shareholders. Without a register, or list of current holders, some companies have resorted to share blocking, in which a bearer shareholder will deposit company shares with his or her broker for a number of days before the meeting, promising not to trade the shares for the duration. This process also is called share freezing. Share blocking or freezing forces holders to decide between voting rights on the one hand and the flexibility to sell shares on the other hand.

If the company has an overseas listing via a depositary facility (for example, U.S. American Depositary Receipts), the provisions of the depositary agreement can vary as well, with corresponding effects on shareholder rights. For example, some agreements allow the depositary or even a management designee to vote shares on behalf of investors who have not submitted voting instructions to the depositary bank. Other agreements have been designed to accept votes only from beneficial owners who have provided voting instructions. Similarly, in the United States some companies allow brokers to vote in the assumed interests of beneficiaries even if the beneficiaries have not sent voting instructions (see Table 6-5).

Table 6-5 ADRs

Voting without Consent: Depositary Receipts	If there is an overseas listing via depositary receipts, the deposit agreement prevents the depositary or management designees from voting shares on which they have received no instructions. Other custodians also do not vote without beneficial owners' consent.	Very strong to strong
	Depositary banks and other custodians routinely vote their shares without owners' consent.	Moderate to very weak

Voting Rights

Even when shareholder meeting procedures are state of the art, minority shareholders may be unable to appoint or remove directors or otherwise promote their interests in the company. Whether shareholder assemblies are largely ceremonial or shoot real bullets depends on the measure of voting rights that extend to all shareholders.

These rights often define the extent of minority influence. Specific provisions of the national laws and norms defined under corporate statutory documents determine the extent to which shareholders affect the composition of governing bodies and participate in major decisions at the company. Those rights may include the following:

- The right to an equality of economic and voting interests in a company, or one share–one vote provisions.
- The right to equal treatment within share classes. There should be no classes of shares with variable rights, or if variable rights do exist, they should be explicit and some form of economic benefit should offset the lack of specific rights. This is particularly the case with regard to voting rights.
- Preemptive rights, or the right of first refusal over dilutive share issuances, including the right not to be threatened by large issuances of preferred stock (so-called blank-check preferred stock provisions).
- The right of shareholders to convene a special shareholder meeting.
- The right of shareholders to put forward specific shareholder proposals.
- The right of shareholders to nominate directors to the board.
- The right to approve specific corporate actions subject to reasonable threshold levels: mergers, acquisitions, disposals, restructurings, changes in corporate purpose, changes to class rights, share option/incentive plans, poison pills and other

defense measures, related-party transactions, amendments to the corporate bylaws/articles.[3]

- The right to approve routine corporate proposals: financial statements, auditors and auditors' fees, dividends.
- The right to elect or remove all directors—executive and nonexecutive—each year.
- The right of shareholders to control board size and board vacancies. An important question is whether the board has the right to increase or decrease its size between shareholder meetings.

Accordingly, the assessment of the actual scope of voting rights is performed along several dimensions, as shown in Table 6-6.

Cash Flow Rights

Cash flow rights include the right to receive a dividend, the right to have excess cash returned if the company cannot find suitable uses for it, the right to participate in share buybacks at a fair price, and the right to receive proportional payment on liquidation of the company.

Cash flow rights may include the following:

- The right to secure ownership and full transferability of shares.
- Tag-along (cosale) rights, or the right of minority shareholders to receive the same offer accepted by a majority shareholder.

---

3 Different companies and jurisdictions will have different rules on shareholder approval, even of similar items. Share option or incentive plans, for example, require shareholder approval in many markets only if they involve the issuance of new shares or involve grants to directors. In the United States, recent proposals to exchange listing rules now require shareholder approval of all share plans, even if awards will be covered by treasury stock. See "Corporate Governance Rule Proposal," NYSE.

Table 6-6 Voting Rights Standards

Factor	Range of Factor Outcomes	Potential Analytical Assessment
Meeting Notification	Shareholders are notified individually and on the company Web site, and there is evidence of attempts to ensure that beneficial shareholders receive notice (a professional level of proxy services is provided).	Very strong
	Shareholders are notified individually.	Strong
	Notice is posted in a widely read newspaper or on the company Web site.	Moderate to weak
	Notice is posted only in a locally read newspaper (if the notice is sent out, it is sent only to shareholders).	Weak to very weak
Notice Period	The notice period is at least 21 days.	Very strong to strong
	The notice period is less than 21 days.	Moderate to very weak
	There is no notice period.	Very weak
Meeting Accessibility	Meetings are held in the "home city," the company's main region, or a place where the majority of shareholders live. Meetings are held at a venue accessible to most shareholders.	Very strong to strong
	Meetings are held at a venue accessible to most shareholders. Meeting location may be less convenient, but there are no roadblocks to attendance.	Strong to moderate
	Difficulties may be encountered by many shareholders (especially individual minority shareholders) in attending.	Weak to very weak
	Difficulties may be encountered by many shareholders (especially individual minority shareholders) in attending, and they have to pay for attendance.	Very weak
Notice Information	The information distributed includes (1) date and location, (2) agenda, (3) background information on issues to be decided, (4) details of voting procedures, (5) financial statements, (6) director and auditor reports, and (7) information needed to vote on (a) large transactions and (b) candidates for the board.	Very strong to strong

	The information distributed includes at least (1) and (2) and then one or more of (3), (4), and (5).	Strong to moderate
	The information distributed includes at least (1) and (2).	Weak
	No information.	Very weak
Proxy Rights	Shareholders are entitled to appoint a proxy to attend and vote and/or vote by post and/or vote electronically. Voting standards are clearly articulated and independently verified. If there are ADRs, they cannot be voted without instruction. Proxies are sent out in good time.	Very strong
	Shareholders are entitled to appoint a proxy to attend and vote and/or vote by post and/or vote electronically. Cheap, transparent, and simple voting procedures are in place for all shareholders unable to attend. Proxies are sent out in good time.	Strong to very strong
	Cheap, transparent, and simple voting procedures are in place for all shareholders unable to attend. Proxies are sent out in good time.	Moderate to strong
	Cheap, transparent, and simple voting procedures are in place for all shareholders unable to attend, but voting options granted to proxies are unequal (e.g., director elections are bundled into one resolution on the proxy card) or proxies are not sent out in good time.	Moderate
	Voting procedures are not clear, and there are no provisions for voting in absentia.	Weak to very weak
Voting without Consent: Depositary Receipts	If there is an overseas listing via depositary receipts, the deposit agreement prevents the depositary or management designees from voting shares on which they have received no instructions. Other custodians also do not vote without beneficial owners' consent.	Very strong to strong
	Depositary banks and other custodians routinely vote their shares without owners' consent.	Moderate to very weak
Security of Ownership	Secure ownership is guaranteed by a transparent and independent registrar system (where ADRs are in place, the depositary bank is reputable).	Very strong to strong
	The registrar is not independent, but security is generally high.	Moderate
	Registrar is not independent and has no reputation for reliability.	Weak to very weak

(Continued)

Table 6-6 (*Continued*)

Factor	Range of Factor Outcomes	Potential Analytical Assessment
Equality of Voting Rights	There are no distinct classes of common shares: The charter establishes a one share–one vote principle. The rights of preference shares are clearly articulated. There is no provision for block voting, multiple voting power, or supermajority requirements that can interfere with the election of directors or the ratification of corporate actions.	Very strong
	Any classes of common shares or preference shares are clearly articulated. There may be a shareholder agreement, but its contents are clearly disclosed, it does not block minority interests, and there is no evidence of unequal treatment.	Strong to moderate
	There are different classes of common shares, and there is evidence of unequal treatment of minority shareholders.	Moderate to very weak
	There is poor disclosure of shareholder agreements.	Weak to very weak
	There are undisclosed shareholder agreements.	Very weak
Right to Call a Meeting	Shareholders accounting for up to 10% of total shares can call an extraordinary general meeting (EGM). This is specified in both the company charter and other shareholder communications (e.g., company Web site). The company notifies shareholders of this right.	Very strong
	Shareholders accounting for at least 10% can call an EGM. The company does not necessarily notify shareholders of this right.	Strong
	The number of shareholders required to call an EGM is above 10%. The company does not necessarily notify shareholders of this right.	Moderate
	Shareholders cannot call an EGM but may have other methods for calling meetings to address specific issues (e.g., proxy contests) that approximate but do not replace the ability to call a meeting.	Weak
	Shareholders cannot call an EGM.	Weak to very weak

Shareholder Proposals	Shareholders accounting for at least 5% can place items on the agenda. This is specified in both the company charter and other shareholder communications (e.g., company Web site).	Very strong
	The number of shareholders required to place an item on the agenda is above 5%. The company does notify shareholders of their rights.	Strong to moderate
	Shareholders do not have the ability to place an item on the agenda.	Moderate to very weak
	Unless materially detrimental to shareholder interests, shareholders have voted to approve a shareholder proposal, and the board has not implemented the resolution.	Very weak
Decision Rights	Decisions reserved for the shareholder assembly: (1) elect and remove directors, (2) approve the company's accounts and directors' report, (3) appoint and remove auditors, (4) approve changes to the charter and major decisions involving a reorganization in the company or a change in its activities or other extraordinary transactions, (5) approve payments of amount of final dividends, (6) authorize additional non–pro rata issues of shares, creation of new classes of shares, or changes to voting rights, and, (7) material related-party transactions on non–arm's length terms, to be approved by noninterested shareholders.	Very strong to strong
	Issues (1), (3), (6), and (7) are reserved for the shareholder assembly.	Moderate
	The shareholder assembly decides on fewer issues than those above.	Weak to very weak
Director Elections	Director elections are transparent, made by cumulative voting (if desirable), and all nominations are voted on.	Very strong to strong
	Some director nominations/appointments are not voted on by shareholders. Partially transparent or cumulative voting unnecessary or necessary because of ownership structure.	Moderate to weak
	Director nominations and/or appointments are not voted on by shareholders.	Weak to very weak

- The right to receive a bid for all outstanding shares when a large percentage of shares (typically 30%) is bought by a larger shareholder (a mandatory bid).
- The right to receive fair compensation in the event of a legitimate squeeze-out.
- A clearly articulated dividend policy. This is very important for investors seeking current income in addition to long-term capital appreciation.
- Dividend payout procedures that provide for a timely remittance of dividends; interim dividends are a plus.
- Payout procedures to ensure equal treatment of all shareholders.

This element of governance analysis does not address the actual size of company earnings, dividends, and capital gains or account for possible losses caused by blockholder influence (such as asset stripping) or weak board performance. Although decisive for the actual volume of shareholder returns, these possible losses and/or lack of oversight are included in the analytical framework of other components (primarily the first and the fourth components) and therefore are not duplicated here.

Accordingly, the assessment of the actual scope of cash flow rights is performed along several dimensions, as shown in Table 6-7.

Takeover Defenses

In addition to voting procedures, cash flow, and control rights, any discussion of ownership rights will include an analysis of takeover defenses and the market for corporate control. Investors should expect to receive a premium for their shares if there is a change in control or to see significant change in severely underperforming managements, including in the latter case nil-premium takeovers proposed by more competent managers. Beyond the financial benefits that accrue to

Table 6-7 Cash Flow Rights

Dividends and Financial Rights	A dividend policy exists and has been clearly articulated to shareholders (and the company follows it). Further, any declared dividend payments have been made expeditiously. All shareholders are treated equally in takeovers or restructurings.	Very strong to strong
	There is no evidence of unequal treatment of shareholders. Dividend policy may be vague or followed inconsistently.	Moderate
	There is no dividend policy, or existing policy is rarely followed.	Weak
	There is clear evidence of unequal financial treatment of shareholders, whether this relates to dividend payments or treatment in a takeover or restructuring.	Weak to very weak
Preemptive Rights	Shareholders have preemptive rights in proportion to their shareholding and are notified of those rights in company materials.	Very strong
	Shareholders have preemptive rights in proportion to their shareholding.	Strong
	Shareholders have preemptive rights, but there have been problems exercising those rights in the past, or they extend only to specific classes or types of shares.	Moderate
	Shareholders do not have preemptive rights.	Weak to very weak
Mandatory Bids and Squeeze-Outs	In the event of a change in control or the emergence of a new significant blockholding exceeding 30% of equity, minority shareholders are entitled to sell their equity stakes in a company at a fair price. The sale price will be based on the highest of the weighted-average market price and the price paid by the acquirer to any significant shareholder. This right extends to all share classes and is effectively supported by the legislation, regulators, and the judiciary. No exemptions for indirect ownership by the acquirer are allowed. Squeeze-outs are possible only when the blockholder owns over 90% of equity and involve reliable price-setting procedures.	Very strong to strong
	Most of the "very strong" conditions are met; however, there may be concerns about the applicability of tag-along rights to certain classes of stock, the effectiveness of valuation procedures, or the ability of blockholders to avoid the buyout procedures in some situations.	Moderate
	Mandatory buyout procedures do not exist or are poorly enforced. Squeeze-out procedures do not ensure fair valuation.	Weak to very weak

shareholders as they realize premiums on their shares, the possibility of an unwanted takeover can provide short- to medium-term performance pressure on managers.

Although there is room for debate about the extent to which certain decisions should be delegated to the board, the ultimate decision on a change in control, particularly if there is more than one possible bid, should be made by the shareholders. Antitakeover provisions that unreasonably remove this decision-making power from shareholders, taking into account the board's greater knowledge of outstanding bids and shareholders' collective action problems, should be viewed as a negative factor.

Despite this, specific takeover defenses must not be viewed in a vacuum, separately from other governance factors, such as board independence and incentive pay for managers. Majority independent boards are likely to accept reasonable or compelling bids despite pressure from a defensive management or the presence of a poison pill, because they will be aware of their fiduciary duties and outside scrutiny. Similarly, despite the potentially perverse incentives that may exist outside a takeover situation, incentive compensation that pays out on a successful change in control may make managers more amenable to a takeover if they are confident of their eventual financial security.[4]

Companies in which changes of control are unlikely despite a lack of structural defenses also must be considered on a case-by-case basis. This includes companies in which industrial or strategic importance to a particular country would invite interference from the government during a takeover bid. Indeed, majority-held companies are virtually immune to takeovers. Although it may be true that immunity from takeover bids is negative in any ownership situation, the majority owner also has the largest amount of capital at risk and bears the

---

4 Marcel Kahan, and Edward R. Rock. "How I Learned to Stop Worrying and Love the Pill: Adaptive Responses to Takeover Law." *University of Chicago Law Review.* Vol. 69, nr. 3, Summer 2002, pp. 871–915.

largest share of costs in the event of poor performance. With a significant investment at stake, a majority shareholder is relatively more likely to be persuaded to sell out to a prospective bidder than is a controlling shareholder with a minority stake, whose main benefits may come in the form of perks. From this perspective, majority ownership can be seen as the most market-based of the takeover defenses.

Examples of more common takeover defenses in both developed and emerging economies are listed below:

- Double voting rights for long-term shareholders (France and some former colonies).
- Issuance of voting preference shares to voting trusts that are friendly to management (Netherlands).
- Golden shares offering a veto to an important shareholder or stakeholder, including a government (Russia, various other jurisdictions).
- Shareholder agreements offering golden share benefits to a strategic holder or holders or syndicate pacts (Italy, France), in which two or more shareholders agree to vote together with the purpose of preventing a change in control.
- Voting or ownership that caps restricting voting or share ownership at a certain percentage of outstanding shares (various).
- Staggered, or classified, boards (United States, Canada).
- Poison pills (United States, Canada; also called shareholder rights plans). Poison pills take many forms but are typically provisions that give shareholders certain conditional rights that become effective during a takeover and significantly raise the costs of mounting a bid. Typically, a triggered pill automatically will issue new shares in some ratio (e.g., two shares for every one already held) to all shareholders except the one making a bid, thus diluting the potential acquirer's stake in the company and making it more expensive for the

acquirer to buy out the remaining shares. Pills usually are triggered when an acquirer's stake reaches a specified percentage of total shares.

- Dual-class capital structures designed for one shareholder or one family.
- The ability to issue a large number of shares without preemptive rights.
- Greenmail provisions, including "fair price" provisions that place limitations on a company's ability to buy back shares from a particular shareholder at higher-than-market prices (United States).
- Supermajority voting requirements, particularly for approving a change in control. Depending on companies' ownership structures, these can be used to entrench management or protect minority shareholders (various jurisdictions).
- Freeze-out provisions (also called merger moratorium laws) preventing a shareholder from buying more than a certain percentage of shares for a period of one to three years (various U.S. states).
- Control-share provisions that block the purchase of more than a 20% interest in a company unless the acquirer first wins majority approval from holders of the other shares (various U.S. states).
- Restrictions on shareholders acting by written consent (acting by written ballot unconnected with a shareholder meeting).
- Protected board seats, in which no shareholder can remove a director who never stands for reelection.

Table 6-8 analyzes ownership controls.

Table 6-8 Ownership Controls

Takeover Defenses	There are no takeover defenses, whether structural or nonstructural. If there are antitakeover provisions, there are other factors (e.g., a substantial majority-independent board and meetings with directors) that mitigate concerns or provide comfort that bids attractive to shareholders will be accepted. If there are structural defenses, they have been approved by shareholders.	Very strong to strong
	There are one or more takeover defenses, and there is little likelihood that they will be used or triggered. This is confirmed by meetings with the directors.	Strong to moderate
	There are one or more takeover defenses, and there is a moderate likelihood that they will be used or triggered. Shareholders have not approved takeover defenses such as poison pills.	Moderate
	There are one or more takeover defenses, and there is a high likelihood that they will be used or triggered.	Weak
	The company has used a takeover defense in the last two years that was materially against the interests of shareholders.	Very weak
Market for Corporate Control	The company is completely open to potential bids. There is an appropriate amount of oversight by shareholders over takeovers and/or changes in control, including the ability of shareholders to judge the merits (and vote on) potential bids. Takeover protections would not dissuade potential acquirers or increase the costs of mounting a takeover.	Very strong to strong
	The takeover defenses that exist would be mildly frustrating to a potential bidder (including structural defenses that need not be triggered). There is no realistic possibility for a change in control despite an absence of takeover provisions; this may be linked to ownership structure, a public interest role, or government interests.	Strong to moderate
	The takeover defenses that exist would be moderately frustrating to a potential bidder. Structural defenses that need not be triggered are moderately to highly frustrating.	Moderate
	The takeover defenses that exist would be highly frustrating to a potential bidder (including structural defenses that need not be triggered).	Weak to very weak

Chapter 7

Transparency, Audit, and Risk Management: Risk-Averse, Risk-Adjusted, and Just Plain Risky[1]

Issues of transparency and disclosure and audit and risk management are critical to investors in emerging markets. After all, many foreign shareholders invested in those firms in the first place because they believed such firms offer a higher rate of return. If the promised growth of the company is in fact an illusion or if breakneck growth depends on a precarious strategy of excessive risk taking, the advantages of investing in an emerging market may be lost. This chapter will examine in depth the signs of a highly transparent company, what specific disclosures to look for, and which disclosures are signs of a corporate regime to be avoided. For example, companies that open a window into executive compensation are likely to be willing to let outside investors see similarly sensitive financial data. In contrast, companies that do not publish financial statements according to U.S. generally accepted accounting principles (GAAP) or International

---

1 This chapter is based on earlier methodology documents by Amra Balic, Dan Konigsburg, and George Dallas that have been updated by Oleg Shvyrkov.

Financial Reporting Standards (IFRS) may be more interested in gaming the local tax authorities than in becoming more transparent to their shareholders.

Whether a company is a boring, steady-as-it-goes utility or a high-growth technology firm, the way it manages the risk it takes on as a business is another major factor in how well it is governed. Investors should look at the kinds of risk companies deal with (credit risk, market risk, liquidity risk, operational risk, political risk, and even reputational risk) and the way those risks are managed. If a company does not disclose details about its risk management process, how can investors know whether an adequate system is in place? Of course, the board's audit committee also plays a role in risk oversight, and investors can inform themselves about the quality and independence of the committee from a few key disclosures. The following sections provide a clear how-to guide for getting behind the numbers and understanding how closely risks are being watched.

Transparency and Disclosure

Transparency is one of the core principles of corporate governance. It relates to the quality, content, and timeliness of company disclosure. The audit process is essential in this context, as is the underlying rigor and independence of accounting information that a company discloses. However, a robust transparency regime extends beyond financial disclosure to encompass other aspects that are important to investors. This includes disclosure relating to a company's broad strategy and mission, its operational and competitive dynamics, key corporate actions, its ownership structure, its shareholder rights, and its management and board structures. Increasingly, the focus on disclosure is addressing nonfinancial performance, particularly in the realm of social and environmental reporting.

At a very basic level, transparency helps external investors make informed investment decisions—a vital governance strength in its own right. More often than not, investors reward transparent issuers with lower costs of capital, which is an important competitive advantage. In emerging economies, there is a general trend toward stronger disclosure by companies that raise relatively cheap capital on the international capital markets.

Transparency also affects the overall governance architecture in a number of subtler ways. Most important, strong disclosure bridges the information gap between insiders and external investors, allowing them to hold management and the board accountable for company performance. It therefore is not surprising that transparency and disclosure often are seen as leading indicators of a company's overall governance standards, as companies that have a higher level and higher quality of disclosure tend to be more open and investor-friendly.

In many emerging markets, relatively generic and superficial information disclosure is the norm and fails to meet the information needs of investors and other users. Standards of statutory disclosure vary significantly among countries, as does the effectiveness of their enforcement. Increasingly, leading companies in emerging markets are developing disclosure programs that exceed the domestic regulatory norms. At the same time, the leading international exchanges have become increasingly important in setting disclosure standards in the emerging world, as the number of companies raising capital on the international markets has increased.

Ownership and Governance Disclosure

Understanding the ownership structure of a company is essential, especially when there is a possible blockholder with significant voting power or when de facto majority holdings may exist on the basis of collusive shareholding arrangements. It is difficult if not impossible to assess the influence of a company's blockholders if the identity or exact size of their stake is not clear. Moreover, when blockholders exist, transparency of ownership goes beyond identifying the size of their stake. Other pertinent information is important in assessing existing or potential blockholder influence, such as the blockholders' other interests, the register of related-party transactions, and the relationship of the blockholders to the individual company managers.

It is also important to know the exact amounts held by a company's senior managers and directors regardless of whether those individuals have large equity positions. Information on the backgrounds of executives and board members is also important from the perspective of analyzing their affiliations and possible loyalties.

A particular problem is getting behind the beneficial holders of nominee accounts, as it is the beneficial holders who hold the control rights in an individual company. Even the most transparent companies in the most advanced markets cannot know all the beneficial holders behind nominee holdings. Some companies address this issue by engaging a shareholder tracking service—a service offered by proxy solicitation firms—to track down the details of the beneficial holders to the greatest extent possible.

Disclosure standards on ownership structure can vary from jurisdiction to jurisdiction; however, the requirement to disclose individual owners who have at least 5% of a company's shares is the most common. In most cases, this is sufficient to analyze meaningful shareholder influences. However, a greater level of detail becomes desirable in situations in which there is a risk of consolidated ownership stakes emerging without the company's knowledge to account for the magnitude of such potential concentrations on the basis of the available ownership information.

Table 7-1 lists the most important shareholder disclosure criteria.

Accounting Standards

IFRS, U.S. GAAP, and several other accounting systems generally are recognized in international financial markets as world class on the basis of their approach and comprehensiveness. However, there are

Table 7-1 Shareholder Disclosure Criteria

Factor	Range of Factor Outcomes	Potential Analytical Assessment
Disclosure of Beneficial Ownership and Control	Full disclosure identifying major and majority beneficial owners and/or control right holders, *and* disclosure of holdings in excess of 5%, *and* disclosure of all outstanding options over shares. There should be no shareholding structures that obscure ownership (pyramids, shell, or holding companies).	Very strong
	Disclosure sufficient to ascertain de facto majority holder or major holder with veto power *and* disclosure of holdings in excess of 5%. Disclosure of beneficial ownership and control right holders in excess of 10%.	Strong Moderate
	Some but inadequate reporting on beneficial ownership, voting control of board, and management.	Weak
	No reporting.	Very weak
Disclosure of Indirect Structures	Disclosure enumerates and explains indirect shareholding structure, including ADRs.	Very strong to strong
	Indirect shareholding structure not disclosed; there is no information on managerial shareholdings; shareholders are unidentifiable private corporations and possibly are in tax havens.	Weak to very weak
Minority Interests and Intrafirm and Related-Party Transactions	There is detailed disclosure of minority interests and intrafirm and related-party transactions. No evidence of transfer pricing, hidden transfers, special treatment of arrears with related companies, or omissions in financial reporting. No evidence of noncommercial transactions.	Very strong to moderate
	Some omission of minority interests but no omission of related-party and intrafirm transactions.	Moderate to weak
	Significant omission of minority interests and/or omission of related-party and intrafirm transactions.	Weak

(Continued)

Table 7-1 *(Continued)*

Factor	Range of Factor Outcomes	Potential Analytical Assessment
	No disclosure of related-party transactions and minority interests.	Weak to very weak
Governance-Related Disclosure	There is detailed disclosure of key governance-related information, including ownership information, shareholder rights, takeover defenses, management backgrounds and structures, board member backgrounds and structures, a code of ethics, and a company mission statement.	Very strong to strong
	There is some disclosure of key governance-related information, but several components may be incomplete or missing.	Moderate
	There is little, if any, disclosure of relevant governance-related issues.	Weak to very weak

many individual accounting standards on a global basis that may vary widely in quality and orientation. Some are robust and comparable with world-class standards. Others may be narrow or incomplete in scope, often driven by the desire to minimize corporate income tax. Even for the most sophisticated financial analysts operating with a multinational perspective, it is difficult if not impossible to master the intricate details of numerous accounting systems.

Accordingly, convergence in accounting principles has become a global trend. Many companies in emerging economies report under IFRS or U.S. GAAP standards in addition to local standards or at least provide a reconciliation with internationally recognized accounts. Indeed, regulators in most countries have agreed to abandon national standards in favor of the IFRS. Thus, in 2007, shortly after the European Union converted to IFRS, China adopted new accounting principles that are very close to IFRS. Brazil is set to convert to IFRS in 2010, and India in 2011. Russia, however, has not committed to a specific timeline for such conversion despite the fact that its domestic accounting rules are by far the weakest among the national standards in the BRIC pack.

Even within the well-established accounting frameworks such as U.S. GAAP, there is room for discretion. Analysts should not be satisfied simply because a company's accounts are compiled according to globally recognized accounting standards. In this regard, controversial issues such as the expensing of options and the treatment of company pension earnings and expenses or reporting practices for cash flow have to be scrutinized from the perspective of insights that the existing reporting practices provide into the economic processes they describe. Table 7-2 lists the elements of accounting disclosure.

Table 7-2   Accounting Disclosure

Accounting Standards	Company financial statements are produced according to local country accounting requirements and according to at least one internationally recognized set of accounting standards (U.S. GAAP, IFRS, or near equivalent), and both former and latter are audited.	Very strong to strong
	Company financial statements are produced according to local country accounting requirements, and the company provides a reconciliation of its accounts according to an internationally recognized set of accounting standards (U.S. GAAP, IFRS, etc.).	Strong to moderate
	Company financial statements are produced according to local country accounting requirements and according to at least one internationally recognized set of accounting standards (U.S. GAAP, IFRS); the former are audited, and the latter are not.	Moderate to weak
	Company financial statements are produced, but there is clear evidence of noncompliance with local country accounting standards. Audit may not have been performed or may not have been accepted. No attempts to produce accounts in accordance with international accounting standards.	Weak to very weak
	Company financial statements are produced, but there is no attempt to provide information that is useful to shareholders. Reports are for tax compliance purposes only.	Very weak

Operating Disclosure

Unlike financial disclosures, which generally are mandated by accounting principles, the scope of operating disclosure to a great extent remains at the discretion of companies. Industry-specific indicators, information on the competitive environment, strategy guidelines, and forecasts are important for external assessment of company performance and growth potential and often are provided by transparent companies above and beyond the regulatory norms. Table 7-3 summarizes the disclosure of operating information.

Fair and Continuous Disclosure

The concepts of fair and continuous disclosure have been adopted into legislation in many jurisdictions (such as Regulation FD in the United States) and provide a framework and discipline for companies to disclose material developments on a "continuous" basis, that is, when those developments occur as opposed to waiting for the next quarterly or semiannual reporting cycle to come around. For example, if a senior executive sells shares or exercises options, this can be an important signal to investors that warrants prompt communication.

Table 7-3 Operating Information

Operating Disclosure	There is a detailed discussion of the company's operating strategy and the nature of its operations and competitive environment. The company actively and objectively compares its operating standards with those of its peers.	Very strong
	There is a detailed discussion of the company's operating strategy and the nature of its operations and competitive environment.	Strong
	There is disclosure of some of the company's operating strategy and the nature of its operations.	Moderate to weak
	There is little, if any, meaningful operating disclosure.	Weak to very weak

The example of Enron senior management selling its own shares while encouraging its employees to buy company shares is a notable example of this.

The notion of fair disclosure means that information should be provided to the market as a whole via newswires or other communications platforms, not disclosed selectively to a privileged group of analysts or other shareholders. The concepts of fair disclosure and continuous disclosure in principle provide a basis for timely and equitable disclosure above and beyond normal reporting cycles. However, to the extent that the materiality of what needs to be disclosed on this basis remains a matter of discretion, there is the risk that companies may choose a very high materiality threshold, with the result that the effectiveness of a fair and continuous disclosure regime may be less robust in practice than it may appear to be in theory (see Table 7-4).

Table 7-4   Disclosure Requirements

Fair and Continuous Disclosure	The company discloses public information in a continuous and fair manner, based on its own internal guidelines or prevailing regulations. Continuous disclosure means that key corporate actions or events are communicated as they happen, not subject to periodic reporting cycles. Fair disclosure means that corporate communications are distributed fairly to the market as a whole, not to selected individuals or institutions.	Very strong to strong
	The company does not disclose public information in a continuous and fair manner, but it does practice fair disclosure.	Moderate to weak
	The company does not disclose public information continuously and does not practice fair disclosure.	Very weak
Corporate Actions	Shareholders have been notified of all major corporate events occurring in the last 12 months.	Very strong to strong
	Shareholders have been notified of major events, although there may be some borderline omissions.	Moderate
	Some efforts to notify shareholders of major corporate events.	Weak
	No or little effort to notify shareholders of major corporate events.	Weak to very weak

Frequency and Timing of Disclosure

In light of the development of the Internet and the strong regulatory disclosure requirements in various jurisdictions, the role of the annual report as an information tool can be a matter of company discretion. Many companies that are subject to stringent regulatory requirements on disclosure provide only minimal disclosure in annual reports and present the annual report as a glossy public relations document. Regulatory filings often are bound together with the annual report to provide a more complete basis of disclosure. Although many companies have adopted cursory annual reports, deferring to regulatory filings as the main platform of informational disclosure, other companies opt for more complete annual reports even if they may not be required to do so.

The argument for relying on regulatory filings is that it is ultimately less costly and prevents repeating the same information in the regulatory document and the company's annual report. For sophisticated institutional investors this typically is not viewed as a problem. However, particularly for retail investors, regulatory filings may be more difficult to access and very technical; there are counterarguments calling for more complete corporate disclosure presented in a format that is readily accessible and easier to read.

The frequency of reporting cycles is a hotly debated issue, particularly with regard to the question of quarterly reporting. Proponents of quarterly reporting (compared with semiannual reporting) maintain that more disclosure is better than less. This is particularly important in companies with blockholders who may be in a position to have more frequent access to information (owing to managerial or directorial positions) than minority shareholders have. Detractors point to both the incremental costs involved with quarterly reporting and the concern that the time frame of quarterly reports is too short to have great relevance and can lead to a dysfunctional short-term perspective on the part of both managers and analysts. Standard & Poor's takes a nuanced view of this debate in its governance scoring. Although on balance quarterly reporting is viewed as preferable, particularly for

Table 7-5 Reporting Requirements

Frequency of Reporting	The company reports quarterly and the conditions listed below apply *or* the company does not report quarterly and the conditions below do not apply.	Very strong to strong
	The company reports quarterly, and conditions listed below do not apply.	Moderate to weak
	The company does not report quarterly, but conditions listed below do apply.	Weak to very weak
	Conditions: (1) short business cycles, (2) existence of large blockholders, (3) particularly unpredictable revenues or expenses, (4) recent management changes, (5) a nonmature industry, (6) unpredictable external influences and/or governments, (7) cases in which cash flow is a more critical indicator, (8) recent changes in strategy, (9) recent mergers and/or restructurings.	
Filing Record	Public reports are always filed on time.	Very strong to strong
	There has not been more than one instance of late filing in the previous year.	Strong to moderate
	Public reports generally are filed on time.	Moderate
	The company regularly files public reports late.	Weak to very weak
	The company has failed to file one or more of the required public reports.	Very weak

companies with significant blockholdings by managers and directors and companies in volatile sectors, it may be less important for widely held companies that operate with a policy of fair and continuous disclosure (see Table 7-5).

Accessibility

The timing and content of public disclosure should be viewed in conjunction to its accessibility. Disclosure that is timely and of high quality may be of little value if it is difficult to access. In some jurisdictions, regulatory disclosure filed with regulatory authorities may be used for the regulators' own purposes but not be accessible to the wider public. In other cases, prospectuses may contain ample amounts of disclosure for public dissemination; however, the public may be able to access information of this nature only as and when a company makes an issue for new capital.

Technology and the Internet provide a means for unprecedented access to public disclosure. Regulatory Web sites such as the U.S. Securities and Exchange Commission's (SEC) EDGAR system can provide a comprehensive and accessible basis of company disclosure. Companies also are improving in terms of their use of technology to communicate to the public. Increasingly, company Web sites contain not only annual reports but considerable additional information, including regulatory filings, social and environmental reports, operational discussion, and profiles of company managers and directors. The investor relations function in many companies uses the Web to provide supplemental information on a company. This can include the publication of broker reports and the use of Webcasts to communicate more directly to investors and other external analysts. Many companies also employ newswire services to ensure that key corporate actions are communicated directly to a wide universe of users. A key issue for companies with international investors is the language of disclosure both in company materials and on the Web. Web sites that have a preponderance of information in a company's local language as opposed to English (as an international standard) can create an asymmetry in favor of local investors. Conversely, companies that provide 20-F reports to the U.S. SEC but do not provide that disclosure for local investors may be creating an unfair advantage for U.S. investors. Table 7-6 analyzes access standards.

Social and Environmental Reporting

The main thrust of company reporting is focused on the interests of a company's financial stakeholders, in particular its shareholders.

Table 7-6 Access Standards

Access to Public Information	Public information is sent to shareholders in a timely manner and via formal distribution mechanisms. There is some evidence of extra effort made by the company to ensure widest possible access, including use of analyst presentations and conference calls and a presence on the Web. A Web site is available with comprehensive financial and nonfinancial information.	Very strong to strong
	Public information is sent to shareholders in a timely manner and via formal distribution mechanisms and is available on request from the company. A Web site is available that addresses most of the elements of financial and nonfinancial disclosure.	Strong
	Public information is distributed to shareholders via formal mechanisms, although there may be some question about the timeliness of information for shareholders and therefore its usefulness. A Web site is available that addresses many of the elements of financial and nonfinancial disclosure, though there may be some gaps.	Moderate
	Channels through which information is disseminated are inadequate to ensure that the information reaches all shareholders, or it may not be clear to all shareholders where or how to access information. There is no evidence of extra effort made by the company to ensure widest possible access to its disclosure. A Web site is available, but it may have limited information or address few of the elements of financial and nonfinancial disclosure.	Weak
	There are no formal channels through which information is distributed, resulting in information not reaching all shareholders. There is no Web site available, or there is a placeholder Web site of limited value or use.	Weak to very weak

(Continued)

Table 7-6 *(Continued)*

Access to Company Legal Document-ation and Shareholder Information	Shareholders are sent information on where and how to access corporate records of shareholder meetings. Shareholders are sent publicly filed financial statements and reports. Company bylaws, statutes, and/or articles are available on the Web at no cost. Corporate records of shareholders' meetings are available for inspection at the corporate head office or on the company Web site.	Very strong to strong
	Shareholders are sent information on where and how to access corporate records of shareholders' meetings. Shareholders are sent publicly filed financial statements and reports. Company bylaws, statutes, and/or articles are available for inspection at the company's corporate head office upon request by any shareholder.	Strong to moderate
	Company bylaws, statutes, and/or articles are available for inspection, although there may be some evidence of difficulty of access.	Moderate
	It is difficult to obtain public reports from the company.	Weak to very weak

However, the growing emphasis on corporate social responsibility and sustainable development is resulting in increasing calls for more robust disclosure related to broader elements of performance, particularly with regard to the company's own workforce, its involvement with local communities, and its environmental impact. The United Nations–sponsored Global Reporting Initiative represents a major effort to develop more systematic reporting practices on a company's environmental and societal impact and is being adopted increasingly in Europe and to a lesser extent in other parts of the world. Table 7-7 discusses the quality of reporting.

Table 7-7   Quality of Reporting

Stakeholder Engagement and Disclosure	There is good public reporting on key areas of employee, community, and environmental activities that addresses the concerns of nonfinancial stakeholders, and the company maintains an active policy of engagement with diverse investor and stakeholder interests.	Very strong to strong
	There is some public reporting on key areas of employee, community, and environmental activities that addresses the concerns of nonfinancial stakeholders, and the company maintains an active policy of engagement with diverse investor and stakeholder interests.	Strong to moderate
	There is some public reporting on key areas of employee, community, and environmental activities that addresses the concerns of nonfinancial stakeholders. The company does not maintain an active policy of engagement with diverse investor and stakeholder interests.	Moderate
	There is no meaningful communication on nonfinancial stakeholders' interests and no policy of engagement with stakeholders.	Weak to very weak

The Audit Process

The quality, integrity, and independence of the audit process are key elements in recent efforts at governance reform. The role of the audit committee is particularly focused on providing greater integrity in the preparation of a company's financial statements and providing more generally a robust system of internal control that reflects both operational and financial risks. A number of new guidelines on corporate governance are proposing more stringent rules and procedures in regard to auditor independence and the audit process as a whole. As many of the recent corporate failures have resulted to a great extent from accounting irregularities, the need for more structured monitoring of the process has become an obvious requirement.

Both the U.S. Sarbanes-Oxley Act of 2002 and the Smith Report in the United Kingdom are prominent and extensive examples of new and tighter rules governing the audit process and ensuring auditor independence. The policies regarding auditor independence and the controversial issue of the engagement of external audit firms for nonaudit work are detailed prominently in both documents. Although neither set of rules and recommendations completely prevents companies from using their auditors for nonaudit work, both require rigorous oversight of the whole process and include guidance on situations in which the use of an auditing firm for nonaudit work is prohibited. With regard to ensuring the independence of the auditor, these reforms have brought several new features, including having the independent audit committee "own" the relationship with the auditor, having the internal audit committee report directly to the audit committee chair, and ensuring a transparent and accountable process for auditor selection, along with mandatory periodic rotation of audit partners and audit firms. Table 7-8 covers audit standards.

Increasingly, best practice is defined as having an entirely independent audit committee with an engaged and financially literate board team. Definitions of a financial expert have been framed to ensure that audit committee members have the requisite financial skills. In many cases, meaningful and precise definitions of financial expertise can be problematic. However, in light of the particular role of the audit committee in overseeing the preparation of financial statements, the committee would be strengthened by having at least one director with some background or experience in the preparation of financial statements. Although director training is desirable generally, the need is arguably greatest for audit committee members. In addition, the effectiveness of audit committees often can be enhanced by means of reasonable access to external consultants or advisors. Table 7-9 lists the elements of audit independence.

Table 7-8 Audit Standards

Factor	Range of Factor Outcomes	Potential Analytical Assessment
Auditor Choice and Audit Process	The company's choice of an outside auditor is appropriate to the company's size, scope, and business conditions. The auditor is experienced and reputable, and the audit fees are commensurate with the size and complexity of the audit. The auditor does not designate the client a high-risk client. The auditor has significant interaction with *both* members of the audit committee *and* members of the internal audit function. If the auditor uses a risk-based approach to the audit, he or she is able to justify why this does not compromise the integrity of the audit. The auditor does not question the integrity of management. The auditor confirms that he or she receives full cooperation from management in terms of quality, availability, and timeliness of information provided.	Very strong to moderate
	The company's choice of an outside auditor is not appropriate to the company's size, scope, and business conditions. The auditor still may be experienced and reputable.	Weak
	The company's choice of an outside auditor is not appropriate to the company's size, scope, and business conditions. The auditor is less experienced and/or reputable.	Very weak
Auditor Appointment	There should be some evidence that explicit consideration has been given to auditor independence in the appointment process (in public reports and internal board documents).	Very strong to strong
	There is no evidence of potential collusion between management and auditor and no evidence that independence is compromised by a large amount of nonaudit consulting work, but there is very little explicit consideration of auditor independence.	Strong to moderate

(Continued)

Table 7-8 *(Continued)*

Factor	Range of Factor Outcomes	Potential Analytical Assessment
	There is evidence of potential collusion between management and auditor.	Weak to very weak
Nonaudit Services	No professional services are provided by the auditor that are unrelated to the audit. If the audit firm also is paid for other services, those services should be related directly to its work on the audit, they should be transparent and not material in amount, and there should be a good reason, backed up by audit committee members. The audit committee approves all nonaudit fees. Auditors are not indemnified out of the assets of the company.	Very strong
	If the audit firm also is paid for consulting work or other professional services, this is made transparent and is not material in amount. The audit committee has approved all nonaudit fees. Auditors are not indemnified out of the assets of the company.	Strong to moderate
	If the audit firm also is paid for consulting work or other professional services, this is made transparent. The fees *may be* material in amount or may have not been approved by audit committee members in every instance. Auditors are not indemnified out of the assets of the company.	Moderate to weak
	The audit fees are not separated from the nonaudit fees or are not made transparent. The level of nonaudit consulting work is material and/or excessive. The audit committee has limited oversight over nonaudit fees. Auditors are indemnified out of the assets of the company.	Weak to very weak
Definition of Nonaudit Services	The company has a clear definition of audit and nonaudit services and/or adopts the accepted definition of the relevant regulatory authority.	Very strong to moderate
	No clear definition.	Weak to very weak

Table 7-8 *(Continued)*

Auditor Selection	There is an explicit, transparent, and accountable process for selecting the auditor. Auditor is selected by board or by a committee of the board, with significant effort to ensure that independent outside directors lead the decision process, and auditor selection is put to the vote at a general shareholders' meeting.	Very strong
	There is a transparent and accountable process for selecting the auditor. Auditor is selected by board or by a committee of the board, with some effort to ensure that independent outside directors are involved in the decision process, and auditor selection is put to a vote at a general shareholders' meeting, although there may be evidence that this is merely a formality.	Strong
	Process by which auditor is selected is transparent, although there may be some question about the extent of involvement of independent outside directors and shareholders in the selection process.	Moderate
	Auditor is appointed via a nontransparent process over which management presides.	Weak to very weak
Rotation Policy	The company has a clearly articulated policy regarding rotation of auditor firm and/or lead audit partner and (1) the senior partner in charge of the account is rotated every 5 years or (2) the audit firm is rotated every 10 years. If there is senior partner rotation, there is evidence of appropriate rotation of more junior auditors as well.	Very strong to strong
	The company has a policy on rotating the audit partner every five years. There is evidence that there is appropriate rotation of more junior auditors as well.	Strong
	There is no policy on rotation, but the same audit partner has been in place for less than 5 years and the audit firm has been in place for less than 10 years.	Moderate to weak
	There is no policy on audit rotation. The same audit partner has been in place for over 5 years, and the same audit firm has been in place for over 10 years.	Weak to very weak

Table 7-9   Audit Independence

Audit Committee Independence and Skill Sets	The audit committee is made up solely of independent directors, all of whom are financially literate. There is at least one audit committee member with experience with financial statement preparation and one member with experience in risk management and internal control.	Very strong
	The audit committee is made up of a majority of independent directors, all of whom are financially literate. There is at least one audit committee member with experience in financial statement preparation.	Strong
	The audit committee includes several independent directors, most of whom are financially literate. Alternatively, there may be no audit committee and there is evidence of alternative structures with similarly appropriate skill sets and oversight ability.	Moderate to weak
	The audit committee does not exist, and there is no evidence of alternative structures with similarly appropriate skill sets and oversight, or the audit committee is dominated by management or blockholder members. Audit committee members do not have strong financial literacy.	Weak to very weak
Audit Committee Resources and Training	Audit committee members have *considerable* access to funds for independent advice and training; audit committee members have an *explicit* right of access to company information as well as to executive directors, employees, and the external auditor. Audit committee members exercise the right to meet on their own. The committee truly owns the internal and external audit relationships.	Very strong to strong
	Audit committee members have *some* access to funds for independent advice and training; audit committee members have an *implicit* right of access to company information as well as to *many of the following*: executive directors, employees, and the external auditor. Audit committee members exercise the right to meet on their own. The committee truly owns the internal and external audit relationships.	Strong

Table 7-9 *(Continued)*

The audit committee has some resources available to it but does not receive much support from external advisors or undergo training. Some access to company staff and auditors. The committee does not truly own the internal and external audit relationships.	Moderate
The audit committee has few or limited resources for outside support services or training. It has limited access to company officials, staff, and internal or external auditors. The committee does not truly own the internal and external audit relationships.	Weak to very weak

Audit charters are important for the articulation of the specific duties of the audit committee, including review of financial statements, approval of the audit and nonaudit services, engaging with the auditor, and monitoring internal controls. The nature of audit committee work means that the committee often meets more frequently than the board as a whole, either formally or informally. Many companies have six to eight formal audit committee meetings a year, and some audit committees meet with greater frequency. The committee members often receive monthly reports comparing company performance measures to budget and internal control parameters. Table 7-10 describes audit committee procedures.

Enterprise Risk Management

The question of transparency and disclosure is not limited to matters that are external to the company. The scope and breadth of a company's internal control and risk management systems are critical in this context. Internal disclosure is crucial in allowing the senior executives and board directors (particularly audit committee members) to perform their duties appropriately. The ability of directors and senior managers to identify and effectively mitigate risks related to the company is often

Table 7-10 Audit Committee Procedures

Audit Committee Charter	There is a clear and updated charter or terms of reference for the audit committee.	Very strong to strong
	Terms of reference are not clearly articulated.	Moderate to weak
	There is no audit committee charter.	Very weak
Audit Committee Engagement	Audit committee meetings are held at least quarterly, with monthly reports or communications and evidence of more informal meetings and ability to meet more frequently as required. Attendance records for all audit committee members are satisfactory. Audit committee meets regularly with outside auditor. There is evidence of engagement that is above average and of oversight that is led by the committee, not by management. There is evidence that the audit committee members are able to devote a significant amount of time to the work of the committee, for example, there is evidence that audit committee members meet regularly with internal and external auditors outside of regular meetings.	Very strong to strong
	Audit committee meets quarterly. Limited informal communications or interim reporting. Audit committee meets with auditor two to four times per year.	Moderate
	Infrequent meetings and poor attendance record. Audit committee does not meet with auditor.	Weak to very weak
Audit Committee Accountability	The chair of the audit committee is present at the AGM to answer questions on the report and matters within the scope of audit committee's responsibilities.	Very strong to moderate
	Chair not present at the AGM.	Weak to very weak
Internal Control and Internal Audit	The audit committee is actively involved in the internal control process, establishing and monitoring control procedures. It is kept informed on a monthly basis with reports and engages in an annual qualitative review of the effectiveness of internal controls. The audit committee oversees the work of	Very strong

Table 7-10 *(Continued)*

the external auditor. The audit committee has direct lines of communication and a reporting relationship with the internal audit function. There is a system in place to facilitate whistle-blowing. There is evidence that the information the committee receives is thoughtful, of high quality, and neither too much nor too little. The internal audit function is properly staffed and resourced and reports to the chair of the audit; i.e., the chair of the audit committee is responsible for the hiring, firing, and salary of the head of the internal audit function. There is some evidence that the audit committee has reviewed the quality of the internal audit process and its resources.	
The audit committee is involved in the internal control process, establishing and monitoring control procedures. The audit committee oversees the work of the external auditor and interacts regularly with the internal audit function. There is a reporting system in place on major financial performance parameters. There is evidence that the information the committee receives is of variable quality. The internal audit function is properly staffed and resourced and reports to the chair of the audit committee; i.e., the chair of the audit committee is responsible for the hiring, firing, and salary of the head of the internal audit function.	Strong to moderate
The audit committee has only a limited or superficial engagement with the internal control process. There is limited engagement or interaction with the outside auditor, and there are no or inadequate reporting mechanisms to inform the committee about financial performance and compliance with internal controls. There is evidence that the information the committee receives is of a poor quality or is inadequate.	Weak to very weak
The audit committee does not appear to be involved with internal control issues. The internal audit team reports to management and does not meet with the audit committee.	

what differentiates successful companies from less successful ones. Increasingly, operational risk management systems that are particular to the nature of individual companies' unique circumstances provide executives and directors with information systems that define key parameters of risk relating to both financial and nonfinancial risk factors. Inadequate internal controls may result in errors of judgment, product failures, operating losses, and legal actions, all of which can have a substantial negative effect on shareholder value.

Our review of risk management focuses predominantly on the board of directors and its role of providing oversight of the risk management process. Our review of board oversight is centered not on the strength of oversight of particular risks (e.g., credit risk, market risk, liquidity risk, reputational risk) but on the quality of oversight of all risks, or what we call risk culture or risk governance. In addition to risk governance, our analysis has a particular interest in the extent to which strategic decisions are informed by considerations of risk. We call this process strategic risk management.

The main focus is on a company's approach to monitoring and minimizing risk across the entire firm, not just in one or two businesses. This firmwide approach to risk sometimes is called enterprise risk management (ERM). ERM often is misunderstood as a rigid system that applies to all companies in the same way. This could not be farther from the truth.

What a Firmwide Approach to Risk Is

- An approach to assuring that the firm is paying attention to all risks
- A set of methods for steering away from situations that might result in losses that would be outside the tolerance of the firm
- A method to shift from thinking in terms of cost-benefit to thinking in terms of risk-reward

- A language for communicating employees' efforts to keep the risk profile of the firm on track
- A set of expectations among management, shareholders, and the board about what risks the firm will take and what risks it will not take
- A tool kit for trimming excess risks and a system for intelligently selecting which risks need trimming
- A way to move over time toward lower losses compared to average earnings

What a Firmwide Approach to Risk Is Not

- A way to eliminate all risks
- A haphazard collection of longstanding practices placed under one roof
- A guarantee that the firm will avoid losses
- A rigid set of rules that must be followed in all circumstances
- Exactly the same for all firms in all sectors
- Exactly the same from year to year
- A passing fad

Finally, it is of vital importance to distinguish between an assessment of risk management at industrial or manufacturing companies and an assessment at a bank or financial institution. Industrial companies accumulate risk as they manufacture, sell, and distribute products and services; financial institutions trade risk by buying and selling financial instruments. In other words, financial institutions are in the business of risk, whereas industrial companies encounter risk as a by-product of their main activity. This has consequences for risk analysis and increases the responsibility for directors of financial firms to oversee risk (see Table 7-11).

Table 7-11   Risk Governance Standards

Factor	Range of Factor Outcomes	Potential Analytical Assessment
Risk Management Culture and Governance	There is evidence that risk and risk management considerations have a major influence on daily corporate judgment. There is an organized process that involves identification, measurement, and communication of corporate-level risks and assignment of responsibilities for specific risks. Risk management staff members coordinate the process; however, they request and account for expert judgment by line-level managers in risk assessments and prioritization. In financial organizations, risk managers have considerable status and authority. Senior executives perform regular reviews of corporate risk profile and keep the board-level committee on risks or the audit committee updated on exposures and risk policies. A risk specialist is present on the risk and/or audit committee.	Very strong to strong
	Risk governance practices show many of the above attributes and allow the executives and the board to have an adequate understanding of significant corporate-level risks. However, certain elements of the risk management process, such as the quality of communication on risk exposures and tolerances and involvement of line-level managers in the assessment and management of relevant risks, may be missing.	Moderate
	There is no organized risk management process. Executives may have an incomplete understanding of several risk areas. Risk analysis is limited to basic issues such as safety and fraud prevention. Operational risks are handled by production and operating units on a stand-alone basis.	Weak to very weak

Table 7-11 *(Continued)*

Strategic Risk Management	Strategic decisions are influenced by risk management considerations and involve assessments of diversification benefits in the context of comprehensive measure of risk. Risk considerations affect strategic processes such as capital budgeting, strategic asset allocation, product and new venture risk-reward standards, risk-adjusted financial targets, and executive compensation plans.	Strong
	Risk considerations are not demonstrably linked to strategic processes.	Weak

Chapter 8

Board Effectiveness, Strategy, and Compensation: Boards of Directors versus Potemkin Villages[1]

For shareholders, the last line of defense against a range of corporate governance problems—poor management, excessive risk taking, value-destroying related deals, and outright corruption—is the board of directors. When the board fails, the costs to investors and other stakeholders can be devastating. The current financial crisis, for example, is at least in part attributable to boards' limited understanding of risk exposure at many financial institutions around the world.[2] After all, the board is in place to oversee management and strategy and to sign off on all major transactions. How can investors tell the difference between a good board and a bad one, especially in the BRIC

1 This chapter is based on earlier methodology documents by Nick Bradley and Dan Konigsburg that have been updated by Oleg Shvyrkov.
2 *Corporate Governance and the Financial Crisis.* OECD Consultation Document. March 18, 2009.

countries, where boards often do not look like boards elsewhere? This chapter will focus on how boards operate and what they look like in emerging markets.

The board is important not only as a defensive measure. The right combination of directors can make the difference between an adequate board and a board that builds value. There is no single right way to build an effective board, yet there are certain common denominators: appropriate size, a strong and diverse mix of skills and backgrounds, a sophisticated committee structure, and a culture of open discussion in which little is off limits. All these factors can lift a board from good to great.

This chapter also will review the board's role in setting the strategic direction for the firm, looking in some detail at the hot-button issue of executive compensation. We will consider why companies in emerging markets generally have avoided problems with stock options and option backdating and why, in fact, the hidden danger in BRIC countries' pay policies lies in paying too little.

The Board of Directors: The Heart of Corporate Governance

Board structure and board effectiveness are focal points of corporate governance. The board acts as a bridge between the owners, or principals, of a business (the shareholders) and their agents (the management), some of whom may sit on the board in their capacity as executive or employed directors. The senior managers of the company are appointed by the board to run the business on a day-to-day basis and ensure that the company achieves its strategic and financial objectives and that shareholders and other stakeholders receive their fair share of the company's earnings and assets. In turn, director and senior executive compensation policies are intended to provide alignment between managers', directors', and shareholders' interests.

Board structure plays a key role in framing the balance of power between company managers and directors, but ultimately board effectiveness is more than a matter of structure or architecture. The "tone at the top" is a reflection of the integrity, independence, and teamwork of individual board members and a company's executive management. For a board to be truly effective, not only must an appropriate structure be in place but individual board members should be engaged and well informed and represent diverse skill sets and perspectives. The "human side" of the board process suggests that the board should demonstrate true independence of mind vis-à-vis the chair, the chief executive officer (CEO), and other board members. The ability to work as a cohesive team must mesh with the ability to offer constructive criticism of senior executives or other board members.

Effective boards have overall accountability for the strategy, performance, and internal control of the company. An analysis of the effectiveness of boards will establish the extent to which the board determines or influences the direction of the company, sets performance objectives for management, and places limits on the discretion of management. The board also should have overall accountability for the performance and internal controls of the company. In a more qualitative sense, the board should ensure the presence of the proper tone at the top to establish an overarching culture of integrity and business ethics throughout the company.

In emerging economies in which many companies have been created from the privatization of state-owned enterprises and in countries where family-controlled companies are prevalent, the board typically is dominated by management directors or owner-appointed directors. This can lead to problems for minority shareholders in situations in which controlling shareholders have little regard for their interests, as there are no or few independent directors to provide checks and balances. In recent years, however, tightening regulatory requirements and pressure from investors have contributed to a general trend of improving board structures and processes in the BRIC countries.

In many cases, the decision to appoint reputable independent directors and formalize board procedures was made around the time of a public placement, driven by a need to meet regulatory requirements or provide a degree of comfort to international investors.

Progress in board structures and procedures can be driven internally if there is recognition of boards' potential in creating value. We have observed cases in which strong appointments were made to a board and procedures were implemented at closely held companies without any specific plans for an initial public offering (IPO). This reflected the awareness of founder shareholders that their companies had grown beyond the stage of entrepreneurial development and that further growth would be best assured by professional management and solid governance structures. In a similar vein, governments in many emerging economies are becoming increasingly alert to their own limitations in the role of shareholders, particularly when state-owned enterprises are governed like ministries. In 2008, Russia embarked on a program (albeit not without controversy) that increased the role of independent directors at state-owned enterprises. In contrast, Singapore has been supporting independent directors with the government's votes for years.

Structural Issues

The size of the board can be an important governance consideration, as boards with too many directors can be unwieldy, making decision making inefficient because of poor communication among directors. Boards with too few directors may lack the appropriate skills and backgrounds or may be dominated by management and thus not be representative of all shareholder groups. Particularly in light of the tendency for increased use of individual board committees, it may be difficult for small boards to accommodate a wide range of committees with independent directors. Table 8-1 discusses the issue of board size.

Table 8-1   Board Numbers

Factor	Range of Factor Outcomes	Potential Analytical Assessment
Board Size	Appropriate for the size and nature of the company (as a guide, boards will typically have between 7 and 15 members).	Very strong to moderate
	Much too big/small.	Weak to very weak

Boards with high accountability typically include a strong base of independent nonexecutive directors who look after the interests of all shareholders—both majority and minority holders. Conversely, companies that have a strong majority shareholder or are dominated by a few shareholders may have boards with limited accountability to all shareholders.

Independence of judgment is one of the most important contributions that directors can make to the board. Therefore, the extent to which the board is composed of truly independent directors serves as one of the most distinguishing factors in a company's entire governance framework.

For the purposes of this chapter there are three principal categories of directors:

1. *Executive directors* (sometimes referred to as employed directors). These are senior employees of the company who are elected to the board. They are responsible for the day-to-day operation of the company and by definition are nonindependent.

2. *Nonindependent and nonexecutive directors* (often referred to as nonemployed or outside directors). These directors usually are elected to the board by the shareholders but are not

classified as independent of management, possibly because of close commercial ties with the company or previous employment with the company.

3. *Independent nonexecutive directors.* These directors usually are elected to the board by shareholders and have no previous ties to or commercial relationships with the company. They often are viewed as the most objective in terms of taking minority shareholders' interests into account.

However, even as definitions put forward by regulators become more sophisticated and detailed, defining "true" independence may be very difficult in practical terms. An active and assertive independence of mind vis-à-vis a company's chief executive, chair, or blockholder representatives is not necessarily assured by directors who simply satisfy specific independence criteria. Also, it is clear that in many cases directors who may not satisfy these independence criteria are quite able to exercise an independent voice.

In the context of the emerging economies, affiliations with blockholders are the most common impediment to true independence, and these links may not be obvious from biographical records. In our experience, personal interviews of the directors in question as well as their peers are the most helpful means of understanding the existing commitments and potential biases (see Table 8-2).

Board composition and independence need not be addressed only at the level of the whole board; the balance of power and the composition of key board committees can be significant, particularly for audit committees. Best practice in many jurisdictions is increasingly recognized as entailing 100% director independence in audit committees. In other key committee areas, notably nomination or remuneration committees, there is also an increasing focus on substantial or complete director independence (see Table 8-3).

The debate regarding the combined or split roles of the chair and the CEO warrants particular mention. With different practices in

Table 8-2 Board Member Criteria

Factor	Range of Factor Outcomes	Potential Analytical Assessment
Director Independence	At least two thirds of board members are independent: directors are defined as independent if they have no material relationship with the company or the company's shareholders that could compromise objectivity or judgment. There is clear evidence that the role of the independent director is recognized as distinct from executive directors and other nonindependent nonexecutives. E.g., there is a separate committee for nonexecutive directors (such as a chairman's committee) and/or special meetings organized for nonexecutive directors only — enabling them to discuss control issues separate from executive directors. Directors play a meaningful role on the board and exercise true independence of mind in discussions and decision making.	Very strong
	Independent directors form a majority on the board, and there are industry experts as well as specialists in relevant functional areas among them. Directors play a meaningful role on the board and exercise true independence of mind in discussions and decision making.	Strong
	At least one-quarter of directors are independent. Independent directors possess relevant expertise and hold separate consultations. Jointly, they have an ability to veto major transactions, related-party deals, and strategic decisions under the company charter.	Moderate
	There may be no clear recognition of the distinct role of independent directors. Those few independent directors that are present on the board may lack industry or functional knowledge to challenge management or nonindependent nonexecutives.	Weak
	There are no independent directors on the board. Nonindependent nonexecutives do not have freedom and/or expertise to challenge management and representatives of blockholders.	Very weak
Director Tenure	Nonexecutives should not have served for so long they have been "captured" by management. No bright line rule, but there should not be too many directors who have served for more than 10 years.	Very strong to moderate
	Nonexecutives may have served for so long they have been "captured" by management. There are a number of very long-serving directors.	Moderate to very weak

Table 8-3 Committee Best Practices

Board Committees	There are board committees for all the main control functions—i.e., audit, remuneration, and nomination. There must be an audit committee; in some cases the nomination and remuneration functions can be dealt with effectively via other structures. There are committees or task forces for other appropriate functions (e.g., risk and governance).	Very strong
	There are board committees for all the main control functions—i.e., audit, remuneration, and nomination. There must be an audit committee; in some cases the nomination and remuneration functions can be dealt with effectively via other structures.	Strong
	There is a board committee for audit only. The board is able to carry out its duties effectively without formal committee structures.	Moderate
	There is a board committee for audit only. The lack of committee structures in other areas means that key functions are not effectively or consistently managed.	Weak
	There are no board committees and there are no meaningful alternative methods or structures for the board to carry out its basic duties.	Very weak
Composition of Board Committees	Each of the control function committees are composed only of independent directors. (The nomination committee may include an executive; management should meet with directors before they join the board.) The audit committee consists *entirely* of financially literate members, including some who have put together financial statements. Committee members have solid functional and industry skills to enable them to challenge management.	Very strong
	Each of the control function committees are composed only of independent directors. The audit and remuneration committees are each comprised solely of independent directors (the nomination committee may include an executive; management should meet with directors before they join the board). The audit committee is comprised of financially literate members.	Strong to moderate
	The audit and remuneration committees are each comprised of a majority of independent directors.	Moderate
	The audit committee comprises a majority of nonexecutive directors and includes at least two independent directors.	Moderate to weak
	There are no board committees.	Weak to very weak

place globally, this area has received considerable scrutiny in the post-Enron era of governance reform. The governance scoring criteria used at Standard & Poor's do not explicitly endorse one approach or the other in this regard. The analytical process focuses on board dynamics and seeks evidence to characterize the balance of power between the chair, the CEO, and other board members. This evidence comes from director interviews and the inspection of board papers.

The split of the chair and CEO roles is "cleaner" in many ways. In such cases, the analytical process is used to identify the existence of fractious or divisive factions. When the chair and CEO roles are combined, the focus is on whether independent directors can exercise their voices meaningfully. This has to be monitored on an ongoing basis. In structures in which there is concentrated power in the form of a combined chair and CEO, the introduction of alternative structures such as a presiding or lead independent director can establish a constructive mechanism to support the independent voice of the directors. Table 8-4 analyzes senior executive ties.

The pool of resources available to the board reflects the professional experiences of the individual members. Relevant industry expertise helps a director understand the company's business and assess the performance of management. Experience in executive positions, particularly at leading international companies, is similarly important and is also instrumental in gaining the respect and trust of executives. At many well-governed companies in the BRIC countries, directors with international expertise are an important source of management know-how and their advice is valued highly by executives. It is therefore not surprising that industry expertise and experience in executive positions are becoming a primary criterion for director nominations (see Table 8-5).

Expertise in key functional areas has become critical for effective boards. Regardless of the industry a company is in, experts in audit and finance are needed for effective oversight of the audit process. The growing recognition of the importance of risk oversight calls for risk specialists on the boards of financial institutions and increasingly at nonfinancial companies as well. Further, as executive compensations

Table 8-4 Senior Executive Ties

Chair/CEO Split	There is very strong, formal, well-led, independent oversight of the CEO and other senior executives. This may be in the form of either a split CEO/Chair OR lead director OR other strong independent element on the board. If there is a combined Chair/CEO role, there is formal, independent, and specific leadership for the nonexecutives that is shown to be effective and not divisive.	Very strong
	There is strong, formal, well-led, independent oversight of the CEO and other senior executives. This may be in the form of either a split CEO/chair OR lead director OR other strong independent element on the board. There is some form of leadership for the nonexecutives.	Strong
	There is moderate oversight of the CEO and other senior executives. This may be in the form of either a split CEO/chair OR lead director OR other strong independent element on the board. Oversight may be informal in nature and may only be partially independent.	Moderate
	There is limited oversight of the CEO and other senior executives.	Weak to very weak

structures have become increasingly complex in North America and Western Europe and some companies in the BRIC countries have begun to follow suit, expertise in compensation and human resources has become crucial for effective oversight of executive incentive systems and succession policies.

It is important that the external commitments of board members not prevent them from being actively involved in the board process; for example, someone with a full-time executive position elsewhere probably would not have enough time for active nonexecutive service on more than one or two boards. Also, many companies in emerging markets find it difficult to involve directors fully in the board process when the directors reside several time zones away. This can be

Table 8-5 Experience Standards

Skill Mix	There is a strong diversity of background and skills that adds breadth and depth to the board and there is evidence that the selection process takes the professional qualifications of the proposed directors into account in order to ensure they have the required skills/experience to contribute in a meaningful way to the board's functioning. There are people on the board with industry experience relevant to the company.	Very strong
	There is some diversity of background and skills. There are people on the board with industry experience.	Strong to moderate
	Skill mix/diversity of background inappropriate. There are no directors on the board with industry experience.	Weak to very weak

particularly challenging when the directors do not speak the local language and their communication with other nonexecutive directors and management is constrained. Prominent well-governed companies around the world make these considerations part of a formal director selection process. Table 8-6 discusses board composition.

Board Authority and Process

An effective board delegates the day-to-day management of the company to the executive management of the company, which may include a number of executive directors, and emerging economies are no exception in this respect. However, do board members and senior management clearly understand lines of responsibility and have clearly defined duties? To avoid confusion and ensure transparency, a board should articulate clearly a set of matters reserved for its own discretion, and those matters should be understood clearly by board members and executive management. These board-reserved matters

Table 8-6   Board Composition

Director Selection	The company has a formal articulated policy with respect to nonemployed director selection, revealing a concern for the amount of time, quality, and independence of involvement that the director will be able to give to the board and there is clear evidence that these criteria have been used in making board appointments.	Very strong to strong
	There are no formal articulated policies on independence or qualification but there is clear evidence that the board has made nonemployed director appointments with considerations of independence and qualification/capability as the main criteria.	Strong to moderate
	There is no evidence that the board has made nonexecutive director appointments with reference to considerations of independence and qualification/capability	Weak to very weak

vary widely from company to company and typically include approval of the company's long-term objectives and commercial strategy:

- Executive appointments and succession planning
- Executive pay decisions
- Approval of budgets and financial statements
- Approval of large transactions and related-party deals
- Oversight of the company's risk management strategy
- Changes in accounting policies and dividends

It is also important that directors, particularly outside directors, receive regular and comprehensive information about the company's operations and important strategic issues. Table 8-7 analyzes board responsibilities.

The corporate secretary plays a very important role in organizing the information flows and keeping records of board decisions. Table 8-8 discusses board information.

Table 8-7 Board Responsibilities

Factor	Range of Factor Outcomes	Potential Analytical Assessment
Board Role	There is evidence that the board has clearly articulated for itself a set of matters reserved for its discretion and put these in its articles. Evidence that the board has thought seriously about its own role.	Very strong
	The board has articulated for itself a set of matters reserved for its discretion (and listed in its articles) but lines of responsibility are not entirely clear.	Strong
	The board's role is only somewhat defined, but the role should be reflected somewhere in the company's articles or public documents.	Moderate
	Poorly defined. Far too much or far too little responsibility is delegated to management.	Weak
	Poorly or not defined or there is substantial disagreement on the board on its role. Far too much or far too little responsibility is delegated to management.	Very weak
Internal Control	The board demonstrates a strong commitment to articulating, implementing, monitoring, and reviewing internal control procedures. A sound system of internal control is in place. Financial and operational risk management systems are also in place and have proven to operate effectively. There are independent directors with experience in internal control and risk management.	Very strong
	The board demonstrates a strong commitment to articulating, implementing, monitoring, and reviewing internal control procedures. A sound system of internal control is in place.	Strong
	Although the board may not have an explicitly articulated set of internal control procedures, it nevertheless achieves control by requiring regular financial information for performance monitoring purposes.	Moderate

(Continued)

Table 8-7 (*Continued*)

Factor	Range of Factor Outcomes	Potential Analytical Assessment
	No evidence of monitoring	Weak to very weak
Succession	There is a formal succession plan in place for the CEO and key executives. The board meets regularly with the CEO to review plans for executive directors and senior managers and the board also meets regularly with senior management with a view to assessing their capability to lead the management of the company.	very strong
	There is an informal succession plan in place for the CEO and key executives. The board meets regularly with the CEO to review the succession plans for the executive directors and senior managers.	Strong strong to
	The board meets regularly with the CEO to review the succession plans for the executive directors.	Moderate
	The board does not appear to play any role in succession planning.	Weak to very weak

In setting the tone at the top, the board plays a crucial role by providing clear guidance in regard to business ethics. Leading by example may not be enough in this area, and formal guidelines are important in shaping attitudes and behavior throughout the organization (see Table 8-9).

Increasingly, boards conduct regular self-evaluations in addition to evaluations of the CEO. Training also can be an effective way to ensure that board members have the appropriate skills in directorship, particularly as the roles of boards and board committees recently have been subject to new rules of compliance and best practice (see Table 8-10).

Table 8-8   Board Information

Access to Information	From discussions with management, it is apparent that the board receives quality information memoranda on a timely basis and acts on a fully informed basis. Timely basis may mean more than several days in advance of meetings. Audit committee members in particular receive financial and internal control reports on a monthly basis. The board is in a position to commission studies or reviews by internal staff or external consultants.	Very strong to strong
	Information and reporting systems provide updates on a regular basis; board briefing papers provide for meaningful contributions to board discussions.	Strong to moderate
	Information and reporting systems are informal, incomplete, and are not timely. Board members are inadequately briefed for board meetings.	Weak to very weak

Table 8-9   Code of Ethics

Ethical Boundaries	The ethical boundaries of the business are clearly defined. The board oversees and endorses a company code of ethics that defines ethical standards of behavior that have been specifically adapted to the nature of the company's business. This code is applied to all employees of the company and an annual verification of compliance is required for all employees.	Very strong to strong
	A code of ethics exists but it is generic and poorly communicated.	Moderate to weak
	There is no code of ethics.	Weak to very weak

Effectiveness is also a function of the level of engagement and the quality of interaction at the board level. Directors must be actively involved both at the board level and in individual committees. This requires regular attendance (see Table 8-11), keeping informed, and ensuring that the board process is conducted with the appropriate level

Table 8-10 Performance Monitoring

Evaluations	The board carries out regular evaluations of the performance of executive directors (and the executives are willing to discuss these). The board carries out regular evaluations of its own performance, facilitated by an independent evaluator.	Very strong
	The board carries out regular evaluations of the performance of the executive directors but the executives are not willing to discuss these. The board carries out collective evaluations of itself, though these may be conducted internally or informal in nature.	Strong to moderate
	No evidence of any formal evaluations.	Weak to very weak
Training	The board has a formal training program for new directors and provides for ongoing training (internal and external) for existing directors.	Very strong to strong
	The board has an informal/ad hoc training program for new directors and ongoing training for existing directors.	Strong to moderate
	The board does not have a formal training program for new directors or ongoing training program for existing directors.	Weak to very weak

Table 8-11 Attendance Policies

Director Attendance	90–100%. While there are no bright-line rules on director attendance, a red flag is often attendance less than 75% by all directors.	Very strong
	75–90%. Adequate (at least 75% attendance by a significant majority of directors).	Strong to moderate
	50–75%. This may include meetings that do not occur in person (excessive use of video conferencing, postal meetings, etc.).	Weak
	Less than 50%.	Very weak

of constructive criticism. Collegiality must be balanced with readiness to challenge the chair, the CEO, or other directors. The board members learn to work as a team and avoid fractious behavior but not necessarily to avoid conflict or expressions of differences in opinion. Table 8-12 analyzes director commitments.

Strategic Process

In any company, strategic process is a crucial tool for value creation. Clarity of strategic objectives, alertness to changes in the market environment, and formalized planning and implementation tools are paramount for long-term growth in shareholder value. In emerging economies, this issue is particularly relevant, since the quality of oversight and planning tools vary significantly from company to company. Indeed, there is always a risk that a strategy exists only in the head of a controlling shareholder or, in the case of state-controlled companies, cannot be formulated at all because of vague goals and indecision in government agencies.

It is important to make a distinction between an analysis of the content of strategy and an evaluation of the strategic process. Assessment of the content of business strategy usually is performed as a part of equity or credit research along with the company's financial profile. The strategic process, in contrast, involves board-level and management-level activity and falls within the realm of governance analysis. In analyzing the strategic process, we focus on three main areas: governance of the strategic process, planning procedures, and implementation tools. Table 8-13 analyzes the issue of strategy and execution.

Board and Management Compensation

It can be difficult to construct executive compensation schemes in a way that allows the interests of directors and senior executives to be aligned with those of shareholders so that senior management is

Table 8-12 Director Commitments

External Directorships	The external directorships of the CEO and other executive directors are minimal. The CEO has one or two directorships at most. All have been approved by the board. Nonexecutive directorships are also not excessive given individual circumstances of directors. No firm and fast bright-line rule, but closer examination of individual circumstances is warranted if individual directors chairing committees have more than three other directorships.	Very strong to strong
	The external directorships of the CEO and other executive directors are not excessive (and have been approved by the board). Nonexecutive directorships are also not excessive given individual circumstances of directors. No firm and fast bright-line rule, but closer examination of individual circumstances is warranted if individual directors have five or more other directorships.	Strong to moderate
	The CEO and other executive directors have a large number of external commitments (and discussions with the board have not revealed any good explanation for this). Nonexecutive directorships may appear excessive given individual circumstances.	Moderate to weak
	The CEO and other executive directors have an excessively large number of external commitments (and discussions with the board have not revealed any good explanation for this). Nonexecutive directorships are excessive; e.g., there are several directors with more than six to eight directorships.	Very weak
Meeting Frequency	While there are no bright-line rules for meetings, the board meets an appropriate number of times per year. At least eight times per annum, or less if the board provides a legitimate reason for doing so and there is evidence that effectiveness has not been affected. Meetings should be in person.	Very strong
	The board meets an appropriate number of times per year. At least six times per annum, or less if the board provides a legitimate reason for doing so and there is evidence that effectiveness has not been affected. Meetings should be in person.	Strong
	The board meets an appropriate number of times per year. The board meets less than six times per annum or less if the board provides a legitimate reason for doing so and there is evidence that effectiveness has not been affected.	Moderate to weak
	The board does not meet frequently enough. The board meets less than four times per annum.	Weak to very weak

Table 8-13 Strategy and Execution

Factor	Range of Factor Outcomes	Potential Analytical Assessment
Governance of the Strategic Process	The board-level strategy committee enjoys substantial industry expertise and is active in discussing and assessing strategy in joint sessions with executives. There is evidence that open vertical lines of communication exist allowing the executives to capitalize on initiatives from line management. The strategic planning department within the company keeps executives up-to-date on industry and macroeconomic trends and engages in scenario planning. There is a good external disclosure of strategic targets and timelines.	Strong to very strong
	Governance of the strategic planning process shows several of the above attributes, however, certain weaknesses are present with respect to quality of vertical communication, industry expertise of the strategy committee, and/or staffing and expertise of the internal strategic planning department.	Moderate
	There is little in-house planning capability or structured decision-making process.	Weak to very weak

motivated to deliver long-term and sustainable returns to shareholders and is compensated appropriately for achieving that goal. The guiding principles in this context are that pay should be linked to performance and that the executive compensation should be determined with appropriate independence: Managers should not set their own pay levels.

Executive compensation has to be designed to enable companies to recruit, retain, and motivate senior staff. Increasingly, shareholders require transparency in the reporting of the remuneration of directors and senior executives, but this transparency is anathema in certain countries. For example, in many emerging economies, it is unusual to find disclosure of directors' and senior executives' pay in companies' annual reports or annual statutory filings. Indeed, when there is disclosure, this is often an aggregate amount covering all directors and senior executives of a company that is not useful to investors.

Executive compensation policies featured prominently in the public debate over the causes of financial crisis in 2007–2009 and even drew the attention of key political figures around the world. According to the OECD report on governance in the banking sector,[3] aggressive short-term performance stimuli often associated with poor risk oversight were principle causes of excessive risk taking. The issue of executive compensation featured prominently on the agendas of the G20 summits in 2009. At the request of this group of world leaders, the Financial Stability Board, an international association of financial regulators, produced a report titled Principles for Sound Compensation Practices. This report calls for a greater focus on long-term corporate achievement as a basis for incentive rewards (as contrasted to quarterly or annual results). This document also urges corporate boards to include claw-back provisions in the executive contracts; these provisions allow companies to recover bonuses paid to executives on the basis of manipulated or unsustainable results.

The leaders of the BRIC countries have joined the G20 debate on executive pay, indicating that this element of governance has a global relevance. And yet, aggressive compensation arrangements are far less common in these economies than in the developed world. Why? Recall the concentrated ownership structures of BRIC companies. Controlling families or governments typically have a long-term view of business, keep a close eye on performance of executives, and are unlikely to allow extravagant pay packages or "pay-for-failure" awards. In fact, you are more likely to see the opposite problem, particularly at government-controlled companies. Taking a civil servants' perspective of fair pay levels, governments may be reluctant to allow market-rate pay at companies under their control.

---

3 OECD. *Corporate Governance Lessons from the Financial Crisis.* 18.03.2009.

Therefore, in the realities of the BRICs, analysts need to be alert to overly conservative compensation plans that lack incentives, as well as to aggressive, risky plans that the developed economies are currently trying to move away from.

See Tables 8–14 and 8–15.

The use of options as a component of executive pay has become the subject of considerable scrutiny, particularly after megagrants of options to CEOs and other senior executives, most notably in the United States. Although options have been viewed traditionally as a mechanism to bring about an alignment of interests between executive management and minority shareholders, the granting of excessive amounts of options has the potential to encourage a performance time frame (given exercise dates) or aggressive strategies that are not always consistent with the goals of core long-term shareholders. Option repricing and the providing of corporate loans to executives to cover tax payments upon the exercise of options also have been abuses of the system. This has led many critics to call for companies to expense options in the income statement or, in more extreme cases, to reject the use of options as a form of compensation. See Table 8-16 on compensation mix.

Option plans for nonemployed directors, which are common in the United States, are particularly controversial. Although paying nonexecutives in shares can make good sense, with options the incentives are different. As Sir Adrian Cadbury has noted, the figure for reported profits in any year is a matter of judgment but one that influences option values. The effect of a rise in share price on option values is, of course, leveraged. It is therefore helpful, says Sir Adrian, to have some board members whose judgment on the subjective elements of accounting is entirely disinterested.

Significant option grants are relatively rare in the emerging economies, and when they exist, there is usually a blockholder present to make sure the system is not abused. However, bonus payments to nonexecutives based on annual results are not uncommon in several markets and can create harmful short-term incentives (see Table 8-17).

Table 8-14 Compensation Standards

Factor	Range of Factor Outcomes	Potential Analytical Assessment
Performance-Based Pay	Clearly articulated policy linking pay to performance. For employed directors and other senior executives, there are performance-contingent elements representing at least half of total compensation (if performance targets are reached), with many of the following characteristics: (1) criteria based on performance measures that are related to shareholder value, (2) criteria that are adequately stringent in terms of both metrics and goals (analysts will compare goals with actual past performance), (3) at least one half of annual incentive payment is deferred, fully vests no earlier than in five years, and is subject to performance criteria, (4) at least one share-based performance metric, (5) some evidence of peer group benchmarking in assessing performance, (6) some evidence of awards for meeting more qualitative objectives, and (7) there is a claw-back provision that applies in specific cases of misstatement or misconduct.	Very strong
	Clearly articulated policy linking pay to performance. There is a meaningful performance-contingent element linking the performance targets to shareholder value and at least one half of incentive pay is deferred. Pay levels are assessed objectively relative to peers.	Strong
	There is a performance-contingent element and some evidence of linking the performance targets to shareholder value.	Moderate
	There is no performance contingent-element, or incentive payments are not made with specific performance criteria.	Weak to very weak
Executive Contracts	Notice periods for executive contracts are reasonable and as short as possible. Often they are no more than one year.	Very strong

	Notice periods for executive contracts are reasonable and as short as possible. Often these are two years, but compensation payments are limited to one year's remuneration.	Strong
	Notice periods for executive contracts should be reasonable and as short as possible. Often they are two years.	Moderate
	Notice periods for executive contracts may be more than two years in length or are unreasonable.	Weak to very weak
Independence of Executive Compensation Setting	Executive compensation is decided on by a board committee composed exclusively of independent directors. This committee receives independent advice regarding salary and pay structures and has established its own guidelines and benchmarks for senior executive compensation.	Very strong
	Compensation is decided by a majority of independent directors. This committee receives independent advice regarding salary and pay structures and has established its own guidelines and benchmarks for senior executive compensation.	Strong
	A near majority of independent directors is involved in the process of compensation setting. There is evidence that the committee does not passively accept management proposals vis-à-vis pay.	Moderate
	Executive compensation appears not to be subject to a formal internal assessment and review process. There is no compensation committee on the board. Management directly controls its own level of pay.	Weak to very weak
Compensation Consultant Relationship	Committee owns the relationship with the outside compensation consulting firm, including the ability to hire and fire.	Very strong to strong
	Committee shares the relationship with the outside compensation consulting firm with management, including the ability to hire and fire, *or* if there is no compensation committee,	Strong to moderate

(Continued)

Table 8-14 (*Continued*)

Factor	Range of Factor Outcomes	Potential Analytical Assessment
	there are appropriate processes and/or structures in place that can ensure private engagement between independent directors and compensation consultants.	
	Committee shares the relationship with the outside compensation consulting firm with management but not the ability to hire and fire, *or* if there is no compensation committee, management attempts to involve outside directors in the process.	Moderate to weak
	No compensation committee. Management controls the relationship with the outside compensation consulting firm.	Weak to very weak
Compensation Disclosure	Compensation disclosures for each executive director and the most highly remunerated executives below board level (often the management board or executive committee). Compensation is broken down into all the main components: salary, incentive, equity-based awards, and other benefits or perquisites. Documented performance measures, performance targets, and actual performance and associated pay.	Very strong to strong
	Disclosure of senior management compensation in aggregate, isolating individual pay levels in "bands" or ranges, on an anonymous basis.	Strong to moderate
	There is some disclosure of compensation policy at the board level and some disclosures on executive and director compensation.	Moderate to weak
	There is no disclosure of compensation whatsoever.	Very weak

Table 8-15   Shareholding Policies

Executive and Director Shareholdings	Executive and nonexecutive directors have meaningful shareholdings relative to individual financial positions (i.e., equivalent to at least one year's total remuneration or some other relevant measure). There should be no excessive shareholding requirements that could lead to perverse incentives (i.e., requirements to hold 20 times salary).	Very strong to strong
	Executive and nonexecutive directors have meaningful shareholdings relative to individual financial positions.	Strong to moderate
	Executive directors do not possess any meaningful shareholdings.	Moderate to very weak

Table 8-16   Compensation Mix

Stock Option Usage	Executive stock options: A balanced part of compensation mix, along with other components. No megagrants: reasonable in volume, phased over time, and no discounting or repricing.	Very strong to moderate
	Executive stock options: Heavy use of, poorly phased, and considerably discounted or repriced.	Weak to very weak
Compensation Plan Dilution	Total overhang (which includes expected dilution) for all plans is either less than 5% or is reasonably in line with peers. Dilution and overhang should be analyzed separately, as well as repurchase rates and the value of outstanding options as determined by Black-Scholes.	Very strong to strong
	Total overhang (which includes expected dilution) for all plans is not more than 5–7% higher than peer average.	Moderate
	Total overhang (which includes expected dilution) for all plans is significantly out of line with peers. Or: shareholders cannot easily determine total overhang or total payout (evergreen plans, or opaque performance criteria).	Weak to very weak

Table 8-17 Options and Incentives

Nonexecutive Options	Nonexecutive directors do not receive options.	Very strong
	Nonexecutive directors may receive options but they should not be excessive or discretionary: grants should have fixed prices and fixed exercise dates. Options/shares resulting from option exercises should be held until directors leave the board.	Strong to moderate
	Nonexecutive directors may receive options but they should not be excessive or discretionary: Grants should have fixed prices and fixed exercise dates.	Moderate
	Nonexecutive directors receive options and they may be excessive or discretionary.	Weak to very weak
Incentives and Other Issues	There are no excessive perks or retirement benefits, or other structures affecting incentives. Non-executive directors do not receive compensation linked to short-term results.	Very strong to strong
	There are no excessive perks or retirement benefits, or other structures affecting incentives OR there are some reasonable exceptions which have been fully disclosed. Nonexecutive directors may be entitled to moderate annual bonus grants.	Strong to moderate
	There is evidence of excessive perks or retirement benefits, or other structures affecting incentives. These are either not disclosed or well hidden. Significant part of nonexecutive compensation consists of short-term performance awards.	Weak to very weak

In conclusion, directors and executives should be remunerated fairly and motivated to ensure the success of the company. Directors and executives should be compensated in a fashion that rewards excellent service, not marginal performance, and enhances directors' links to shareholders. The board's role is to ensure appropriate rigor, fairness, and independence in the setting of compensation policies and the determination of specific compensation awards.

PART THREE

CASE STUDIES

Chapter 9

Wimm-Bill-Dann Foods OJSC

Russian Federation

Oleg Shvyrkov and Anna Grishina

This report, summarizing the status of Wimm-Bill-Dann Foods as of June 29, 2009, begins with Table 9-1.

Table 9-1   Wimm-Bill-Dann Foods at a Glance OJSC (Russian Federation)

Overall Company Score*STRONG	7+		
Maximum is 10		NYSE:	WBD
Component Scores:*		MICEX/RTS	WBDF
Shareholder influence	7+		
Shareholder rights	7+	S&P credit rating	BB–/Stable/—
Transparency, audit, and risk management	7	12M P/E	34.1
Board effectiveness, strategic process, and incentives	7+	Market cap (ADRs)	U.S.$2.4 billion

Standard & Poor's has affirmed a GAMMA score of GAMMA 7+ for Wimm-Bill-Dann Foods OJSC (WBD).

Strengths

The founding shareholders play a positive role in WBD, and the independent directors provide checks and balances in the governance system. WBD provides a high overall level of disclosure, and its shareholder meeting procedures are consistent. The scope of shareholder rights is broad by international standards. Solid procedures for strategic planning are in place.

Weaknesses

There are certain weaknesses in the scope, timing, and accessibility of disclosure. There are also issues regarding board composition, including the presence of a competitor's representative among the directors and a limited skill mix among the independents. Figure 9-1 outlines the shareholding structure of the company.

Executive Summary

Standard & Poor's Governance Services has affirmed its Governance, Accountability, Management Metrics, and Analysis (GAMMA) score

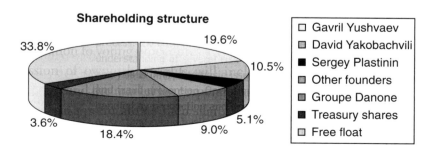

Figure 9-1   Shareholding Structure of Wimm-Bill-Dann Foods OJSC

of "GAMMA 7+" for the Russian food producer Wimm-Bill-Dann Foods OJSC (WBD). See "About GAMMA," below, for general details about GAMMA scores.

WBD is a Russian producer of dairy products, baby food, juice, and mineral water. A group of entrepreneurs founded the company in 1992. Together, they currently own 44.2% of the company and remain important shareholders. WBD is a market leader in Russia's dairy products segment, controlling about 30% of the market, and has a market share of 18% in the baby food segment. The company is also the third largest Russian producer of juice products, with a market share of 18%. WBD has maintained a Level 3 American Depositary Receipt (ADR) program on the New York Stock Exchange (NYSE) since 2002. WBD reported consolidated net income of $102 million on revenues of $2.8 billion in 2008 [using U.S. dollars and generally accepted accounting principles (GAAP)].

Strengths

The founding shareholders are committed to promoting strong governance practices at WBD and are motivated to seek growth in shareholder value. Their external investments do not expose them to material conflicts of interest.

Reputable independent directors play a significant role on the board. The board is well balanced, as the group of founders is in the minority. The effectiveness of the board is supported by four active committees.

WBD is open to the investment community and has a high degree of financial and operational transparency. This is supported by WBD's obligation to comply with the Sarbanes-Oxley Act and other U.S. Securities and Exchange Commission (SEC) regulations.

Generally solid procedures for strategic planning are in place. The board-level investment and strategic planning committee is active in providing oversight of the strategic process.

Shareholder meeting procedures are robust, and minority shareholders have a wide range of rights under Russian law.

Weaknesses

The role of Groupe Danone, a competing company and minority shareholder in WBD's governance system, is ambiguous. Its representative on WBD's board is not active, though.

There is room for improvement in terms of board composition and processes. Independent directors have not had a majority of board votes since 2007. Specific expertise in human resources and compensation is not represented on the board, and only one independent director has relevant industry expertise. The overall frequency of meetings is moderate.

There are some weaknesses in the scope and accessibility of disclosure. They include limited information on executive pay and weak governance-related disclosure on the company's Web site.

An integrated approach to risk management is just being developed. Despite a generally sound approach to risk, function-specific risks are managed within separate silos.

Full Report, Shareholder Influence: Component Score 7+

Key Analytical Issues

Founding shareholders support strong governance. The founding shareholders, who jointly hold 44% of shares, are committed to separating ownership from management, involving independent directors in strategic decisions, and exercising their influence on the company through transparent corporate procedures.

Independent directors provide checks and balances. Five of 11 board seats and the majority of seats on two board-level committees belong to independent directors. There is a culture of open discussion and consensus-based decision making. However, the founding shareholders' undertaking to elect an independent board majority, which was included in the shareholder agreement, has not been fully observed since June 2007.

Founders have no significant conflicts of interest.   Although several members of the controlling group have business interests outside WBD, some of which are in related industries, the scope of transactions with those affiliated entities is negligible (U.S.$15,289 in 2008), and those transactions are subject to the board's scrutiny. These external businesses are individual initiatives rather than joint enterprises owned by all the members of the controlling group, thus creating internal checks and balances within the group.

Blockholder Groupe Danone plays an ambiguous role.   Groupe Danone, WBD's direct competitor in the dairy segment, holds an 18.3% stake in WBD. Since 2007, Danone has had one seat on WBD's board. The long-term goals of Danone are not clear, and its current role in the WBD's governance is ambiguous.

Founders serve on subsidiaries' boards.   Some of the founders continue to serve on the boards of WBD's subsidiaries. This runs counter to the notion of separating ownership from management or delegating authority.

Separating Ownership from Management

The entrepreneurs who founded the company in 1992 and remain in control of it have demonstrated their commitment to strong governance procedures on numerous occasions. Most important, around the time of the initial public offering (IPO) in 2002, they adopted a hands-off approach to WBD's operations and made a commitment to appoint a significant number of reputable independent directors to the board. Furthermore, in 2006, one of the founders, Sergey Plastinin, stepped down as chief executive officer (CEO), and an external international executive, Tony Maher, was hired with the active involvement of the independent directors.

The mutual obligations of the founders and key governance principles are formalized in the shareholder agreement. This agreement, which originally was concluded in 1997, was amended and restated in 2002 when it was filed with the SEC. Members of that group agreed to concerted voting at shareholder meetings (but not at board meetings) and agreed to coordinate share sales to parties outside the group. The shareholder agreement specifies shareholders' commitment to elect a majority of independent directors to the board.

Groupe Danone has been a minority shareholder since its unsuccessful bid to take over WBD in 2003. Furthermore, Danone increased its blockholding to 18.4% from 7% between 2003 and 2007; over the last 24 months, its equity position has been stable. This may signal Groupe Danone's continuing interest in taking over WBD. Indeed, a potential acquisition by a major international industry player does not raise concerns from the perspective of WBD's governance. There is also a precedent, set in 2003, of independent directors taking an active role to ensure that minority shareholders are treated fairly in the course of a prospective change in control.

Even though Danone is unlikely to be able to challenge the status quo in WBD's governance structure as long as its blockholding remains under 25%, its current role in WBD's governance is ambiguous. For instance, Danone appointed its senior executive, Jacques Vincent, to WBD's board in 2007. In light of the fact that Vincent has limited time to devote to board service at WBD and limited ability to participate in board discussions because of competition issues, it is not clear why Danone did not choose to appoint an independent director rather than its own executive to protect its interests as an investor in WBD.

Shareholder Rights: Component Score 7+

Key Analytical Issues

Good meeting notification procedures. Shareholders are notified of general meetings through an announcement in the *Wall*

Street Journal and by individual mail. It is an important positive that annual U.S. GAAP statements are available ahead of a meeting. It is a weakness, however, that the agenda and the meeting materials are not made available on the Web site. We also note that meeting materials present limited background information about board candidates. WBD is one of the few public Russian companies that do not publish the minutes of shareholder meetings.

Strong meeting procedures.   Meeting procedures are fairly strong in accordance with Russian law. Voting by proxy is allowed. Votes are cast through ballots and counted by the independent registrar. Neither management nor the ADR depositary can vote the deposited shares at their discretion. About 26% of the total number of shares held by minorities cast their votes in the 2008 board elections; that indicates lack of technical constraints on such voting. At the same time, we note that annual meetings are held in June, which is the norm in Russia but fairly late by international standards.

Broad range of voting rights.   Russian law provides a broad range of voting rights to minority investors. Holders of 2% or more of the company's voting stock may put forward candidates to the board of directors, and holders of at least 10% of voting stock may convene extraordinary shareholder meetings. Cumulative voting is compulsory in board elections.

Independent registrar.   The share registrar, CMD, is the largest and the most reputable in Russia.

Law provides moderate protection of ownership rights.   In theory, Russian law provides many elements of ownership protection found in other jurisdictions, including preemptive rights in new share issues, mandatory buyouts in the event of a blockholding exceeding a 30% threshold, and fair pricing in squeeze-outs. In

practice, however, certain legal loopholes and the country's ineffective judicial system create risks that blockholders may circumvent such protections. Although those risks are unlikely to affect
WBD's shareholders, we note them as a general attribute of the
legal environment in Russia.

No dividend policy available. There are no articulated guidelines or policies for dividend payout. The company has made
dividend announcements after the official record date in recent
years.

Fair payout procedures. In 2007, the last time a dividend was
paid, WBD announced and respected a 60-day payout period,
which is shorter than that of most Russian companies.

Transparency, Audit, and Enterprise Risk Management: Component Score 7

Scope, Timing, and Accessibility of Public Disclosure

Key Analytical Issues

**Ownership information is complete, but accessibility can be
improved.** Ownership disclosure is fairly complete. Detailed ownership information and group structure are presented in the statutory filings to the SEC and to Russian authorities. There is room for
improvement in terms of accessibility of such information, however.
WBD's Web site does not contain a section on ownership structure,
for example. Comprehensive ownership information is filed with
the SEC only once a year, in the 20-F report. Filings to Russian regulators are more up to date, yet they have a cumbersome structure
and usually are not translated into English in full.

Solid financial and operational disclosure. WBD prepares U.S. GAAP financial statements on a quarterly basis and hosts quarterly conference calls. Management presentations containing financial, operational, and strategic data are available on the Web site. At the same time, there is room for improvement in terms of interim disclosure: Quarterly U.S. GAAP accounts currently do not contain notes on the financial statements.

Adequate timing of disclosure. Unaudited annual U.S. GAAP results were released on March 18, 2009 (March 28 a year earlier). This is significantly earlier than such announcements by most Russian public companies but about three weeks later than the international norm. Results for the third quarter of 2008 were released on December 18, almost two months after such disclosures by international peers. Audited annual results under U.S. GAAP, complete with notes, are presented in the 20-F filing to the SEC published on June 22 in 2009 (June 26 in 2008).

Proactive investor relations. WBD follows proactive investor relations policies, including maintenance of an ongoing dialogue with major non-Russian investment funds. The company's top management engages in non-deal road shows and is open to meetings with investors and analysts.

Governance-related disclosure is moderate. It is a positive that the auditor's fees and the specifics of services provided are disclosed and that the charter, corporate governance code, and key bylaws are available online in Russian and English. At the same time, the composition of board committees is not available on the Web site, and meeting attendance rates by board members are not published. The compensation of individual managers and directors is not disclosed. Information on the terms of related-party transactions is not specified in the notes for the U.S. GAAP accounts. The investor events calendar is updated irregularly.

Limited social and environmental disclosure. Despite WBD's substantial participation in social activities, public disclosure of social and environmental information remains limited.

The Audit Process

Key Analytical Issues

Reputable external auditor. WBD employs Ernst & Young, an established international auditor that was chosen via open tender. Ernst & Young does not provide any nonaudit services to WBD.

Audit committee has strong composition. The audit committee, which is composed solely of independent directors, provides close oversight of the external auditor and the internal audit. The chairperson of the committee has a strong background in audit, but only one other committee member has a background in finance.

Audit committee procedures are robust. The audit committee regularly interacts with the internal audit department and conducts meetings with the external auditor without members of management present. The committee also is involved in finance-related risk management issues, though an integrated risk management system has not been developed. The committee conducts quarterly face-to-face meetings, which we consider only a moderate frequency, however.

Internal audit fully staffed but has limited experience. The internal audit department is headed by an audit expert and is fully staffed. Most internal auditors have limited experience, however, and this constrains the effectiveness of the department. The statutory audit board is composed of staff from the internal audit department. The internal audit department reports to and regularly interacts with the audit committee.

Enterprise Risk Management

Key Analytical Issues

Risks managed within functions. Line management and functional management are aware of relevant risks and exposures. These risks are analyzed and managed within the respective functional units. The respective board-level committees, most importantly the audit committee and the investment and strategic planning committee, are involved in reviewing risk controls within their respective areas of expertise.

Risk management activities are not integrated. Management and the board believe that in view of the relatively homogeneous geographic base of the operations (the former Soviet Union) and limited industry diversification (dairy foods and beverages), the structure of risks is relatively straightforward and does not warrant complex risk management techniques. In accordance with this view, function-specific risks currently are managed within separate silos. Some elements of an integrated risk management system are at the initial stage of development.

Audit committee analyzes financial risks. The audit committee is active in reviewing risks pertaining to the audit process and finance. The internal audit department provides a map of these relevant risks.

Elements of strategic risk management are present. There is evidence that risk considerations, although not systematized, have links to strategy, such as the diversification into dairy farms. This was motivated by the need to hedge against a possible shortage of supply and price fluctuations.

Board Effectiveness, Strategic Process, and Incentives: Component Score 7+

Board Composition

Key Analytical Issues

Board has a significant proportion of independent directors. The board has a significant degree of independence from management and the controlling shareholders. It consists of 11 members, all of whom are nonexecutive directors. Five directors are independent. The independent directors are high-profile figures, and three of them are non-Russian professionals. One director represents Danone, and another five are part of the founding shareholder group. Members of the controlling group are not obligated to coordinate their votes at board meetings as they are required to at shareholder meetings. This allows all directors to contribute to decision making individually.

Board-level committees. The independence and effectiveness of the board are reinforced by a sophisticated committee structure. This enhances the role of the independent directors.

Executive of a competitor is on the board. We have reservations about Danone representative Jacques Vincent's ability to contribute to board decision making at WBD because of his conflict of interest. We note, however, that the issue of his board presence and involvement in discussions on strategic issues has been handled professionally and amicably. In the last 12 months, the issue generally has been moot as a result of his low attendance at board meetings.

Casting vote of chairperson weakens the balance. The board chairperson has a deciding vote in case of a tie, which technically gives the founders a board majority whenever Vincent (or one of the independents) is absent, as has been often the case in the last

12 months. We note nevertheless that the board has a tradition of consensus-based decision making and that it is very unlikely that the founders will insist on a decision when the independents oppose it.

There is still room for improvement in terms of the skill mix. Only one of the independent directors has industry-specific expertise. Also, none of the board members has a background in human resources and incentives structures.

Four board committees (investment and strategic planning, human resources and compensation, audit, and corporate governance) are chaired by independent directors. Additionally, the audit committee is fully composed of independent directors. Jacques Vincent, the representative of Danone, is not a member of any committees. The corporate governance committee has an independent majority.

Board Effectiveness

Key Analytical Issues

Wide authority of the board. The board of directors has far-reaching authority, including the approval of WBD's strategic and investment plans, budgets, and performance evaluations. The board's mandate is formulated clearly in the charter, bylaws, and corporate governance code. All investments exceeding U.S.$5 million are reviewed by the investment and strategic planning committee and approved by the board. However, for some types of transactions, such as divestments, the practical threshold requiring board approval is rather high at 25% of assets under Russian Accounting Standards (RAS). Also, Russian law does not require that significant transactions performed by subsidiaries be approved by the board.

Solid board process. There is a tradition of open discussion among board members that is encouraged by the controlling shareholders. The frequency of face-to-face meetings of the board and committees is intermediate, although there are frequent informal discussions and consultations between directors. The overall attendance level is reasonably high.

Professional corporate secretary. A corporate secretary facilitates the functioning of the board and committees. The corporate secretary reports directly to the board and has sufficient staff to ensure timely review, translation, and distribution of documents for board and committee sessions.

Self-appraisal routine to be launched. The board has decided to start performing annual self-appraisal procedures, which we view positively. These procedures will include a survey and one-on-one interviews by the board chairperson.

Strategic Planning Process

Key Analytical Issues

Solid planning process. A thoroughly structured strategic planning process has been in place since 2006. There are regular executive-level strategy sessions and meetings with the board-level investment and strategic planning committee.

Planning performed internally. Strategic planning extends to five years and builds on internally developed industry forecasts. There are direct links to budgeting processes and incentives plans. The planning guidelines have not been formalized in a specific document, however.

Communication of strategic goals limited. In view of the relatively short history of the strategic process in its current shape, several elements that take time to build have not been developed fully. They include communication of strategic goals, values, and culture throughout the organization as well as encouragement of strategic initiatives at the line management level. As part of the effort to develop open strategic communication, the CEO and other executives frequently visit manufacturing sites. External communication of strategic objectives is limited.

Adequate implementation tools. There is a management accounting system in place that provides monthly reports containing data on key strategic indicators and year-end outlooks. There is a clear link between strategic targets and executive compensation systems.

Board and Executive Compensation

Key Analytical Issues

Clear executive compensation plan. There is a clearly structured, objective compensation plan for executives that provides a link between performance targets and bonus payments. The individual performance targets include a healthy mix of top-line and bottom-line targets, with earnings before interest, taxes, depreciation, and amortization (EBITDA) being the most important bottom-line indicator.

Balanced equity-based incentive plan. In addition to short-term performance bonuses, the company uses an equity-based incentives plan. There is a phantom stock plan that extends to senior executives and includes phantom stock with a three-year vesting period.

Conservative board compensation. Board compensation is transparent and conservatively structured. Directors receive a fixed salary and additional fixed compensation for committee memberships. The aggregate amount of board compensation is approved annually by the shareholders. The phantom stock plan developed for executives does not extend to directors.

Committee provides compensation oversight. The human resources and compensation committee of the board reviews the compensation policies on a quarterly basis. An overview is presented to the board. It is a weakness, however, that none of the committee members is a compensation expert. There is also room for improvement in terms of the board's overall involvement in the oversight of compensation policies.

Limited compensation disclosure. The disclosure of executive pay is limited. As a foreign issuer on the NYSE, WBD is exempt from any requirement to disclose the compensation of its five highest-paid executives. Furthermore, like most other Russian companies, it does not provide an individual pay breakdown. The aggregate compensation of the management board is disclosed in the 20-F filing to the SEC and other public documents.

Golden parachutes are not an issue. We are not aware of the existence of any significant golden parachutes or similar arrangements with respect to senior executives.

About GAMMA

A company Governance, Accountability, Management Metrics, and Analysis (GAMMA) score reflects the opinion of Standard & Poor's Equity Research Services' GAMMA department on the relative strength of a company's corporate governance practices as an investor protection against potential governance-related losses or failure to create value. The governance practices and policies of an individual company are measured against Standard & Poor's corporate governance criteria, which are based on a synthesis of international codes, governance best practices, and guidelines for good governance practice.

Companies with the same score have, in the opinion of Standard & Poor's, similar company-specific governance processes and practices overall regardless of the country of domicile. The scores do not address specific legal, regulatory, and market environments and the extent to which those environments support or hinder governance at the company level, a factor that may affect the overall assessment of the governance risks associated with an individual company (see "Country Factors," below).

A GAMMA Score Is Articulated on a Scale of GAMMA 1 (Lowest) to GAMMA 10 (Highest).

GAMMA 9 and GAMMA 10. A company that, in Standard & Poor's opinion, has very strong corporate governance processes and practices overall. A company in these scoring categories has, in Standard & Poor's opinion, few weaknesses in any of the major areas of governance analysis.

GAMMA 7 and GAMMA 8+. A company that, in Standard & Poor's opinion, has strong corporate governance processes and practices overall. A company in these scoring categories has, in Standard & Poor's opinion, some weaknesses in certain of the major areas of governance analysis.

GAMMA 5 and GAMMA 6+. A company that, in Standard & Poor's opinion, has moderate corporate governance processes and practices overall. A company in these scoring categories has, in Standard & Poor's opinion, weaknesses in several of the major areas of governance analysis.

GAMMA 3 and GAMMA 4+. A company that, in Standard & Poor's opinion, has weak corporate governance processes and practices overall. A company in these scoring categories has, in Standard & Poor's opinion, significant weaknesses in a number of the major areas of governance analysis.

GAMMA 1 and GAMMA 2+. A company that, in Standard & Poor's opinion, has very weak corporate governance processes and practices overall. A company in these scoring categories has, in Standard & Poor's opinion, significant weaknesses in most of the major areas of analysis.

GovernanceWatch

A "GovernanceWatch" designation may be used to highlight the fact that identifiable governance events and short-term trends have caused a GAMMA score to be placed on review. GovernanceWatch does not mean that a change to the score is inevitable. GovernanceWatch is not intended to include all the GAMMA scores under review, and changes to a GAMMA score may occur without that score having first appeared on GovernanceWatch.

Country Factors

Although Standard & Poor's publishes country governance infrastructure analyses from time to time, it is important to note that it does not score individual countries. However, consideration of a country's legal, regulatory, and market environment is an important element in the overall analysis of the risks associated with the governance practices of an individual company. For example two companies that have the same company scores but are domiciled in countries with contrasting legal, regulatory, and market standards present different risk profiles if their governance practices deteriorate;

that is, if there is deterioration in a specific company's governance standards, investors and stakeholders are likely to receive better protection in a country with stronger and better enforced laws and regulations. However, in Standard & Poor's opinion, companies with high GAMMA scores have less governance-related risk than do companies with low scores regardless of the country of domicile.

For a full explanation of Standard & Poor's GAMMA scoring methodology, refer to the latest edition of "Criteria: GAMMA Scores," available online at http://www2.standardandpoors.com/portal/site/sp/en/us/page.article/2,5,13,0,1204838772463.html.

Important Note

The opinions expressed are the independent opinions of Standard & Poor's Equity Research Services' GAMMA department and do not reflect the opinions of other areas of Standard & Poor's. Standard & Poor's GAMMA scores and other analytic services are performed as entirely separate activities to preserve the independence and objectivity of each analytic process.

A GAMMA score is based on current information provided to Standard & Poor's by a company, its officers, and any other sources Standard & Poor's considers reliable. A GAMMA is neither an audit nor a forensic investigation of governance practices. Standard & Poor's may rely on audited information and other information provided by a company for the purpose of the governance analysis. A GAMMA score is neither a credit rating nor a recommendation to purchase, sell, or hold any interest in a company, as it does not comment on market price or suitability for a particular investor. Scores may be changed, suspended, or withdrawn as a result of changes in or unavailability of such information.

Chapter 10

EuroChem Mineral and Chemical Co. OJSC

Russian Federation

Oleg Shvyrkov and Anna Grishina

This report, summarizing the status of EuroChem Mineral and Chemical Co. as of July 20, 2009, begins with Table 10-1.

Table 10-1 EuroChem Mineral and Chemical Company at a Glance

Overall Company Score* MODERATE	6+		
Maximum is 10			
Component Scores*			
Shareholder influence	6+		
Shareholder rights	6	S&P credit rating	BB/Stable–
Transparency, audit, and risk management	6	12M P/E	Not available
Board effectiveness, strategic process, and incentives	6+	Market cap (GDRs)	Not available

Standard & Poor's has assigned a score of GAMMA 6+ to EuroChem Mineral and Chemical Co. OJSC (EuroChem). This score addresses the relative strength of the governance structures and practices at EuroChem from the perspective of potential minority shareholders' interests. (See "About GAMMA" in Chapter 9 for general details about GAMMA scores.)

Strengths

EuroChem is the only large company under the control of Andrey Melnichenko, and that limits the potential for conflicts of interest. Melnichenko has encouraged improvements in governance structures. The EuroChem board is active, and its composition is strong in terms of independence, level of expertise, and the skill mix of its members. Transparency is high overall, and Russian law provides a wide scope of voting rights to potential minority shareholders. Strategic decision making is solid.

Weaknesses

The ability of independent directors to balance the controlling shareholder's influence in the interests of external investors has not been tested. The volume of related-party financing transactions is significant. The internal audit department is relatively small and has a short history. A holistic approach to risk management is just starting to be developed. EuroChem has a mixed record in terms of minority relations with its formerly public subsidiaries. Figure 10-1 shows the shareholding structure of EuroChem.

Executive Summary

Standard & Poor's Governance Services has assigned a Governance, Accountability, Management Metrics, and Analysis (GAMMA) score

Shareholding structure

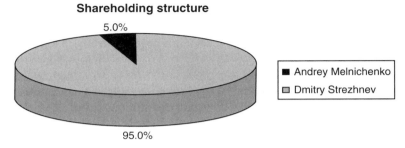

Figure 10-1 Shareholding Structure of EuroChem

to Open Joint Stock Company (OJSC) EuroChem Mineral and Chemical Co. (EuroChem) of GAMMA 6+.

Established in 2001, EuroChem is Russia's largest fertilizer producer and one of the top 10 globally. Although there is a possibility of an initial public offering (IPO) in the medium term, EuroChem remains a privately held company and is majority owned by Melnichenko. The company's principal activities include mining (apatite, iron ore, and baddeleyite) and the production and distribution of fertilizers. EuroChem's major markets are Western and Eastern Europe and the United States, but it also exports its products to Asia and Latin America. In addition to five plants in Russia and Lithuania and a mining site in Russia, the group has extensive transportation and marketing structures, including its own railway cars and seaport terminals. EuroChem is developing a potash fertilizer division and has acquired licenses at two potash-mining sites in Russia. It is attempting to acquire a license for the development of a phosphorous deposit in Kazakhstan.

EuroChem's sales rose from U.S.$2.9 billion in 2007 to $4.9 billion in 2008, of which about 80% was derived from nitrogen and phosphate fertilizers, 6% from organic chemicals, and 10% from mining by-products. The earnings before interest, taxes, depreciation, and amortization (EBITDA) margin was a healthy 39%. Despite the increase in financial leverage over 2008, the ratio of net debt to EBITDA was at the moderate level of 0.6× at the year end.

The GAMMA scoring methodology approaches the analysis of governance from the perspective of existing and potential minority shareholders' interests. In line with this approach, the GAMMA score and the current commentary address EuroChem's corporate governance practices as if the company were about to be publicly traded and widely held.

Strengths

Melnichenko, the ultimate controlling shareholder, is committed to raising the shareholder value of EuroChem and supports improvements in governance mechanisms. He is not involved in executive functions at EuroChem.

Board composition is vigorous in terms of balance, level of expertise, and the members' skill mix. Three active board-level committees contribute to the board's effectiveness.

A clear and effective incentives plan for executives and a sound compensation plan for nonexecutive directors are in place.

There is a high overall level of transparency. The company prepares its International Financial Reporting Standards (IFRS) statements quarterly and discloses them sooner than most Russian companies do. A reputable international audit firm audits those accounts. EuroChem is one of the few companies that present social and environmental reporting under the internationally recognized standards.

EuroChem's charter sets forth a wide measure of shareholder rights.

The strategy-making process is clear and well managed.

Weaknesses

The board's ability to stand up for the interests of minority investors has not been demonstrated in practice.

The scope of related-party transactions involving the parent company, including loans to and purchase of shares from the parent, has been significant in recent years.

Because of loopholes in Russian law, the board has incomplete control over transactions carried out by subsidiaries, including related-party transactions.

The scope and timing of disclosure and the audit process could be improved further. The internal audit department is relatively small and has limited experience.

Enterprise risk management (ERM) procedures are just being developed.

EuroChem has a mixed record in its relations with minority shareholders in subsidiaries.

Full Report

Shareholder Influence: Component Score 6+

Key Analytical Issues

Majority shareholder supports governance improvements. There is a clear differentiation between the roles of the controlling shareholder, the board, and management at EuroChem. The ultimate majority owner, Melnichenko, refrains from taking an executive or semiexecutive role. He supported the election of an independent majority to EuroChem's board and encourages improvements in transparency.

No history of independent directors' ability to balance majority shareholders' influence. The existing governance structures, although sophisticated, have not faced the task of protecting the interests of minorities in EuroChem. Also, there are reasons to believe that the board makes concessions to the current private status of the company in endorsing some of the shareholders' initiatives. Loans extended to the parent in 2007 and 2008 might have raised questions from minority shareholders if EuroChem had been a public company, for example.

Positive consequence of majority stake in EuroChem. Although Melnichenko's interests were fairly diverse in the past and included banking, metalworks, energy, and mining, he divested most of his external stakes in 2007 and raised his beneficial equity position in EuroChem to 95% from 50%. EuroChem is now the only large company in which Melnichenko holds a majority stake. This reduces the potential for a conflict of interest. We note, however, that although information about Melnichenko's external industrial assets is available to the external auditors and EuroChem's board, it is not disclosed publicly.

Significant volume of related-party financing transactions. EuroChem's exposure to related-party transactions in its operations is negligible. However, financing transactions with the parent were a regular occurrence in the period 2006–2008 and were significant in scope. They included providing loans and acquiring shares in K+S from the parent. Transactions were reviewed by the board, and there is no reason to believe that they were disadvantageous to EuroChem; however, their significant volume represents a concern from the perspective of the conflicts of interest they may entail.

Support for Improvements in Governance

In recent years, Melnichenko has been consistent in implementing elements of strong governance at EuroChem and other companies in which he has been a significant investor. First, this reflects Melnichenko's interest in overseeing his investment in EuroChem without being personally involved in executive functions. Second, the presence of strong governance structures creates opportunities for a public placement of shares. This option is valuable to the company because it has ambitious investment plans.

Ultimate Ownership Structure

A company that holds Melnichenko's business interests owns 95% of Cyprus-registered MCC Holding Ltd. (MCC), EuroChem's parent company. EuroChem's chief executive officer (CEO), Dmitry Strezhnev, has beneficially owned 5% of shares in MCC since 2007.

Recurrent Related-Party Transactions

The scope of recurrent related-party transactions is relatively small. In 2008, sales to related parties [as defined under International Accounting Standard (IAS) 24] were U.S.$18.3 million, less than 0.5% of total sales ($0.1 million and less than 0.1% in 2007). Purchases from related entities were U.S.$14.1 million, less than 0.8% of the cost of goods sold ($10.4 million and less than 0.9% in 2007). Moreover, most of those transactions involved NF HimAgro, a nonconsolidated Ukraine-based trading affiliate with significant outsider ownership.

Loans to Parent Company

On several occasions in the past and most recently in October 2008, EuroChem provided loans to its parent, MCC. In some cases, those loans were extended in advance and in the expected amount of the upcoming dividend. In April 2006, EuroChem provided MCC with a six-month U.S. dollar–denominated unsecured loan in the amount of $50 million at LIBOR plus 2%. Another $100 million was provided in September 2006 at 8% annual interest. That loan came due on December 31, 2006, but was extended and eventually was repaid in February 2007.

In October 2008, EuroChem provided MCC with an unsecured U.S. dollar–denominated loan in the amount of $195 million at LIBOR plus 2.5%, maturing on April 21, 2009. That loan was made in connection with the acquisition of K+S shares, which MCC was expected to acquire in the open market. It was repaid on schedule.

Investments in K+S Shares

In 2007, MCC started acquiring the stock of K+S AG, a German producer of potash fertilizers, salt, and chemicals, based on the shareholders' assessment that K+S was significantly undervalued. According to K+S disclosures, MCC had accumulated 10.4% of its shares by the end of June 2008. In the second half of 2008, shareholders concluded that it would be more logical for EuroChem rather than MCC to hold those shares, since it would allow the company to explore strategic opportunities in the investment. K+S is an experienced producer of potash fertilizers and has moderate reserves—exactly the opposite of EuroChem's situation. However, it is not clear at this point whether there are tangible synergies to be explored and whether a strategic partnership between producers is feasible from the organizational perspective.

According to the IFRS statements for the first three quarters and the full year 2008, EuroChem purchased in October and November 2008 around 5% of K+S's shares, of which about half was purchased from MCC.

As of June 26, 2009, EuroChem held 12.5% of K+S shares with a market price of 830 million euros. About 9.4% of K+S shares had been purchased from MCC, and the rest were purchased in the open market. The combined shareholding of MCC and EuroChem currently amounts to 16.3% of outstanding shares. Overall, EuroChem invested about 31.3 billion rubles in K+S shares between October 2008 and April 2009.

Shareholder Rights: Component Score 6

Key Analytical Issues

Solid voting rights. Russian law and EuroChem's charter provide for a wide measure of direct voting rights that would apply automatically to all new equity investors. There is a one share–one vote principle, and any shareholder or any group of shareholders jointly holding over 2% of shares may put forward candidates for the board. Holders of at least 10% of the voting stock may convene extraordinary shareholder meetings. Cumulative voting must be used in board elections, and the entire board slate must stand for reelection annually.

Shareholder meeting procedures thoroughly regulated by law. Although EuroChem remains a private company and does not have experience in catering to the needs of a wide shareholder base at the corporate level, we do not believe this creates risks for potential minority shareholders in EuroChem. Russian law is very prescriptive in terms of procedures for shareholder meetings, and EuroChem can draw on the experience of its formerly public subsidiaries. EuroChem has an independent registrar chosen through a tender, which is a positive factor. Also, the full text of meeting minutes is published on the company's Web site.

Mixed record in minority relations with subsidiaries. There are indications that the interests of minority shareholders in EuroChem's subsidiaries did not always receive sufficient consideration in the past. For several years the public subsidiaries were not distributing profits, whereas EuroChem was paying out a substantial dividend. This effectively caused a redistribution from minorities in subsidiaries to EuroChem's shareholders. After EuroChem increased its equity interest in formerly public subsidiaries to 100%, it required them to make significant dividend payments. Also, some of the squeeze-out procedures at subsidiaries raise concerns.

The law provides moderate protection of ownership rights. In theory, Russian law provides many elements of ownership protection found in other jurisdictions, including preemptive rights in new share issues, mandatory buyouts in the event of a blockholding exceeding a 30% threshold, and fair pricing in squeeze-outs. In practice, however, certain legal loopholes and the country's ineffective judicial system create risks that blockholders may circumvent such protections. Also, some of these rights do not extend automatically to holders of depositary receipts (e.g., preemptive rights in new share issues). Although these risks are not relevant in the current ownership setting, we note them as a general attribute of the legal environment in Russia.

Dividend Policy Is Sound but Raises Questions
EuroChem has an internal dividend policy that specifies several meaningful criteria for the payout ratio. It is positive that the policy provides for quarterly dividend payouts, which is unusual in Russia, and requires that payment be made within 30 days after the approval of a dividend at the shareholders' meeting. There remains the question, however, of whether the company would manage to follow the payout timeline after an IPO. Quarterly dividends require quarterly shareholder meetings under Russian law, for example, which may not be realistic at a public company.

Squeeze-Out Procedures in Subsidiaries

EuroChem squeezed out the minority shareholders in its major subsidiaries in 2007 and 2008, shortly after that kind of move became possible under Russian law. This led to a simpler structure of the group, which we see as a governance positive. At the same time, there are indications that at least in some cases, the interests of minority shareholders in EuroChem's subsidiaries did not receive sufficient consideration in the course of the squeeze-outs.

Thus, local appraisers, rather than international companies, were invited to perform valuations at all the subsidiaries involved. Russian law requires that all such valuations undergo third-party reviews by the national association of appraisers; that assures a certain level of quality. Nevertheless, expertise available to—and research independence policies followed by—reputable international companies, such as the major audit firms, allows these companies to produce valuations of consistently high quality, leading to greater protection of the parties affected by a squeeze-out. We believe that by recruiting an international appraiser instead of or in addition to a local firm, EuroChem could have strengthened the ownership rights of shareholders in its subsidiaries.

In February 2008, squeeze-out procedures were completed at Kovdorskiy GOK, a mining subsidiary. We note that the independent appraiser's valuation that was based on the commodity prices and price forecasts as of July 1, 2007, was not updated at the time the squeeze-out was initiated in November 2007. The price of the subsidiary's products had risen by then, and price projections were revised upward, making the earlier valuation conservative. Nevertheless, EuroChem's management and board chose not to call off the squeeze-out, requesting an updated appraisal in November 2007 because the earlier valuation was still valid under the applicable regulations.

It is a positive that EuroChem's management took a different approach at two large production subsidiaries, Nevinnomysskiy Azot and Novomoskovskiy Azot, where a squeeze-out was completed in July 2008. As in the case of Kovdorskiy GOK, the initial appraisal was performed in August 2007, and the price of the products rose spectacularly during the autumn. Unlike in the case of Kovdorskiy GOK, however, EuroChem's management chose not to proceed with the squeeze-out based on the mid–2007 valuations and requested an updated appraisal of those two subsidiaries in February 2008. Nevertheless, a group of former shareholders of Nevinnomysskiy Azot is challenging the fairness of the buyout prices in court.

Squeeze-outs also were performed at a trading subsidiary, Agrocenter EuroChem Ust-Labinsk.

Transparency, Audit, and Enterprise Resource Management: Component Score 6

Scope, Timing, and Accessibility of Public Disclosure

Key Analytical Issues

Good ownership disclosure. Although EuroChem is a private company, its ownership structure is disclosed and easily accessible. EuroChem is in effect a holding company, and it is therefore positive that a full list of subsidiaries and affiliates is presented in the annual report. A complete list is not presented in the IFRS statements, however. Information about the key production entities and the largest trading subsidiaries is listed on EuroChem's Web site.

IFRS statements accessible online; timing is fair. The IFRS statements are produced in addition to statutory statements under Russian Accounting Standards that have limited value to international investors. EuroChem produces its IFRS statements quarterly and releases them earlier than do most companies in the Confederation of Independent States (CIS) yet later than do some well-governed international peers. It is a plus that annual and interim IFRS statements are published in full and include notes. At the same time, there is room for improvement in terms of the level of detail presented in the IFRS statements. In terms of the scope of information contained in the statements, we note that only the aggregate volume and balances for related-party transactions are presented, whereas a breakdown by the largest counterparties is lacking. The list of all related counterparties is not provided, and the structure of the group is not presented in detail.

Clear and informative annual report. The scope of disclosure in the annual report is substantial. The 2008 report, which is available in English, presents significant operational and financial details, including the analysis of global industry trends, strategic priorities, governance information, and full IFRS statements. The report contains a section titled "Management Discussion and Analysis" that provides additional details on revenue and cost structure as well as on financing decisions.

Web disclosure strong overall. EuroChem has an informative bilingual Web site on which it publishes its charter, bylaws, financial statements under IFRS and Russian Accounting Standards (RAS), statutory filings by the company and its subsidiaries, agendas and overviews of shareholder meetings, information on the structure of the group, and the composition of the governing bodies. It is also a positive that with the exception of some statutory filings, all information and downloadable documents are translated and presented on the English version of the Web site. If EuroChem were a public company, we would expect a regularly updated events calendar to be present on the site, along with management presentations and transcripts of conference calls.

Strong social and environmental disclosure. EuroChem is one of the few Russian companies that produce social and environmental reports in compliance with internationally accepted standards. EuroChem published a Global Reporting Initiative (GRI)–based report for the years 2001–2005, a GRI-compliant report for the year 2006, and an audited GRI 3.0 report for the year 2007, with the application level of B+ (on a scale from C to A+). Both the English and the Russian versions of the report are available on the company's Web site. EuroChem came out second on the Accountability Rating–2008, a social responsibility ranking of the 50 largest Russian companies produced under an international accountability franchise.

Weaknesses in governance disclosure. Although there are several strong elements of governance disclosure, there are weaknesses as well. Like most Russian companies, EuroChem does not disclose an individual breakdown of compensation paid to senior executives. Only the aggregate figures are presented in the IFRS statements. Data on compensation paid to nonexecutive directors are not disclosed in the IFRS statements or in the English version of the annual report. The aggregate figures for board compensation are presented on the Web site, yet the compensation guidelines are not available in the public domain. Also, statistics on meeting attendance by individual directors are not reported.

Investor relations focused mainly on creditor banks. Since the $300 million issue of Eurobonds in March 2007, an investor relations department has been established, with several quarterly conference calls for bondholders held. However, in view of limited interest on the part of investors, EuroChem suspended the conference calls. It must be noted, however, that the executives regularly present operational and financial results to participant banks in the $1.5 billion syndicated loan.

Timing of IFRS Statements

Annual audited IFRS accounts for 2008 were released on March 20, which is reasonably timely by international standards and earlier than such publications by most companies in Russia. It is, however, a weakness that EuroChem does not release preliminary (unaudited) annual results, as most international public companies do. Interim reviewed reports are released 60 to 75 days after the end of the reporting period, which is commonplace in Russia yet significantly behind the practice of the leading transparent international companies (21 to 30 days).

The Audit Process

Key Analytical Issues

External auditor is a reputable firm. EuroChem employs a reputable international audit firm, PricewaterhouseCoopers, to audit its statements under IFRS (RAS statements are audited by a local firm). PricewaterhouseCoopers provides certain nonaudit services to EuroChem, but on a very limited scale (less than 5% of audit fees in 2008). The latest tender for audit services (IFRS) was conducted in February 2008.

Strong audit committee. The audit committee is composed of three board members, of whom two, including the chairperson, are fully independent. The committee chairperson has an extensive background in audit and risk management. The committee convenes on average once a month; approximately 75% of those meetings are held in person, with the rest in the form of conference calls. The head of internal audit and EuroChem's chief financial officer (CFO) are present at each committee meeting, and representatives of the external auditor are present at most meetings.

Internal audit department has limited experience. Like many other Russian companies, EuroChem has been facing difficulties in recruiting experienced personnel and building a full-fledged internal audit structure since such efforts started in 2005. Difficulty in hiring audit professionals in Moscow was one of the reasons EuroChem chose to adopt a decentralized structure of internal auditing in 2009 by moving a majority of internal audit positions to the main production sites. The effectiveness of the new structure remains to be demonstrated. Most of the internal audit positions (13 of 16) are currently filled, but at 13 members, EuroChem's internal audit group appears small in relation to the scope of operations. It is positive that the internal audit department has the status of a statutory audit board at EuroChem as well as at its subsidiaries.

Independent Committee Members

One of the three directors, Pilipenko, cannot be considered fully impartial since he served as the CFO of EuroChem between 2006 and 2008. We note that Pilipenko no longer is employed by EuroChem, however, and that with the passage of time he might be considered independent along with the other committee members.

Enterprise Risk Management

Key Analytical Issues

Development of integrated ERM system just starting. The integrated risk management system is at the initial stage of development, with function-specific risks currently managed within separate silos. There are at present no overall policies on risk tolerances or guidelines for specific risks, such as a clear criterion for selecting risks of corporate or business-unit importance. No integrated database on identified risks and risk management activities is maintained. The board and management recognize the need to introduce a more holistic approach to risk and are set to build formalized risk governance structures in the coming months. An integrated approach of that type appears better suited for the company in view of the wide geographic span of operations, complex and environmentally impactful technologies, and sophisticated product mix.

Disjointed risk analysis is part of decision making. But risks are discussed routinely at management meetings, and function heads effectively act as risk managers within their areas of responsibility. Board-level committees are involved in reviewing risk controls within their respective areas of expertise.

Links to strategy still informal. Explicit ties between risk analysis and strategic planning (strategic risk management) have not been formalized. However, risk considerations influence strategic decisions informally. EuroChem's entry into the potash fertilizer segment, for example, was motivated in part by the need to reduce exposure to the risk of fluctuations in the price of natural gas, an important element of costs in the nitrogen fertilizer segment.

Board Effectiveness, Strategic Process, and Incentives: Component Score 6+

Board Composition

Key Analytical Issues

Balanced board composition. The board structure creates the potential for a balancing influence by independent directors. The board includes eight members, a moderate but hardly constraining size. With the exception of one director, who serves as EuroChem's CEO, all board members are nonexecutive directors. Four of eight board members are independent of the controlling shareholder and management, and one more director, the former CFO of EuroChem, potentially could be considered independent in the future.

Strong skill mix. The board has a rich skill mix, with expertise in finance being particularly well represented. One of the board members, Vladimir Stolin, is a specialist in human resources and incentive systems. Keith Jackson has extensive international experience in the fertilizer industry. It is a weakness, however, that he is the only board member with a relevant industry background.

Sophisticated committee structure. There are three board-level committees, and independent directors play an important role in each committee. The governance and human resources committee is composed entirely of independent directors. The audit committee has an independent majority. The strategy committee includes an independent director and Mr. Cardona, the advisor to Melnichenko.

Chairperson has tie-breaking vote. It is a positive that the positions of CEO and board chairperson are separated, as required by Russian law. At the same time, the board chair has a deciding vote in case of a tie, which increases the influence of the chair. In practice, this means that for checks and balances to be solid, at least a simple majority of directors must be independent.

Board Effectiveness

Key Analytical Issues

Board has wide authority under company's charter. The board's mandate is defined in accordance with the Law on Joint Stock Companies and is clearly formulated in the charter and bylaws of EuroChem. It includes the approval of strategic and investment plans, budgets, related-party transactions, changes to bylaws, executive appointments, and other issues. The threshold for large transactions requiring board approval is set at a relatively high level of 25% of assets; many well-governed international companies set those thresholds at lower levels, such as 1% of assets. There are weaknesses regarding control over subsidiaries' operations, as detailed below.

Board has never faced task of protecting minorities' interests in EuroChem. The ability of the board to balance the influence of the controlling shareholder in the interest of external investors has not been demonstrated in practice.

Board meetings are frequent and well organized. The board demonstrates a moderately high—but not excessive—level of involvement in management oversight. Board members receive management accounting information monthly. There were six face-to-face meetings in 2008, and each of the board committees held seven to nine face-to-face meetings. Board processes are facilitated by a corporate secretary who has rich experience in this function and sufficient resources at her disposal to ensure smooth organization of board and committee sessions. According to comments from directors, the quality of background materials, the timing of their circulation, and the quality of their translation are high.

Board has incomplete control over transactions performed by subsidiaries. Although Russian law is fairly prescriptive in terms of transactions requiring board approval, it takes a stand-alone perspective on a company (i.e., it addresses the core legal entity only). As a consequence, the above requirements do not extend to transactions conducted by subsidiaries. In practice, this arrangement gives wide discretion over subsidiaries' operations to the group's CEO. The fact that the board reviews consolidated budgets and financial statements (which is beyond the requirements of the law) significantly mitigates this problem but does not solve it entirely.

Regular executive and board performance evaluation. It is a positive that the board performs a self-evaluation annually. The board also reviews the performance of executives and conducts succession planning.

Strategic Planning Process

Key Analytical Issues

Clear strategy exists, updated annually. EuroChem uses a five-year planning horizon and formulates an overall strategy, covering all segments and functions as well as the more detailed segment-level and function-level strategies. These internal strategy documents present a clear discussion of global competitive trends and industry dynamics, threats and opportunities to EuroChem's business, and base-scenario financial models under the expected market conditions. These documents are developed internally, are clearly written, and detail the assumptions behind the projections. We note, however, that scenario analysis is not part of those documents. No formal guidelines for the annual cycle of strategic planning have been developed.

Board and management agree on strategic objectives. On the basis of our interviews, board members have a shared view on the long-term strategic direction of the company. We see this as a sign of a solid strategic decision-making process at the board level.

Implementation tools largely in place; further improvements expected. There is a mature budgeting process in place, and the management accounting system saw significant improvements with the implementation of the El Compas proprietary framework. This framework provides management and the board with the primary tools of strategy implementation. Further improvements in budgeting and accounting are expected with the full deployment of the Oracle enterprise resource planning software. The performance indicators for about 200 senior managers have formalized links to strategic priorities.

Competent board-level strategy committee. Strategic decision making at the board level is strengthened by the active role of the strategy committee.

Solid external communication. The annual report presents detailed information on the overall strategy and segment-level strategies. The Web site does not have a section dedicated to strategy.

Horizontal strategic communication is mainly informal. At the management level, strategy making is performed largely in a top-down manner, with the CEO setting the main targets and priorities and the CFO coordinating the planning. There is no formal procedure for soliciting inputs from line management, although EuroChem's open culture does not preclude bottom-up initiatives. Significant efforts are made to promote values and develop a companywide identity across the production units of EuroChem through internal media, sports, and cultural events.

Board and Executive Compensation

Key Analytical Issues

Sound compensation policies for nonexecutive directors. Board compensation is set by a general shareholder meeting with a binding vote. Compensation for independent directors includes a flat annual fee as well as further compensation for additional functions in board committee meetings and for acting as committee chairpersons. It is a positive that board compensation does not create any adverse incentives, as some aggressive short-term focused arrangements can. However, the existing plan does not provide motivation to increase shareholder value since it does not include any long-term incentive components or equity-based pay.

Robust structure of executive compensation. The executive compensation plan is based on strong principles. The plan includes a significant at-risk component, which includes annual and strategic or project-based elements. The board assumed a greater role in setting the performance targets for executives in 2008.

Moderate compensation disclosure. Board compensation is not presented in the notes to IFRS statements, although the aggregate figure is provided on the Web. These figures also are provided in the notes to annual accounts according to RAS, yet they are presented in a way that is not easy to interpret and the statements are available only in Russian. The aggregate figures for compensation of senior executives are presented in the IFRS statements and in the annual report. Like most companies in Russia, EuroChem does not disclose an individual breakdown of executive pay.

Appendix A

Transparency and Disclosure by Russian Companies 2008: Insignificant Progress Along with Fewer IPOs[1]

Introduction and Executive Summary

Russian Firms' Transparency Improves Steadily, If Slowly, Year by Year

Our Transparency Index, which is calculated as the average score for the 90 largest public Russian companies, increased to 56% in 2008 from 55% in 2007, according to this study. In the group of 71 companies covered by the study in both 2007 and 2008, the score grew by 2.5 percentage points (p.p.) to 57.7% in 2008 versus 55.2% in 2007. Fifty companies improved their scores, and the scores of 21 companies dropped. Thus, the transparency of Russian companies continued to grow steadily, if slowly, year over year. Growth in 2008 should be attributed to the 71 companies already covered in the 2007 survey,

1 Editor's Note: The authors would like to express their profound gratitude to the RTS Stock Exchange.

as the average newcomers' score was lower than the previous year's average score of the companies in the survey that were dropped from the sample. As in previous years, the greatest progress was registered by the less transparent companies. However, the 20 most transparent companies in 2007 improved their scores by more than 2 p.p. The gap in transparency between the leaders and the outsiders remained substantial: The 2008 scores ranged from 78% for the top company to 28% for the bottom one. It is notable that the growth occurred in spite of the considerable slowdown of companies placing their shares on foreign exchanges through initial public offerings (IPOs).

After several years of leadership by Mobile TeleSystems OJSC (MTS), CTC Media, which was in third place in 2007, gained the top standing with an improvement of 3 p.p. in its score. In 2008 Novolipetsk Steel (NLMK) and TMK made it into the top 10, with NLMK placing third (versus 20th place in 2007) with an improvement of 12 p.p. in its score and TMK (18th place in 2007) placing sixth with a gain of 9 p.p. Practically all of the top 20 companies increased their scores compared with 2007. Some companies progressed more than others, and this largely accounts for changes in the upper tier of the rankings. The fact that the leader in the previous three years, MTS, dropped to fourth place can be attributed to improvements by NLMK and OAO Rosneft Oil Co. and moderate progress by CTC Media while the transparency score of MTS remained stable at its original high level. At the same time we noted the small spread of scores among the top 10 companies, with the average gap between neighboring companies being just 0.57 p.p. Thus, the real difference in transparency between the leaders in the ranking was negligible.

On the positive side, companies made some progress in the area of the worst-disclosed criteria compared with 2007. In particular, more companies published their business conduct and ethics codes in 2008, and the calendars of important shareholders' events. Early publication of audited financial reports became more common, and more companies disclosed their auditor rotation policies. The disclosure of investment plans and earnings forecasts improved significantly. However, the

level of disclosure on key issues such as the terms of related-party transactions, terms of the contract with the auditor on nonauditing services,
and remuneration of the chief executive officers (CEOs) left much to
be desired and even declined on average. Fewer companies announced
the dividends recommended by their boards of directors before the
record date.

The breakdown of transparency by sector showed that the telecommunications sector remained the most transparent, with an average
capitalization-weighted transparency score of 74%, up 3 p.p. over 2007.
The engineering sector, the outsider in 2007, became noticeably more
transparent (by 7 p.p.) and outstripped the information technology (IT)
sector. The food, consumer goods, and retail sector demonstrated a
noticeable improvement of transparency, with an increase of 6 p.p. By
contrast, the utilities sector became less transparent, falling 7 p.p.; this
can be attributed largely to the newcomers' low transparency and the
fact that RAO UES, one of the leaders on the list in 2007, was liquidated as part of Russia's power sector liberalization.

Earlier studies showed that IPOs tend to increase a company's transparency significantly. Our analysis showed that companies listed in
London (the main market) or New York were substantially more transparent than were the others. Companies that traded only in Russia had
an average transparency index of 50%, whereas the transparency index
for companies listed on the London Stock Exchange (LSE) was 63%;
the number was 74% for New York Stock Exchange (NYSE)–listed
firms. The Russian exchange quotation list level had little bearing on
transparency: Companies not traded abroad that were on the A1 and
A2 lists of the Russian Trading System (RTS) and the Moscow Interbank Stock Exchange (MICEX)—there were 16 such companies in
our study—were on average just 3 p.p. more transparent than were
companies traded only in Russia (there were 49 such companies).

Concentration of ownership declined somewhat but was still high.
In our sample 62% of companies had a controlling shareholder, compared with 71% in 2007. Controlling stakes represented 45.5% of the
aggregate market capitalization versus 49% in 2007. This was partly

because we defined the ownership structure of ownership of Evraz Group S.A. (Evraz) in a more "liberal" manner in which members of a controlling group of shareholders were viewed as separate shareholders. However, the concentration level would have gone down even without the revision, although not as much.

We found some worsening of ownership structure disclosure. The aggregate capitalization of all disclosed stakes in 2008 was 56.5% of the total capitalization in the sample versus 59.3% in 2007. Disclosure of controlling stakes decreased as well: from 81.8% to 80.4% of the total number of companies that had a controlling shareholder. The number of companies disclosing all their blockholders (over 25% stake) went down by 3.4 p.p. and was 75% of the total number of companies that had blockholders in 2008. To a large extent, the worsening of disclosure occurred because some companies in the power-generating sector were slow in updating their ownership structures after the liquidation of RAO UES.

Transparency Score Should Not Be Compared with Corporate Governance Score

This survey was a joint research project of Standard & Poor's and the Centre for Economic and Financial Research (CEFIR) at the New Economic School (NES). It used only publicly available information that rendered incorrect any comparison of a company's transparency score with its corporate governance score (CGS) and GAMMA (Governance, Accountability, Management Metrics, and Analysis) score or its interpretation as an integral indicator of corporate governance quality. A CGS (or GAMMA) is our assessment of a company's corporate governance practices and is not limited to information disclosure. In addition, these scores are assigned on the basis of an in-depth, interactive analytical process that involves both public and nonpublic data. However, we view corporate transparency as an important factor in a firm's attractiveness to investors and an important element of corporate governance.

Study Covered Largest Public Corporations

This study looked at the 90 largest and most liquid publicly traded Russian companies. In 2007, we analyzed 80 companies. Seventy-one companies were included in both studies. We enlarge our sample from year to year as a result of the increasing listing activity of Russian companies and their greater involvement in international markets. According to a global IPO trends survey conducted in 2008 by Ernst & Young, in 2007 Russian companies raised U.S.$19 billion, which represented 7% of all IPO proceeds globally, versus $18 billion (7.3% of all proceeds) in 2006 and about $5 billion (2.9%) in 2005. Relative to other nations, in 2007 IPOs of Russian companies raised the fourth largest amount of capital after companies from China, the United States, and Brazil.

We used two criteria to select the companies in the study: size and liquidity. As a rule, the liquidity of stocks is positively correlated with the size of a company, but there are exceptions, especially in cases of minor free float. There are more than 300 public companies in Russia, and this sample may not be representative of all Russian public companies. As the larger companies tend to be more transparent than are the smaller ones, our sampling method is likely to cause an upward bias in assessing the transparency of the entire population of public Russian companies. However, as the companies included in the survey account for about 80% of the cumulative capitalization of the Russian stock market, they represent the major part of the Russian economy in terms of assets and operations.

Methodology: Keeping in Mind the International Investor's Perspective

Our analysis accounted for information included in the three major sources of public information: annual reports, Web-based disclosures, and public regulatory reporting. The first group included annual reports published by the company (with financial statements and accompanying notes if a company stated that it was an integral part of the report), Forms 20-F (20-F/A) and 10-K for companies that are obliged to report under these forms, and proxy statements. The second group consisted of all the information on the company's Web site, including hyperlinks to lists of documents related to the company (e.g., hyperlinks to the lists of regulatory reporting forms located at www.edgar.com). The regulatory reporting included the following sources: publicly available statutory filings with the Federal Financial Markets Service (FFMS), Frankfurt Stock Exchange, U.K. Financial Services Authority (FSA), U.K. Listing Authority (UKLA), and U.S. Securities and Exchange Commission (SEC) for companies listed on the NYSE or Nasdaq. In addition, this group includes information contained in prospectuses on bonds, Amercian Depositary Receipts (ADRs), and Global Depositary Receipts (GDRs) issued after January 1, 2008, and available on the company's Web site or that of the stock exchange or the regulatory authority involved in the placement. Moreover, we consider as regulatory filings annual International Financial Reporting Standards (IFRS) financials for the companies listed on the London Stock Exchange and annual reports for the companies listed on Alternative Investment Market (AIM), a small funds branch of the LSE that offers a waiver for some of the disclosure requirements associated with a listing on the exchange's main trading floor, as these documents are filed with regulatory authorities and are made public.

According to our weighting system, public disclosure, regardless of the source through which it was made, yields 80% of the maximum score on each part of the questionnaire. The remaining 20% of points are awarded if this information is present in the other two sources as well (10% to each). This scoring system reflects the notion that replication of information in various sources has value for investors, as it makes the information more easily accessible. The value of replication is, however, incremental compared with the fact of disclosure.

We analyzed the information available as of August 11, 2008.[2] Information published after that date was considered irrelevant for the assessment of transparency related to the annual results because it appeared more than seven months after the end of the reporting year (2007). We believe that information published after that time was of little value to a company's stakeholders (shareholders, creditors, analysts, etc.) who wished to analyze information pertaining to that year to get insight into the current situation. Similarly, any changes or updates that occurred after this date were not accounted for.

This survey analyzed disclosure from the perspective of the international investor. This approach was factored into the list of criteria used for the survey and the fact that we accounted for disclosure in English as well.

The checklist method consists of 108 items relating to three blocks:

1. Ownership structure and shareholder rights
2. Financial and operational information
3. Board and management structure and process

The complete list of items is presented in Table A-8 on pages 273–278.

Additional Analyses

As a part of the Transparency and Disclosure (T&D) Project, we also updated our study of the ownership concentration in Russian corporations and the disclosure of those corporations' ownership structures. This research complements the questionnaire-based T&D study by providing an in-depth view of ownership concentration in Russian companies and their ownership disclosure practices. In addition, we explored the relationship between transparency and company value.

2   In past years the limit date was August 10; in 2007 August 10 was a Sunday.

Findings

Less Transparent Companies Were Gaining Gradually on the Leaders; Overall Progress Was Insignificant

The results of our survey revealed that the level of transparency of 90 major Russian companies was 56% (see Table A-1), representing an increase of 1 p.p., in absolute terms over 55% in 2007. The average score for the 71 companies covered in both the 2007 and 2008 samples grew 2.5 p.p. Among those 71 companies, 50 improved their scores and 21 saw their scores worsen. Thus, Russian companies were steadily, if slowly, becoming more transparent year in and year out. Growth in 2008 was due primarily to the companies also covered in the 2007 survey: The average score of the newcomers in our sample was 49.7%, whereas the average score of the companies dropped from the sample was 52.5% in 2007. As in earlier years, the best progress, on average, was reported by the companies with lower transparency scores in 2007, but even for the 20 most transparent companies in 2007 the index improved by over 2 p.p. The spread in transparency between the leaders and the outsiders was substantial: The score of the companies in 2008 varied from 78% for the top company to 28% for the bottom one. Still, the gap was narrowing. In 2007, in spite of the smaller number of companies, the spread was between 77% and 20%. The average gap between neighboring companies on the list is 0.56 p.p., compared with 0.7 p.p. in 2007. The difference between the average score of a top 10 company and the 50th company was about 20 p.p. in 2008, compared with 22 p.p. in 2007. Thus, the less transparent companies were slowly catching up with the more transparent ones.

Entry into foreign public equity markets is an important factor in a company's transparency. It is worth noting that transparency improved over 2007 in spite of the significant decline of Russian companies' IPO activities on foreign stock exchanges. At the end of 2007 the number

Table A-1 Transparency Scores of Most Transparent Russian Companies, 2008

2008 Rank	2007 Rank	2006 Rank	Company	2008 Score (%)	Ownership Structure & Shareholder Rights (%)	Financial & Operational Information (%)	Board & Management Structure & Process (%)	2007 Score (%)
1	3	N/A	CTC Media	78	80	74	82	75
2	10	12	Rosneft	78	81	79	70	70
3	20	11	Novolipetsk Steel	77	78	83	66	65
4	1	1	Mobile Telesystems	77	92	72	69	77
5	6	2	Mechel	76	89	76	60	71
6	18	39	TMK	75	86	71	69	66
7	4	7	Vimpelcom	75	87	72	64	75
8	9	5	Wimm-Bill-Dann Foods	74	80	76	65	70
9	8	42	Evraz Group	74	59	83	74	71
10	7	16	LUKOIL	73	66	82	62	71
			Top 10 average	75.5	79.7	76.7	68.1	72.9
			Whole sample average	56.0	55.2	59.4	49.8	54.9
			Average for 71 companies included in both 2007 & 2008	57.7	57.2	61.4	50.8	55.2

of Russian IPOs (including those made abroad) dropped sharply, and in the first half of 2008 only three Russian companies conducted IPOs, compared with 14 companies in the same period in 2007. Two of the IPOs in 2008 were conducted abroad.

The most transparent company in 2008 was CTC Media, which improved its indicator by 3 p.p. over 2007. In 2008 Novolipetsk Steel and TMK made it to the top 10. NLMK placed third, up from 20th in 2007, improving its transparency score by 12 p.p., and TMK, which was in 18th place in 2007, placed sixth with growth of 9 p.p. NLMK owed its progress mainly to better disclosure of its ownership structure. The company also improved disclosure in a number of areas, including the results of the annual meeting of shareholders and detailed earnings forecasts. TMK's success is due to two factors. First, the company issued Eurobonds in 2008, which called for a detailed prospectus in English. Second, the company improved disclosure in a number of components, such as the auditor's remuneration, investment plans, and information on board of directors' meetings.

Among the top 10 companies in 2007, Rosneft should be noted. Since its IPO in 2006 the company improved its transparency for the second year in a row. In 2008 Rosneft rose to second place from 10th place in 2007, with an improvement of 8 p.p. in its score. The company's annual report was much more informative, disclosure of the ownership structure improved, and the company published its audited IFRS financials before the end of April.

Practically all the top 20 companies improved their scores over 2007. As noted, changes in the top tier of the rankings were due mainly to the faster progress of some companies. Thus, MTS, the leader over the previous three years, dropped to fourth place because of the substantial progress of NLMK and Rosneft, coupled with moderate progress for CTC Media, although the transparency score of MTS remained high. Two companies that were in the top five in 2007, Golden Telecom and RAO UES, were not present in our survey in 2008. Golden Telecom was bought out by Vimpelcom in February

2008 and ceased to be a public company. RAO UES ceased to exist on July 1, 2008, as a result of the restructuring of the Russian power sector. It has to be mentioned that the gaps between neighboring companies in the top 10 were small, with an average gap of just 0.57 p.p. versus 0.89 p.p. in 2007. To reiterate, the real difference in transparency between the leaders was insignificant.

Higher Market Capitalization Associated with Above-Average Disclosure

The results of our survey indicate that there is a link between market capitalization and transparency. The breakdown of the total market capitalization of the 90 Russian companies by scores (see Figure A-1) shows that almost 85% of capitalization was represented by companies with disclosure levels above 50% (in 2007 the share of such companies was 90%).

There was measurable growth in the aggregate market capitalization of companies with more than 70% of the criteria disclosed (there were 11 such companies): 27% of total capitalization from 18% in 2007 (see Figure A-1). This growth was due mainly to NLMK, TMK, and Rostelecom, which improved their transparency and got scores above 70%.

Figure A-1 shows the relationship between transparency and the aggregate market capitalization of the companies in a band of transparency scores. To understand the link between capitalization and transparency at the level of an individual company, we devised Figure A-2, which reveals a positive correlation between the two values (the correlation coefficient was 0.41). Major companies more frequently trade in foreign exchanges where transparency requirements are more stringent. The reverse causality also may be relevant: Increased transparency often leads the market to upgrade its valuation of a company.

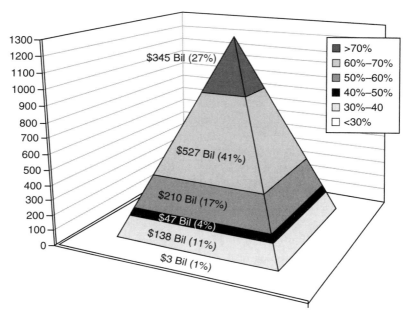

Figure A-1   Disclosure pyramid, 2008.*

*The market capitalization numbers were computed based on the market capitalization of the companies averaged for the period from January 18, 2008 to June 19, 2008. (Dollar amounts are in U.S. dollars.)

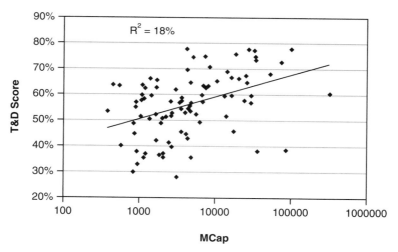

Figure A-2   Market capitalization (logarithmic scale) and transparency.

Companies Improved Disclosure in Annual Reports and on Web Sites

As mentioned above, we analyzed what was disclosed via three main sources of information: annual reports, company Web sites, and public regulatory reporting. Year to year, we find that Web sites are the most informative source. The average score for Web site disclosure in 2008 was 59.5%, up from 58% in 2007. Our weighting system implies that public disclosure, regardless of the source through which it is made, yields 80% of the maximum score. Many companies publish annual reports and reports submitted to regulatory agencies as well as additional information on their Web sites. Hence, as a rule a Web site ensures the highest disclosure score. As a result, that source is more indicative of the dynamics of the transparency index than are other sources. The level of disclosure in the reports submitted to the regulatory agencies, which had risen to 43% in 2007 thanks to companies that conducted IPOs, was back to the 2006 level (40%) in 2008. At the same time the disclosure level in annual reports increased to 40% compared with 38% in 2006 and 2007.

Insignificant Changes in Disclosure by Component

One aspect of our study is analysis of disclosure by component (see note to Table A-2). Disclosure of the companies' operational information registered the biggest improvement (+5 p.p.) and reached 66% in 2008. This was due largely to better disclosure of detailed information on investment plans and compliance with environmental laws as well as on functional relationships between key operating units. Interestingly, the companies included in the sample in 2008 for the first time received a rather high average score on the operational information component: 62%.

Disclosure of the companies' financial information and the information concerning shareholder rights improved slightly. At the same

Table A-2 Comparative Disclosure by Component by the Largest Russian Companies in 2006–2008*

Components, %						
	1	2	3	4	5	6
90 Russian companies, 2008	57	53	57	66	60	22
80 Russian companies, 2007	59	52	55	61	63	22
70 Russian companies, 2006	56	53	55	63	56	30

*Component 1: Ownership structure. Component 2: Shareholder rights. Component 3: Financial information. Component 4: Operational information. Component 5: Board and management information. Component 6: Board and management remuneration.

time, disclosure for the component that describes ownership structure, which steadily improved in earlier years, worsened by 2 p.p. and was 57% in 2008. Also in 2008 the companies were somewhat worse at disclosing information on boards of directors and top executives. Disclosure on the remuneration of board members and top managers remained at the same low level. This area of companies' life remains the most opaque, and the companies included in the sample in 2008 for the first time demonstrated an especially low level of disclosure: a mere 14%.

Most Critical Opaque Areas Remain Essentially the Same

There are several poorly disclosed areas in each component. The size of our sample allows us to extrapolate our findings about those opaque areas across Russian companies in general. Emphasizing these issues each year allows us to track the trends in their disclosure. Table A-3 shows the opaque areas. The figures in this table reflect the share of companies disclosing this information in relation to all the companies in our sample to which this criterion applies.

Among the elements least disclosed in 2007, the most notable improvements occurred in the disclosure of detailed earnings forecasts and investment plans, both of which are highly important to current

Table A-3   The Weakest Specific Areas of Disclosure by the Largest Russian
Companies, 2008–2007

Component 1. Ownership Structure, %	2008	2007
• The indication that management is not aware of the existence of >5% stake in free float	22	20
• Number and identity of all the shareholders holding more than 10%	29	23
• Disclosure of share of beneficial owners more than 75%	42	43
Component 2. Shareholder Rights		
• Evidence of existence of code of business conduct and ethics	22	24
• Announcement of recommended dividends before the record date	15	29
• Calendar of important future shareholder dates	42	34
• Formalized dividend policy	44	45
Component 3. Financial Information		
• Auditor rotation policy	6	1
• Detailed earnings forecast	14	4
• Nonaudit fees paid to the auditor	7	11
• Indication that related-party transactions are made on market or nonmarket terms	8	15
• Audited IFRS/GAAP financial results published before the end of April	31	26
Component 4. Operational Information		
• Social reporting	8	11
• Detailed information about investment plans in the coming year	50	28
• Overview of compliance with ecology law	55	40
Component 5. Board and Management Information		
• Details of the CEO's contract	2	3
• Policy on assessment of board of directors and on training provided to them	2	1
• Attendance record for board meetings	24	23
• Information about ratio of in-person and in-absentia board meetings	32	23
Component 6. Board and Management Remuneration		
• The specifics of directors' pay	30	33
• The specifics of managers' pay	6	6
• The specifics of performance-related pay for managers	19	18

*The proportion of companies disclosing such information is given in columns.

and potential investors. Shareholders are now much better informed about future important events through company Web sites.

In addition, the disclosure of information on compliance with environmental laws improved. The share of the companies that disclose their auditor rotation policies increased from 1% to 6%, but the disclosure of fees paid to the auditor for nonauditing services decreased.

Although the overall disclosure of the ownership structure worsened compared with 2007, in 2008 the number of companies that disclosed all shareholders owning more than a 10% stake increased 6 p.p.

Early release of IFRS/U.S. generally accepted accounting principles (GAAP) financials is crucial because timely financial information allows investors to make better decisions. Our analysis shows that in 2008, 31% of the companies in our sample published IFRS/U.S. GAAP accounts before the end of April, which was an improvement of 5 p.p. over 2007. The share was still relatively low, meaning that many companies were not conforming to international best practices. However, most annual general meetings (AGMs) of Russian companies are held at the very end of June, which is the legal deadline for those meetings in Russia. Therefore, we consider the release of IFRS financials within the six-month period after the year end more or less acceptable. If the statements are released within this period, the investors can analyze them before the AGM. In 2007, 48 companies (60% of the 2007 sample) released those statements by the time of the AGM. In 2008 the number of such companies was 58 (64% of the 2008 sample).

Although information on the composition, role, and competence of the board of directors, individual directors, and board committees was well disclosed, information on the form of the board meetings and the number of directors attending still was seldom disclosed, although disclosure of the form of the meetings improved after 2007.

Unfortunately, the disclosure of certain elements that are of significant importance to investors remained very low in 2008 and even worsened for some elements. By comparison with 2007, the share of companies that announced recommended dividends before the record date almost halved to 15%. Similarly, the share of companies that disclosed information on the terms of related-party transactions dropped by half to 8%. The level of disclosure of the terms of employment contracts with CEOs and the details of directors' and executives' remuneration remained very low.

Telecommunications and Metallurgical Companies Remain the Most Transparent

Companies in different economic sectors typically have different levels of transparency. This may be due to differences in demand for external financing, greater government participation in some industries, and higher risks of expropriation by the government in certain industries. Therefore, we provide a separate capitalization-weighted transparency index (CWTI) for every industry. Companies in the telecommunications sector remained the most transparent, with a CWTI of 74%, up 3 p.p. over the value in 2007. The CWTI also rose in the metallurgy sector by 5 p.p., which was second place in terms of disclosure. The increase occurred because of improved transparency scores by large companies such as NLMK, Severstal, and Mechel. Engineering, the outsider in 2007, became noticeably more transparent; a 7 p.p. increase placed it ahead of the IT sector. This improvement was due mainly to substantial progress made by AvtoVAZ. One also should note improved transparency in the food, consumer goods, and retail trade sector, which was up 6 p.p. Almost all the companies in that sector became more transparent, with Pharmstandard and X5 Retail Group recording the greatest progress. The utilities sector, in contrast, became 7 p.p. less transparent. This was due to two factors: the relatively low transparency of the newcomers (companies that were on the list in both 2008 and 2007, by contrast, improved their average scores) and the liquidation of RAO UES, which was among the leaders of the list in 2007 and had a capitalization much higher than that

Table A-4   Disclosure by Industry

Industry (No. Companies)	2008 CWTI*, %	2007 CWTI, %	Change in 2008 from 2007, %	Change in 2007 from 2006, %
Telecommunications (10)	74	71	3	(2)
Metallurgy (12)	70	65	5	3
Oil and gas (10)	63	61	2	0
Development (7)	56	55	1	
Food, consumer, and retail (9)	60	54	6	(1)
Utilities (21)	55	62*	(7)*	9
Banking (3)	45	57	(12)	0
Engineering (5)	44	37	7	(6)
IT (2)	40	46	(6)	(10)
Total CWTI*	62	53	9	(1)

*CWTI = capitalization-weighted transparency index. If RAO UES is excluded from the sample in 2007, the CWTI of the utilities sector in 2007 and its change are 50% and +5 p.p., respectively.

of other power companies. If we excluded RAO UES from the 2007 sample, the CWTI of the utilities sector would be 50% in 2007 and, accordingly, in 2008 we would have recorded growth of 5 p.p. in the sector's CWTI. Table A-4 shows disclosure by industry.

Ownership Concentration Diminished Slightly but Was Still High

As in previous years, we looked at the concentration of ownership and its disclosure. In 2008 we continued to use the liberal approach in assessing concentration, in which members of a controlling group are viewed as separate owners.

In 2008 there was a further decline in ownership concentration in major Russian companies. The share of controlling stakes in the aggregate market capitalization (AMC) was 45.5%, compared with 49% in 2007 (see Table A-5). The difference remained virtually unchanged for the sample of 71 companies that were in our list in both 2007 and

2008. The smaller share of controlling stakes to some extent was due to the fact that Evraz had three major beneficial owners and we saw no grounds for considering any one of them as the controlling shareholder. Without this adjustment, the change compared with 2007

Table A-5 Concentration of Ownership in the 90 Largest Russian Companies, in 2008

	Number of Companies	Companies in the Sample, %	Companies in AMC*, %[†]	Stakes in AMC, %[‡]
Widely held companies (largest stake <25%)	10	11.1	7.5	3.8
Companies with at least one blockholder (>25%)	80	88.9	92.5	56.1
...of which: majority owned companies (>50%)	56	62.2	71.4	45.5
Companies with large stakes (>25%) directly or indirectly owned by government	29	32.2	53.2	31.0
...of which: companies with direct government stake >25%	9	10.0	36.6	16.6
Companies with controlling stakes (>50%) directly or indirectly owned by government	20	22.2	49.9	29.8
...of which: companies with direct government stake >50%	4	4.4	10.4	6.6
Companies with large (>25%) private stakes	59	65.6	42.1	28.3
Companies with private stakes >50%	36	40.0	21.5	15.6

*AMC—Aggregate market capitalization of 90 companies included in the survey.

[†]Share of combined market capitalization of the relevant *companies* in aggregate market capitalization of the 90 largest companies.

[‡]Share of the corresponding *stakes* in aggregate market capitalization of the 90 largest companies.

would be smaller, though still remaining negative (-1.5 p.p). If we calculate the percentage of companies with a controlling shareholder in 2008 and in 2007, we find that it went down too, from 71% to 62.2% (from 71.8% to 63.4% for the 71 companies covered by the samples in both 2007 and 2008).

The 2008 study revealed that the share of blocking stakes ($>25\%$) in the AMC dropped by 6 p.p. compared with the previous year. That decline is not connected with the inclusion of newcomers in our sample: In the group of 71 companies that were in the sample in both 2008 and in 2007, the change was virtually the same. The percentage of companies with blocking stakes also went down, falling from 92.5% to 88.9% (94.4% to 90.1% for the 71 companies). The share of companies with dispersed ownership structure increased accordingly: In 2008 small stakes accounted for 3.8% of AMC versus 2.8% in 2007 (11.1% versus 7.5% by calculating the percentage of the number of companies in the sample).

If we divide the companies with a controlling shareholder into those under private control and those under government control, we see that it is the latter that were mainly responsible for the decrease of the ownership concentration. The share of controlling stakes owned by the state dropped from 32.6% to 29.8% of the AMC (the percentage of companies controlled by the government dropped from 30% to 22.2% of the companies in the samples). For privately controlled companies the figures were 15.6% (40% of the companies) in 2008 versus 16.6% (41.2% of the companies) in 2007. Here, counting Evraz as a company with a controlling owner would have resulted in a slight increase of the share of private controlling stakes in the AMC. For 71 companies that were in the sample in both 2008 and 2007, the changes over the year were from 17.5% to 15.1% of AMC for privately controlled companies (the percentage of such companies dropped from 40.8% to 38%) and from 33.1% to 30.4% of AMC for state-controlled companies (the percentage of such companies dropped from 31% to 25.4%).

Ownership Disclosure Worsened Slightly

The 2007 survey revealed a slowdown in the improvement of owner-ship structure disclosure by major Russian companies. The 2008 survey found that the disclosure of beneficial owners worsened compared with 2007. The share of all disclosed stakes in the AMC was a mere 56.5% in 2008 compared with 59.3% in 2007, and the percentage of the companies disclosing at least one beneficial owner was 83.3% versus 91.3%. It has to be said that the decrease is not due to the newly included companies. For the 71 companies that were included in both the 2007 and 2008 samples the share of the disclosed stakes in the AMC dropped from 59.4% to 56.8%, and the percentage of companies disclosing at least one beneficiary owner went down from 90.1% to 85.9%.

As far as disclosure of controlling stakes is concerned, in 2008 such stakes were disclosed by 80.4% of all companies with a controlling shareholder, down 1.4 p.p. from 2007. In the sample of 71 companies included in the study in both 2007 and 2008 the numbers were 82.2% in 2008 versus 84.3% in 2007.

If we examine the share of companies that disclosed all large (over 25%) beneficial owners, we find that it decreased too. Such companies accounted for 75% of the total number of companies with large beneficial owners, down 3.4 p.p. from 2007. Among the 71 companies that were covered in both years, the number was also 75% against 80.3% in 2007. The change results from poorer disclosure of both government stakes (from 93.8% to 82.8% of the total number of companies in which the government had a large stake) and private stakes (from 74.1% to 72.9% of the total number of companies in which there was a private blockholder). Table A-6 shows the transparency of ownership in 90 Russian companies in 2008.

We again point out that to a large extent the worsening of ownership disclosure occurred because a number of companies in the power-generating sector were slow in updating their ownership structures after the liquidation of RAO UES.

Table A-6 Transparency of Ownership, 90 Largest Russian Companies, 2008

Transparency of Ownership	Number of Companies	Share of Companies in the Relevant (sub)Sample, %	Companies in AMC*, %†	Stakes in AMC, % ‡
Companies disclosing at least one owner	75	83.3	90.4	56.5
Companies disclosing all large beneficial owners (>25%)	60	75.0	78.6	46.7
Companies disclosing controlling shareholders	45	80.4	65.5	27.8
Companies disclosing at least one large beneficial owner (>25%)	64	80.0	80.3	50.2
Companies disclosing ALL stakes >25% directly or indirectly belonging to government	24	82.7	51.0	26.8
Companies disclosing ALL large (>25%) private owners	43	72.9	30.2	20.8

*AMC = Aggregate market capitalization of 90 companies included in the survey.

†Share of combined market capitalization of the relevant *companies* in aggregate market capitalization of the 90 largest companies.

‡Share of the corresponding *stakes* in aggregate market capitalization of the 90 largest companies.

IPOs Abroad and Requirements of Foreign Exchanges Are Important Factors That Boost Transparency

IPOs as a rule tend to make a company more transparent. To obtain and maintain listings at any exchange, companies must comply with information disclosure requirements. Companies have to be more transparent if they aim to attract investors and conduct successful IPOs. The number of Russian companies entering public stock markets dropped sharply after several years of sustained growth: Only three Russian companies conducted IPOs in the first half of 2008,[3] compared with 14 in the same period in 2007, as mentioned previously. The most obvious reason was the difficult situation in global financial markets. However, in addition to those three, our sample included six more companies that had an IPO in late 2007, after that year's transparency study was completed.

Because our surveys of previous years included only public companies, we could not trace the impact of IPOs on the changes in the transparency of a company that was never traded before. However, we can trace changes for several companies that previously were traded only in Russia and then had IPOs abroad. Our report in 2007 noted Mechel, MMK, Severstal, and TMK, whose T&D scores improved when they entered Western stock markets. In 2008 we were in a position to monitor the change of transparency of the potash producer Uralkali and the retail supermarket chain Magnit, which were included in the 2007 survey and conducted their IPOs on the LSE at the end of 2007 and the beginning of 2008, respectively. Both companies raised their transparency, with Uralkali registering an especially big improvement.

As in previous years, U.S.-listed companies were considerably more transparent than were their peers listed elsewhere. On average, they scored 75% (see Table A-7). They were followed by companies listed in the main market of the LSE, with an average score of 63%. Companies traded only in Russia had an average score of just 50%, 1 p.p. lower than the average score of Russian companies traded at London's AIM. Thus, the companies listed only in Russia were substantially less transparent than were those which entered Western exchanges. The level of a quotation list of a Russian exchange matters little in terms of transparency: The companies not traded abroad that were on A1

---

3   This includes the IPO on the LSE of the retail chain Magnit, shares of which already had been trading on Russian exchanges.

Table A-7 Breakdown by Exchange Transparency Score, 90 Largest Russian Companies, 2008–2007

Stock Exchange	2008 Average (%)	2007 Average (%)	Number of Companies, 2008
NASDAQ	78	76	1
NYSE	74	72	5
LSE	63	60	29
RTS	50	50	46
MICEX Stock Exchange	50	50	43
Frankfurt Stock Exchange	49	46	1
AIM	51	46	5

and A2 lists of the RTS and MICEX (16 companies in all) were on average just 3 p.p. more transparent than were the companies traded only in Russia (a total of 49 such companies).

The notable differences in transparency between companies listed on various exchanges were due largely to differences in information disclosure requirements (an overview of the disclosure requirements of the world's leading stock exchanges is provided in Appendix B). Companies listed on U.S. exchanges faced the most stringent requirements; the issuers were regulated by the SEC and bound by the Sarbanes-Oxley Act of 2002.

LSE requirements were less demanding, and that contributed to the popularity of this exchange among the foreign issuers planning an IPO. In 2007, LSE-listed companies raised 11% of all global proceeds. On that count, LSE was second only to the Hong Kong Stock Exchange. The dynamics of the growth of the number of Russian companies that held IPOs (or are planning one) on the LSE matched the world dynamic: Thirteen of the 23 Russian companies that held an IPO in 2007 floated their shares on the LSE, and not a single company had an IPO at American exchanges.

For companies listed on AIM, transparency requirements were even less demanding than they were on LSE's main market. The companies in that group were only slightly more transparent than those traded only in Russia.

Of course, the degree of the positive impact of compliance with international disclosure requirements on transparency is impossible to determine precisely because other factors may affect the transparency of companies.[4] However, it is obvious that the disclosure requirements of the Russian stock exchanges were measurably weaker.

Transparency and Company Value

Does increased transparency raise a company's value? For companies that seek outside financing or want to use their shares in merger and acquisition (M&A) deals, it is a highly relevant issue. We made a simple analysis of the link between expected value/sales and the transparency score. An exponential regression yielded a positive correlation (see Figure A-3). The increase in a company's transparency from 40% to 70% was associated with an increase in EV/sales from approximately 2 to 3. However, the fact that the coefficient of determination was a mere 5.5% (the cloud of dots is rather dispersed) indicates that there were probably other factors in addition to transparency that influenced a company's valuation by the market. Even so, the result obtained suggests that transparency is an important intangible asset that enables more transparent companies to increase their market value because by providing more information, they gain investor trust.

---

4 For example, companies listed abroad are generally larger, and firm size per se may affect transparency. Also, independently of the exchange requirements, the desire to attract funds of foreign investors per se creates incentives to improve transparency.

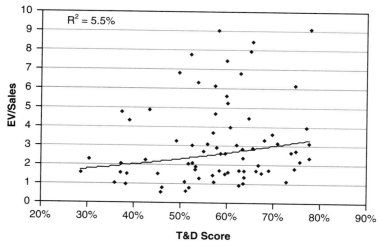

Figure A-3 Relationship between transparency and EV/sales, 2008 (76 observations).

Sources: T&D scores—Standard & Poor's and CEFIR at NES, EV/Sales—Bloomberg.

This study, conducted jointly by Standard & Poor's Governance Services and the Centre for Economic and Financial Research at the New Economic School, builds on and extends the earlier T&D research by Standard & Poor's Governance Services. In 2002, Standard & Poor's published its first T&D study of companies selected from the following indexes:

- S&P/IFC Emerging Asia
- S&P/IFC Latin America
- S&P Asia-Pacific 100
- S&P/TOPIX 150 (Japan)

In April 2003, the study of the S&P Europe/350 companies was released. In addition, in 2004 and early 2005, Standard & Poor's published a number of studies devoted to corporate governance disclosure by companies in various countries in the East Asian region, including

Hong Kong, Singapore, Indonesia, Malaysia, and Thailand. In addition, in June 2005, the Turkish T&D Survey was published. It analyzed the disclosure practices of the 52 largest Turkish companies with the most liquid stock. This research was updated in 2006.

In 2002, Standard & Poor's published its first survey of T&D by the largest Russian public corporations. As a result of the continued interest among investors and analysts, Standard & Poor's has been updating the Russian corporate survey and continuously developing the methodology. The latest annual update of the corporate T&D survey was published on November 14, 2007. Separately, in June 2005, Standard & Poor's published a survey of T&D by Russian state-owned companies at the request of the Organization for Economic Cooperation and Development (OECD) Roundtable on Corporate Governance. In 2005, Standard & Poor's released its first T&D survey of Russian banks. The study was updated in 2006 and in 2007 because of interest among investors and analysts.

About CEFIR at the New Economic School

The Centre for Economic and Financial Research at the New Economic School is an independent economic policy think tank that was established in Russia in 2000. CEFIR's mission is to improve Russia's economic and social policies by producing cutting-edge academic research and policy analysis and helping policymakers and the public make informed choices. Since it was established, CEFIR has conducted more than 40 research projects in research areas such as the following:

- Administrative reform
- Industrial organization and competition policy
- Corporate governance and financial markets
- Macroeconomic policy

- Political economics and federalism
- International trade and foreign investments
- Social policy and labor market
- Migration policy
- Regional economics

CEFIR's work on corporate governance includes research on the composition and functioning of boards of directors, determinants of top executive turnover, interrelations in ownership concentration, corporate governance and firm performance, determinants of corporate governance practices in firms, relationship between corporate governance and company value, and a number of other topics.

CEFIR's critical resources are the high-quality human capital and the academic infrastructure. Research Papers in Economics (www.RePEc.com) has ranked CEFIR a top 10% institution in Europe. CEFIR is closely integrated in the world economic community and has partner relations with leading economic think tanks in many countries. CEFIR researchers have published in top international economics and finance journals, including *American Economic Review, Journal of European Economic Association, Journal of Finance, Journal of Economic Perspectives,* and *Economics of Transition.*

Apart from the current project, CEFIR's project portfolio includes research work done for Russia's central bank, Ministry of Finance, Ministry of Economic Development and Trade, Ministry of Education and Science, Ministry of Health and Social Development, and Presidential Administration; the World Bank; the European Bank of Reconstruction and Development; the Swedish International Development Agency; USAID; the International Finance Corporation; and the United Nations Development Programme.

The CEFIR Web site is at www.cefir.ru, and the New Economic School Web site is at www.nes.ru.

Table A-8 Criteria for the Transparency and Disclosure Survey

Block 1: Ownership Structure and Shareholder Rights

Component 1: Ownership Structure

Disclosure of:

1. Number and par value of issued ordinary shares
2. Number and par value of issued other types of shares disclosed
3. Number and par value of authorized but unissued shares of all types
4. Identity of the largest shareholder
5. Identity of holders of all large stakes (blocking: > 25%; controlling: > 50%)
6. Identity of shareholders holding at least 25% of voting shares in total
7. Identity of shareholders holding at least 50% of voting shares in total
8. Identity of shareholders holding at least 75% of voting shares in total
9. Number and identity of each shareholder holding more than 10%
10. Indication that management is not aware of the existence of any stake exceeding 5% except for those which are reported
11. Shareholding in the company by individual senior managers
12. Shareholding in the company by individual directors
13. The description of share classes
14. A review of shareholders by type
15. Percentage of cross-ownership
16. Information about listings on exchanges
17. Information about indirect ownership (e.g., convertible instruments)

Component 2: Shareholder Rights

Disclosure of:

18. Corporate governance charter or corporate governance guidelines
19. Evidence of existence of a code of business conduct and ethics
20. Contents of the code of business conduct and ethics
21. Articles of association (including changes)
22. Voting rights for each voting or nonvoting share
23. The way shareholders nominate directors to the board

(Continued)

Table A-8 (*Continued*)

24. The way shareholders convene an extraordinary general meeting (EGM)
25. Procedure for initiating inquiries with the board
26. Procedure for putting forward proposals at shareholders' meetings
27. Formalized dividend policy
28. Announcement of recommended dividends before the record date
29. Review of the last shareholders' meeting
30. Full general shareholder meeting (GSM) minutes
31. Calendar of important shareholder future dates
32. GSM materials published on the Web site
33. Detailed press releases covering last corporate events
34. Policy on information disclosure

Block 2: Financial and Operational Information

Component 3: Financial Information

Disclosure of:

35. The company's accounting policy
36. The accounting standards it uses for its accounts
37. Accounts according to local standards
38. Annual financial statements according to an internationally recognized accounting standard (IFRS/U.S. GAAP)
39. Notes to annual financial statements according to IFRS/U.S. GAAP
40. Independent auditor's report on annual financial statements according to IFRS/U.S. GAAP
41. Unqualified (clean) audit opinion on annual financial statements according to IFRS/U.S. GAAP
42. Audited IFRS/U.S. GAAP financial statements published before the end of April
43. Unaudited IFRS/U.S. GAAP financial statements published before the end of April
44. Audited IFRS/U.S. GAAP financial statements published before annual general meeting
45. Unaudited IFRS/U.S. GAAP financial statements published before the end of June

46. Disclosure of related-party transactions (RPTs): sales to/purchases from, payables to/receivables from related parties

47. Indication that RPTs are made on market or nonmarket terms

48. Exact terms of RPTs

49. Interim (quarterly or semiannual) financial statements according to an internationally recognized accounting standard (IFRS/U.S. GAAP)

50. Notes to these financial statements

51. Whether these financial statements are audited or at least reviewed

52. Consolidated financial statements according to the local standards

53. Methods of asset valuation

54. A list of affiliates in which the company holds a minority stake

55. The ownership structure of affiliates

56. A basic earnings forecast of any kind

57. A detailed earnings forecast

58. Segment analysis (results broken down by business line)

59. Revenue structure (detailed breakdown)

60. Cost structure (high degree of detail)

61. Name of the auditing firm

62. Whether the audit firm is a top-tier auditor

63. Auditor rotation policy

64. How much the company pays in audit fees to the auditor

65. Whether auditor renders nonaudit services

66. Nonaudit fees paid to the auditor

Component 4: Operational Information

Disclosure of:

67. Details of the type of business the company is in

68. Details of the products or services the company produces or provides

69. Output in physical terms

70. Description of functional relationships between key operating units within the group

71. Industry indicators that allow comparison with peers

72. Other financial indicators

(Continued)

73. Characteristics of fixed assets employed (including licenses)
74. Efficiency indicators
75. A discussion of corporate strategy
76. Any plans for investment in the coming years
77. Detailed information about investment plans in the coming year
78. An output forecast of any kind
79. An overview of trends in its industry; regulatory environment with regard to industry
80. The market share for any or all of the company's businesses
81. Social reporting (e.g., Global Reporting Initiative)
82. Overview of compliance with ecology law
83. Principles of corporate citizenship

Block 3: Board and Management Structure and Process

Component 5: Board and Management Information

Disclosure of:

84. List of board members (names)
85. Details about the current employment and position of directors
86. Other details: previous employment and positions, education, etc.
87. When each director joined the board
88. The name of the chairperson
89. Details about role of the board of directors at the company
90. A list of matters reserved for the board
91. A list of board committees
92. Names of all members of each existing committee
93. The bylaws on other internal audit functions besides the audit committee
94. Information about the ratio of in-absentia to in-person board meetings
95. Attendance record for board meetings
96. The list of senior managers not on the board of directors
97. The backgrounds of senior managers
98. Nonfinancial details of the CEO's contract
99. Number of shares held in other affiliated companies by managers
100. Policy on assessment of board of directors and training provided to its members

Component 6: Board and Management Remuneration

Disclosure of:

101. Decision-making process for directors' pay

102. Specifics of directors' pay, including the salary levels

103. Form of directors' salaries, such as whether they are in cash or shares

104. Specifics of performance-related pay for directors

105. Decision-making process for determining managerial (not board) pay

106. Specifics of managers' (not board) pay, such as salary levels and bonuses

107. Form of managers' (not board) pay

108. Specifics of performance-related pay for managers

Joint study of Standard & Poor's Governance Services and the Centre for Economic and Financial Research at the New Economic School, supported by the RTS Stock Exchange, conducted on November 13, 2008. The authors are Sergey Stepanov, Olga Lazareva, Igor Salitskity, Ivan Mironets, Evgeny Sidorovskiy, Evgenia Chernina, Elena Pastokhova, and Oleg Shvyrkov.

Table A-9 (on the next page) provides selected requirements for information disclosure at several stock exchanges.

Table A-9 Selected Information Disclosure Requirements at Different Stock Exchanges

	New-York Stock Exchange (NYSE)	Frankfurt Stock Exchange (FSE)	London Stock Exchange (LSE)	Alternative Investment Market (AIM) of LSE	Moscow Interbank Stock Exchange (MICEX)/Russian Trading System (RTS) (lists A1 and A2)
Disclosure of major beneficial shareholders	NYSE rules: Beneficial owners of more than 10% of equity (any class), directors, and executive officers must disclose their shareholdings.	European Commission's regulation No. 809/2004 regarding implementation of the European Prospectus Directive (2003/71/EC of Nov. 4, 2003): disclosure required to the extent known to the issuer. Issue prospectus needs to be registered with the U.K. Listing Authority.		AIM Rules: Disclosure required to the extent known to the issuer.	No requirements.

Appendix B

Transparency and Disclosure 2008: Disclosure Levels for China's Top 300 Companies Lag Far behind Global Best Practices

Introduction and Executive Summary

Study Focuses on Advances in Information Accuracy and Access

This survey of transparency and disclosure to the general public by China's 300 largest companies, which was conducted by Standard & Poor's and Institutional Investor Services, shows that those companies have a considerable gap to close before meeting international standards for timely and accurate disclosure levels. The Transparency Index representing the average level of information disclosure for the companies included in the survey was 46% (a score expressed as a percentage of disclosed items among all relevant disclosure practices listed in the 108-item survey questionnaire). By contrast, overall transparency and disclosure (T&D) scores for other large industrial countries were in the range of 56% to 71%. The survey found that the weakest areas of

disclosure for Chinese companies were business operations, nominations to the board of directors, and performance metrics and compensation for directors and managers. In an effort to improve transparency,
the China Securities Regulatory Commission (CSRC) established a
new disclosure code in 2007.

For our first T&D study of Chinese A share companies, we applied
criteria designed for monitoring the quantity and quality of information disclosed on all material aspects of a publicly traded company's
operations (see "Methodology," "Related Research," and "Criteria"
sections). The 300 companies in the survey (out of more than 1,400
public companies) account for about 80% of the cumulative capitalization of the Chinese stock market. Among those 300, the companies
that have dual listings on China's domestic and Hong Kong markets
presented a far better transparency level (68.6%) than did those listed
only on China's domestic markets (45.7%). Large-cap companies,
mostly central state-owned enterprises (SOEs), demonstrated a generally better transparency level, than did mid- to small-cap companies,
among which the private and local SOEs make up the majority. The
Industrial and Commercial Bank of China (ICBC) far outstripped
others with a strong transparency score of 75.6%. Transparency scores
ranged as much as 40% among the companies measured.

Compared with other countries, China's overall T&D score is
relatively low. In 2003 T&D scores, the United Kingdom ranked
highest at 71% and the United States was a close second at 70%, with
France at 68%, Japan at 61%, and Germany at 56%. The overall T&D
score for the Asia-Pacific region was 48%, slightly better than China's
performance.

We view corporate transparency as a key factor in a company's
attractivess to investors and a significant element of corporate governance that helps protect shareholder value and safeguard the rights of
minority stakeholders. Our survey found that information on Chinese
companies' business operations is rather short and simple and only follows the reporting format. Among those 300 companies, which were

selected on the basis of size of total assets and liquidity, fewer than 10% presented comprehensive and meaningful information on their business economics and dynamics. It is hard for investors, particularly individuals with little industry knowledge, to base sound investment decisions on such terse management discussions and analysis regarding annual results. Investors are left without adequate data on a company's strategic plan, including the next three- to five-year investment plan, and an analysis of the industry's competitive landscape. Except for a few financial metrics required by exchanges, few of China's companies disclose meaningful industry performance metrics in their annual reports. The nomination of directors still is kept far behind the scenes. Since almost every company is controlled by a majority shareholder, the selection of board members is proposed and decided mainly by that controlling shareholder, which often is the government. Even for choosing independent directors, there are no clear rules or procedures that would allow investors to learn how to select the independent director candidates and nominate them.

Further, disclosure of information on remuneration for directors and managers still lags far behind global best practices. However, the listed companies have begun making such disclosures to some degree. All investors require full information on the structure and level of remuneration of senior management, but that information is particularly difficult to obtain about nonindependent directors, since they customarily are paid by a parent company or by controlling shareholders. Information disclosure is particularly scanty on performance metrics. Fewer than 2% of the 300 companies surveyed clearly indicated the factors they use to evaluate the performance of directors and management. Information disclosure regarding ownership concentration is fairly good for these companies. Ownership is extremely concentrated: More than 95% of those companies are controlled by a single largest shareholder, who is called the actual controlling person. Almost all have disclosed the actual controlling person and the shareholders with less than 5% ownership.

Our analysis accounts for information included in three major sources of public information: annual reports, Web-based disclosures, and public regulatory reporting. The study found that regulatory sources provide a far better disclosure level (52.7%) than do annual reports (47.1%) and/or Web sites (12.4%).

China Law and Exchange Requirements on Disclosure

China Moves to Improve Information Disclosure Levels

China's listed companies are not required to submit regulatory reports familiar to international investors (such as the 10-K or 20-F reports filed with the U.S. Securities and Exchange Commission) on market structure or competitors; this explains the CSRC's drive to meet the informational needs of domestic and international investors. Since 1992, the CSRC has been overseeing all securities and futures companies; stock, bond, and futures exchanges; listed companies; fund management companies; and investment consulting firms and other intermediaries involved in the securities and futures business. In an attempt to improve the information disclosure level of publicly traded companies, in February 2007 the CSRC released "Regulations on Information Disclosure of Listed Companies." The new regulations define the information that must be disclosed, the disclosure procedures, the company officials responsible for disclosure, and penalties for violations. The regulations apply to a public company and its directors, supervisors, and management and to the controlling shareholder, potential buyers of the company, investment advisory companies, and media that may play a role in a public company's information disclosure processes.

The CSRC code specifies disclosure content standards for periodical reports, with annual reports considered the most comprehensive compared with quarterly or semiannual reports. The rules also mandate that company bylaws detail the process for information disclosure and for the description of incidents such as changes in management and new acquisitions in ad hoc reports. To ensure full and accurate disclosure, the regulations specify that a company's chair of the board, general manager, and board secretary hold the principal responsibility for the disclosed information's authenticity, accuracy, completeness, immediacy, and fairness. A "fair disclosure" principle states that for the first time a company cannot disclose advance private information to particular investors or media before a public announcement and cannot use investor presentations or media interviews as substitutes for official data release. In 2007 annual reports, a good number of companies voluntarily disclosed meetings with investors, a step rarely taken even in advanced countries.

Ownership Disclosure

Unlike in developed countries, almost every company in China is controlled by one majority-controlling shareholder. Before 2005, it was almost impossible for investors to ascertain who the controlling shareholders were from corporations' public information. The CSRC now requires all listed companies to disclose controlling structures in diagrams that clearly identify the controlling shareholder or shareholder group. In addition, the listed companies must outline the background of shareholders with over 10% ownership. The listed companies also need to issue timely ad hoc reports or press releases on shareholding changes involving shareholders with a stake of 5% or more.

Financial and Operational Information Disclosure

In annual reports, the listed company is required to disclose its financial and operation information by following the reporting format set by stock exchanges. The financial and operation information generally includes key items in financial reports, key ratios, management discussion and analysis, the operation performance of each product line, the company's strategy and key investments, and financial reports with accompanying notes. This structure of information disclosure is similar to the best practice in developed countries, but there is a huge gap in terms of how comprehensive the content is. Without industry knowledge, an investor cannot understand the business economics of a company. The survey shows that few companies have made extra efforts to educate investors about business dynamics such as market structure, the economics of each product line, and competitors, elements that are contained in U.S. 10-K and 20-F reports and other regulatory reporting.

Auditor and Auditing Fees

Information on how and why a certified public accountant (CPA) firm is selected remains confidential within the "insider" circle of top management. To assure auditor independence, when a public company prepares to dismiss a CPA firm, it must inform the auditing firm in a timely manner and allow it to make a statement at the next annual shareholder meeting. There is no requirement for disclosure of nonaudit fees or the auditor rotation policy. However, central SOEs are required to change auditors every five years.

Nomination and Remuneration

Matters involving executive remuneration and nomination have not gained sufficient attention from China's regulators, and the new regulation did not address those issues. Executive nominations normally are decided behind closed doors, since key directors and executive members are appointed by the major shareholder, which most often is the government. Most of the remuneration for corporate executives is in the form of salary and bonuses, with less than 15% of public companies issuing stock options to managers. By the 2006 annual report season, a majority of companies had begun disclosing the compensation details of board and management members in regard to salaries and bonuses. Exposure of the number and value of stock options awarded to executives remains optional. Since the 2007 annual report (AR) season, all companies must make public a report submitted by the compensation committee to the board of directors explaining the compensation process and amounts.

Scope and Methodology

This study covered the 300 largest public Chinese companies listed in the domestic market with the most liquid stock. Among them, 251 companies are listed only in the domestic A share market, with 17 companies listed in domestic A and B share markets, 33 companies listed in domestic A share and Hong Kong H share markets, and one listed in the A, B, and H share markets.

We used two criteria to select the companies in the study: size and liquidity. As a rule, liquidity increases along with the size of a company, but there are exceptions, especially in cases of minor free float. We noted that larger companies tend to be more transparent than smaller ones, and so our sampling method was likely to inflate the scores used in assessing the transparency of the entire population of public Chinese companies. Also, since there are more than 1,400 public companies, this sample may not be representative of the total. However, the companies included in the survey account for about 80% of the cumulative capitalization of the Chinese stock market and therefore represent the major part of the Chinese economy in terms of assets and operations.

Our analysis accounts for information included in three major sources of public information: annual reports, Web-based disclosures, and public regulatory filings. The first group includes annual reports published by the company (with financial statements and accompanying notes if a company states that it is an integral part of the report). The second group consists of all the information on the company's Web site, including hyperlinks to lists of documents related to the company. The regulatory reporting includes publicly available statutory filings with the Shanghai Stock Exchange, Shenzhen Stock Exchange, and Hong Kong Stock Exchange.

According to our weighting system, public disclosure, regardless of the source through which it has been made, yields 80% of the maximum score on each point of the questionnaire. The remaining 20% of points are awarded if this information is present in the other two sources as well (10% to each). This scoring system reflects the understanding that replication of information in various sources has value for investors, as it makes information more easily accessible. The value of replication is, however, secondary to the fact of disclosure.

We analyzed the information available as of August 8, 2008. Information published after that date was considered irrelevant for the assessment of transparency related to the annual results. We believe that information published after that time was of little value to a company's stakeholders (shareholders, creditors, analysts, etc.) who wished to analyze information pertaining to that year to gain insight into current situations. Similarly, any changes or updates that occurred after that date were not accounted for.

This survey analyzes disclosure from the perspective of the international investor. This approach was factored into the list of criteria items used for the survey and the fact that we accounted for disclosure in English as well.

The questionnaire consists of 108 items relating to three blocks:

1. Ownership structure and shareholder rights
2. Financial and operational information
3. Board and management structure and process

The complete list of 108 items is presented in Table A-8 toward the end of Appendix A.

This survey was a joint study by Standard & Poor's and Institutional Investor Services. It used only publicly available information; therefore, a company's transparency report should not be compared with its corporate governance score (CGS) or Governance, Accountability, Management Metrics, and Analysis (GAMMA) reports or otherwise interpreted as a measure of governance standards. CGS and GAMMA reports are our assessments of a company's corporate governance practices and are not limited to information disclosure. In addition, these scores are assigned on the basis of an in-depth, interactive analytical process involving both public and nonpublic data. However, we view corporate transparency as an important factor in a firm's attractiveness to investors and an important element of corporate governance.

Findings

Our analysis shows that the level of transparency of the 300 largest public Chinese companies is 46.1%. The variance is quite significant between the most transparent company and the least transparent one and amounts to 40 percentage points (p.p.). The Industrial and Commercial Bank of China is the best transparent company, with a score of 75.58%. Table B-1 shows the T&D score distribution of those companies.

From the point of view of the types of shares, companies listed both in China (A share) and in overseas markets (H share), mostly

Table B-1   T&D Score Distribution

Distribution					
Number	14	22	14	216	34

in Hong Kong, represent the best class of information disclosure. The average score of the A/H share companies is 68.7%, almost 21 p.p above the general sample average (see Table B-2). The range of score distribution is quite wide, and the majority of companies are in the range of 40% to 49%. The score difference between overseas-listed and domestic-listed companies is due mainly to information disclosure on business operation and board performance and procedures. Also, distribution media have a significant impact since companies listed in overseas markets generally have better company Web sites.

Table B-2   T&D Score by Type of Shares

Share Type	A	A+B	A+H	A+B+H
Number	251	17	33	1
Average	42.9%	45.7%	68.7%	68.1%

From the perspective of the ownership type, the distribution of scores is homogeneous and the difference is marginal. The average score of central state-owned enterprise (C-SOE) is 46.2%, compared with 45.28% and 43% for local government SOE (L-SOE) and private companies (see Table B-3). However, central SOEs account for 8 of the top 10 scoring companies. Except for joint venture (JV) and university-controlled companies, private companies had the lowest transparency level.

Table B-3   T&D Score by Type of Ownership

Ownership	C-SOE	L-SOE	Private	Foreign	JV	University	Total
Number	83	54	51	6	3	3	300
Average	46.2%	45.3%	43.0%	45.9%	41.9%	42.0%	46.1%

A breakdown of transparency by ownership concentration (see Table B-4) indicates that the transparency level was quite similar across all sectors. The highly concentrated sector (>70%) presented the better transparency level; most of those companies were normally SOEs.

Table B-4 T&D Score by Ownership Concentration

Controlling Shareholder	70%	60–69%	50–59%	40–49%	30–39%	20–29%	10–20%	0–9%
Number	12	32	58	55	45	54	34	10
Average	51.60%	45.3%	46.8%	46.7%	47.2%	43.9%	5.2%	45.0%

A breakdown of transparency by sector indicates that the transparency level was very similar across all sectors. The energy sector was the most transparent with a score of 46.86%, and consumer discretionary was the least transparent at 43.10% (see Table B-5).

Table B-5 T&D Score by Sector

Sector	Energy	Material	Industrial	Consumer Discretionary	Consumer Staples	Health Care	Financial	Info. Tech.	Telecom	Utility
Number	20	63	76	38	17	15	36	18	1	16
Average	46.9%	44.85%	45.25%	43.0%	45.4%	42.9%	46.3%	43.6%	44.95%	46.75%

The results of our survey indicate that there is a link between market capitalization and the potential for higher transparency. The score for the largest 100 companies was 53.03%, 10% and 11% higher than the score of the second 100 and bottom 100 companies, respectively, in terms of market capitalization. The breakdown of the total market capitalization of the 300 Chinese companies by scores shows that 94%

Table B-6 T&D Score by Capitalization

Market Cap	Top 100	Mid 100	Bottom 100	Total
Number	100	100	100	300
Average	53.03%	43.20%	42.06%	46.10%

of their capitalization was contained within companies with disclosure levels above 50% (see Table B-6).

There are several poorly disclosed areas in each component. The size of our sample allows us to extrapolate our findings about those opaque areas across Chinese companies in general. Table B-7 shows

Table B-7 The Weakest Specific Areas of Disclosure by the 300 Largest Chinese Companies, 2008

	2008
Component 1: Ownership Structure and Shareholder Rights,%	
Percentage of cross-ownership	0.0
Corporate Governance Charter/CG guidelines	2.3
Evidence of existence of code of business conduct and ethics	0.6
Formalized dividend policy	27.1
Calendar of important shareholders future date	2.0
Component 2: Financial and Operational Information,%	
Detailed earning forecast	4.7
Auditor rotation policy	26.7
Disclosure of the fact whether auditor renders any nonaudit services	13.7
Nonaudit fees paid to auditor	14.0
Social reporting (e.g., GRI)	9.7
Overview of compliance with ecology law	21
Component 3: Board and Management Structure and Process,%	
When each director joined the board	26.7
Details of CEO contract	0.0
The number of shares held in affiliated companies by managers	0.0
Policy on assessment of board of directors	0.0
The specifics on performance-related pay for managers	0.0

the opaque areas. The figures provided there reflected the share of companies disclosing this information in relation to all the companies in our sample to which these criteria apply. Table B-8 lists the top T&D scores for the top 20 companies among the 300 in our survey; Table B-9 provides that information for companies listed only in the A share market.

Table B-8 T&D Scores for Top 20 Companies Among 300 Largest Chinese Companies, 2008

2008 Rank	Company	2008 Score (%)	Ownership Structure and Shareholder Rights (%)	Financial and Operational Information (%)	Board and Management Structure and Process (%)
1	Industrial and Commercial Bank of China Ltd	75.6	74.1	79.4	68.9
2	China Petroleum and Chemical Corp (Sinopec)	75.5	70.2	83.1	65.6
3	China Shenhua Energy Co., Ltd.	72.7	66.8	81.2	61.7
4	Bank of Communications Co., Ltd.	72.7	72.7	75.7	66.0
5	Ping An Insurance (Group) Co of China Ltd.	72.2	71.2	75.9	65.3
6	China Oilfield Services Ltd.	72.1	68.2	79.2	61.3
7	China Merchants Bank Co., Ltd.	71.8	67.9	77.5	64.0
8	Huaneng Power International Inc.	71.6	70.3	75.8	63.9
9	China Construction Bank Corp.	69.9	70.0	71.8	65.6

(Continued)

Table B-8 *(Continued)*

2008 Rank	Company	2008 Score (%)	Ownership Structure and Shareholder Rights (%)	Financial and Operational Information (%)	Board and Management Structure and Process (%)
10	Tsingtao Brewery Co., Ltd.	69.8	69.7	70.0	69.2
11	China COSCO Holdings Co., Ltd.	69.7	72.9	74.5	54.4
12	Yanzhou Coal Mining Co., Ltd.	69.6	68.2	73.8	62.0
13	Huadian Power International Corp Ltd.	69.6	61.8	79.4	58.0
14	Datang International Power Generation Co., Ltd.	69.5	65.9	74.0	64.3
15	Maanshan Iron and Steel Co., Ltd.	69.4	64.4	76.1	61.2
16	China Southern Airlines Co., Ltd.	69.0	69.3	75.3	54.4
17	Air China Ltd.	68.5	64.6	73.4	62.8
18	Guangzhou Shipyard International Co., Ltd.	68.2	65.6	72.9	61.2
19	Shandong Chenming Paper Holdings Ltd.	68.1	66.6	73.0	59.1
20	China Life Insurance Co., Ltd.	68.0	73.1	65.8	66.1

Table B-9 T&D Scores for Top 20 Companies Only Listed in A Share Market, 2008

2008 Rank	Company	2008 Score (%)	Ownership Structure and Shareholder Rights (%)	Financial and Operational Information (%)	Board and Management Structure and Process (%)
1	China Merchants Property Development Co., Ltd.	63.7	58.2	70.3	56.3
2	China Vanke Co., Ltd.	60.4	54.1	65.7	57.0
3	China International Marine Containers (Group) Co., Ltd.	60.4	60.9	63.7	52.1
4	Guangdong Electric Power Development Co., Ltd.	59.0	58.1	64.5	47.4
5	Hainan Airlines Co., Ltd.	56.6	44.3	65.6	52.9
6	Weifu High-Technology Co., Ltd.	56.1	56.0	66.4	33.0
7	Yantai Changyu Pioneer Wine Co., Ltd.	55.3	57.3	59.7	43.0
8	Baoshan Iron & Steel Co., Ltd.	53.9	55.9	55.0	48.7
9	Chongqing Changan Automobile Co., Ltd.	53.8	48.6	61.8	43.0

(Continued)

Table B-9 *(Continued)*

2008 Rank	Company	2008 Score (%)	Ownership Structure and Shareholder Rights (%)	Financial and Operational Information (%)	Board and Management Structure and Process (%)
10	Lu Thai Textile Co., Ltd.	53.8	56.2	58.5	39.8
11	Dazhong Transportation (Group) Co., Ltd.	53.7	58.4	59.0	35.1
12	Offshore Oil Engineering Co., Ltd.	52.6	52.9	53.0	51.1
13	China Yangtze Power Co., Ltd.	52.1	52.6	52.4	50.9
14	Shanghai Fosun Pharmaceutical Group Co., Ltd.	51.9	49.6	51.6	55.7
15	Foshan Electrical and Lighting Co., Ltd.	51.8	45.1	59.7	43.0
16	SAIC Motor Corp Ltd.	51.7	48.6	54.3	50.1
17	Sinochem International Corp	50.9	58.0	49.0	45.5
18	Gemdale Corp	48.9	51.8	45.3	53.3
19	China Merchants Energy Shipping Co., Ltd.	48.4	45.3	53.3	41.5
20	Shanghai Pudong Development Bank Co., Ltd.	48.0	51.3	46.1	48.2

Related Research by Standard & Poor's

This study builds on and extends earlier T&D research by Standard & Poor's Governance Services. In 2002, we published our first T&D study of companies selected from the following indexes:

- S&P/IFC Emerging Asia
- S&P/IFC Latin America
- S&P Asia-Pacific 100
- S&P/TOPIX 150 (Japan)

In April 2003, we released our study of the S&P Europe/350 companies. In addition, in 2004 and early 2005, we published a number of studies devoted to corporate governance disclosure by companies in various countries of the East Asian region, including Hong Kong, Singapore, Indonesia, Malaysia, and Thailand. In addition, in June 2005, we published the Turkish T&D Survey, which analyzed the disclosure practices of the 52 largest Turkish companies with the most liquid stock. That research was updated in 2006.

In 2002, we published our first survey of T&D by the largest Russian public corporations. As a result of the continued interest among investors and analysts, we have been updating our Russian corporate survey and continuously developing the methodology. The latest annual update of the corporate T&D survey was published on November 13, 2008. Separately, in June 2005, we published a survey of T&D by Russian state-owned companies at the request of the Organization for Economic Cooperation and Development (OECD) Roundtable on Corporate Governance. In 2005, we released our first T&D survey on Russian banks. We updated the study in 2006 and in 2007 because of the interest among investors and analysts. Additionally, we published our T&D study of Ukrainian banks in 2006 and in 2007 and our first study on Ukrainian companies in 2007.

Table B-10 provides a complete list of the companies covered by the 2008 survey.

Table B-10   Complete List of Companies Covered by 2008 Survey

	Company
1.	Advanced Technology & Materials Co., Ltd.
2.	Aerospace Information Co., Ltd.
3.	Air China Ltd.
4.	Aluminum Corporation of China Ltd.
5.	Angang Steel Co., Ltd.
6.	Anhui Conch Cement Co., Ltd.
7.	Anhui Heli Co., Ltd.
8.	Anhui Huamao Textile Co., Ltd.
9.	Anhui Jianghuai Automobile Co., Ltd.
10.	Anyang Iron & Steel Inc.
11.	Bank of China Ltd.
12.	Bank of Communications Co., Ltd.
13.	Baoding Tianwei Baobian Electric Co., Ltd.
14.	Baoji Titanium Industry Co., Ltd.
15.	Baoshan Iron &Steel Co., Ltd.
16.	Beihai Yinhe Hi-Tech Industrial Co., Ltd.
17.	Beijing Capital Co., Ltd.
18.	Beijing Double-Crane Pharmaceutical Co., Ltd.
19.	Beijing Gehua CATV Network Co., Ltd.
20.	Beijing North Star Co., Ltd.
21.	Beijing Shougang Co., Ltd.
22.	Beijing Tiantan Biological Products Co., Ltd.
23.	Beijing Tongrentang Co., Ltd.
24.	Beijing Urban Construction Investment & Development Co., Ltd.
25.	Beijing Wangfujing Department Store (Group) Co., Ltd.
26.	Beijing Yanjing Brewery Co., Ltd.
27.	Beijing Zhong Ke San Huan High-Tech Co., Ltd.
28.	Beijinghualian Hypermarket Co., Ltd.
29.	Blue Star New Chemical Material Co., Ltd.
30.	Bright Dairy & Food Co., Ltd.
31.	Chang Jiang Shipping Group Phoenix Co., Ltd.
32.	Changsha Zoomlion Heavy Industry Science & Technology Development Co., Ltd.
33.	Chengde Xinxin Vanadium and Titanium Co., Ltd.
34.	China Construction Bank Corp
35.	China COSCO Holdings Co., Ltd.
36.	China Enterprise Co., Ltd.
37.	China Gezhouba Group Co., Ltd.

	Company
38.	China International Marine Containers (Group) Co., Ltd.
39.	China Life Insurance Co., Ltd.
40.	China Merchants Bank Co., Ltd.
41.	China Merchants Energy Shipping Co., Ltd.
42.	China Merchants Property Development Co., Ltd.
43.	China Minsheng Banking Corp Ltd.
44.	China Nonferrous Metal Industry's Foreign Engineering & Construction Co., Ltd.
45.	China Oilfield Services Ltd.
46.	China Pacific Insurance (Group) Co., Ltd.
47.	China Petroleum and Chemical Corp (Sinopec)
48.	China Railway Tielong Container Logistics Co., Ltd.
49.	China Shenhua Energy Co., Ltd.
50.	China Shipping Development Co., Ltd.
51.	China Southern Airlines Co., Ltd.
52.	China State Shipbuilding Co., Ltd.
53.	China Union Hldgs Ltd.
54.	China United Telecommunications Co., Ltd.
55.	China Vanke Co., Ltd.
56.	China World Trade Center Co., Ltd.
57.	China Yangtze Power Co., Ltd.
58.	China-Kinwa High Technology Co., Ltd.
59.	Chongqing Brewery Co., Ltd.
60.	Chongqing Changan Automobile Co., Ltd.
61.	CITIC Guoan Information Industry Co., Ltd.
62.	CITIC Securities Co., Ltd.
63.	Citychamp Dartong Co., Ltd.
64.	COFCO Property (Group) Co., Ltd.
65.	COSCO Shipping Co., Ltd.
66.	Dalian Daxian Enterprises Holdings Co., Ltd.
67.	Daqin Railway Co., Ltd.
68.	Dashang Group Co., Ltd.
69.	Datang International Power Generation Co., Ltd.
70.	Datong Coal Industry Co., Ltd.
71.	Dazhong Transportation (Group) Co., Ltd.
72.	Dongfang Electric Company Ltd.
73.	Dongguan Development (Holdings) Co., Ltd.
74.	Dongguan Winnerway Industrial Zone Ltd.
75.	FAW Car Co., Ltd.
76.	Feilo Acoustics Co., Ltd. Shanghai

(Continued)

	Company
77.	Financial Street Holding Co., Ltd.
78.	Foshan Electrical and Lighting Co., Ltd.
79.	Founder Technology Group Corp
80.	Fuhua Group Co., Ltd. Zhuhai SEZ
81.	Fujian Expressway Development Co., Ltd.
82.	Fujian Qingshan Paper Industry Co., Ltd.
83.	Fuyao Group Glass Industries Co., Ltd.
84.	Gansu Jiu Steel Group Hongxing Iron & Steel Co., Ltd.
85.	Gansu Yasheng Industrial (Group) Co., Ltd.
86.	GD Power Development Co., Ltd.
87.	Gemdale Corp
88.	Gree Electric Appliances Inc. of Zhuhai
89.	Guangdong Electric Power Development Co., Ltd.
90.	Guangdong Fenghua Advanced Technology (Holding) Co., Ltd.
91.	Guangdong Meiyan Hydropower Co., Ltd.
92.	Guangdong Midea Electric Appliances Co., Ltd.
93.	Guangdong Shengyi Sci Tech Co., Ltd.
94.	Guangdong Yihua Timber Industry Co., Ltd.
95.	Guangshen Railway Co., Ltd.
96.	Guangxi Liugong Machinery Co., Ltd.
97.	Guangzhou Baiyun International Airport Co., Ltd.
98.	Guangzhou Development Industry (Holdings) Co., Ltd.
99.	Guangzhou Shipyard International Co., Ltd.
100.	Hainan Airlines Co., Ltd.
101.	Handan Iron & Steel Co., Ltd.
102.	Hebei Jinniu Energy & Resources Co., Ltd.
103.	Heilongjiang Agriculture Co., Ltd.
104.	Henan Pinggao Electric Co., Ltd.
105.	Henan Shen Huo Coal Industry and Electricity Power Co., Ltd.
106.	Henan Shuanghui Investment & Development Co., Ltd.
107.	Henan Zhongfu Industry Co., Ltd.
108.	Henan Zhongyuan Expressway Co., Ltd.
109.	Hisense Electric Co., Ltd.
110.	Hong Yuan Securities Co., Ltd.
111.	Hua Xia Bank Co., Ltd.
112.	Huabei Expressway Co., Ltd.
113.	Huadian Power International Corp Ltd.
114.	Huafa Industrial Co., Ltd. Zhuhai
115.	Huaneng Power International Inc.
116.	Huawen Media Investment Corp

	Company
117.	Hubei Yihua Chemical Industry Co., Ltd.
118.	Huludao Zinc Industry Co., Ltd.
119.	Hunan TV & Broadcast Intermediary Co., Ltd.
120.	Hunan Valin Steel Tube & Wire Co., Ltd.
121.	Industrial and Commercial Bank of China Ltd.
122.	Industrial Bank Co., Ltd.
123.	Inner Mongolia Baotou Steel Rare-Earth Hi-Tech Co., Ltd.
124.	Inner Mongolia Baotou Steel Union Co., Ltd.
125.	Inner Mongolia Mengdian Huaneng Thermal Power Corp Ltd.
126.	Inner Mongolia Yili Industrial Group Co., Ltd.
127.	Insigma Technology Co., Ltd.
128.	Ji Lin Ji En Nickel Industry Co., Ltd.
129.	Jiangsu Hengrui Medicine Co., Ltd.
130.	Jiangsu Sunshine Co., Ltd.
131.	Jiangsu Zongyi Co., Ltd.
132.	Jiangxi Copper Co., Ltd.
133.	Jiangxi Ganyue Expressway Co., Ltd.
134.	Jiangxi Hongdu Aviation Industry Co., Ltd.
135.	Jiaozuo Wanfang Aluminium Manufacturing Co., Ltd.
136.	Jilin Aodong Medicine Industry (Groups) Co., Ltd.
137.	Jilin Sino-Microelectronics Co., Ltd.
138.	Jilin Yatai (Group) Co., Ltd.
139.	Jinan Iron and Steel Co., Ltd.
140.	Joincare Pharmaceutical Group Industry Co., Ltd.
141.	Jonjee High & New Technology and Industrial Group Co., Ltd.
142.	Kailuan Clean Coal Co., Ltd.
143.	Kingfa Sci & Tech Co., Ltd.
144.	Kweichow Moutai Co., Ltd.
145.	Laiwu Steel Corp
146.	Liaoning Cheng Da Co., Ltd.
147.	Lingyuan Iron & Steel Co., Ltd.
148.	Long March Launch Vehicle Technology Co., Ltd.
149.	Lu Thai Textile Co., Ltd.
150.	Luzhou Lao Jiao Co., Ltd.
151.	Maanshan Iron and Steel Co., Ltd.
152.	Minmetals Development Co., Ltd.
153.	Nanjing Iron & Steel Co., Ltd.
154.	Nanjing Xingang High-Tech Co., Ltd.
155.	NARI Technology Development Co., Ltd.
156.	Ningbo Shanshan Co., Ltd.

(Continued)

	Company
157.	Ningxia Orient Tantalum Industry Co., Ltd.
158.	North China Pharmaceutical Co., Ltd.
159.	Oceanwide Construction Group Co., Ltd.
160.	Offshore Oil Engineering Co., Ltd.
161.	Orient Group Inc.
162.	Panzhihua New Steel & Vanadium Co., Ltd.
163.	PetroChina Co., Ltd.
164.	Ping An Insurance (Group) Co of China Ltd.
165.	Pingdingshan Tianan Coal Mining Co., Ltd.
166.	Poly Real Estate Group Co., Ltd.
167.	Qingdao Haier Co., Ltd.
168.	Qinghai Salt Lake Potash Co., Ltd.
169.	SAIC Motor Corp Ltd.
170.	Sany Heavy Industry Co., Ltd.
171.	SDIC Huajing Power Holdings Co., Ltd.
172.	Searainbow Holding Corp
173.	SGIS Songshan Co., Ltd.
174.	Shandong Chenming Paper Holdings Ltd.
175.	Shandong Dong-E E-Jiao Co., Ltd.
176.	Shandong Expressway Co., Ltd.
177.	Shandong Gold-Mining Co., Ltd.
178.	Shandong Haihua Co., Ltd.
179.	Shandong Huatai Paper Co., Ltd.
180.	Shandong Nanshan Aluminium Co., Ltd.
181.	Shanghai Ace Co., Ltd.
182.	Shanghai Aerospace Automobile Electromechanical Co., Ltd.
183.	Shanghai Airlines Co., Ltd.
184.	Shanghai Bailian Group Co., Ltd.
185.	Shanghai Bashi Industrial Co.
186.	Shanghai Construction Co., Ltd.
187.	Shanghai Datun Energy Resources Co., Ltd.
188.	Shanghai Dazhong Public Utilities (Group) Co., Ltd.
189.	Shanghai Electric Power Co., Ltd.
190.	Shanghai Feilo Co., Ltd.
191.	Shanghai First Provisions Co., Ltd.
192.	Shanghai Fosun Pharmaceutical Group Co., Ltd.
193.	Shanghai Haixin Group Co., Ltd.
194.	Shanghai Industrial Development Co., Ltd.
195.	Shanghai Industrial Pharmaceutical Investment Co., Ltd.
196.	Shanghai International Airport Co., Ltd.

	Company
197.	Shanghai International Port (Group) Co., Ltd.
198.	Shanghai Jinling Co., Ltd.
199.	Shanghai Lujiazui Finance and Trade Zone Development Co., Ltd.
200.	Shanghai Mechanical & Electrical Industry Co., Ltd.
201.	Shanghai Municipal Raw Water Co., Ltd.
202.	Shanghai New Huang Pu Real Estate Co., Ltd.
203.	Shanghai New World Co., Ltd.
204.	Shanghai Oriental Pearl (Group) Co., Ltd.
205.	Shanghai Pharmaceuticals Co., Ltd.
206.	Shanghai Pudong Development Bank Co., Ltd.
207.	Shanghai Shenhua Holdings Co., Ltd.
208.	Shanghai Tunnel Engineering Co., Ltd.
209.	Shanghai Wanye Enterprises Co., Ltd.
210.	Shanghai Yimin Commercial Company Ltd.
211.	Shanghai Yuyuan Tourist Mart Co., Ltd.
212.	Shanghai Zhangjiang Hi-tech Park Development Co., Ltd.
213.	Shanghai Zhenhua Port Machinery Co., Ltd.
214.	Shanghai Zijiang Enterprise Group Co., Ltd.
215	Shantui Construction Machinery Co., Ltd.
216.	Shanxi Guoyang New Energy Co., Ltd.
217.	Shanxi Lanhua Science-Tech Venture Co., Ltd.
218.	Shanxi Lu'an Environmental Energy Development Co., Ltd.
219.	Shanxi Taigang Stainless Steel Co., Ltd.
220.	Shanxi Xinghuacun Fen Wine Factory Co., Ltd.
221.	Shanxi Xishan Coal and Electricity Power Co., Ltd.
222.	Shenergy Co., Ltd.
223.	Shenyang Machine Tool Co., Ltd.
224.	Shenyang Neusoft Co., Ltd.
225.	Shenzhen Agricultural Products Co., Ltd.
226.	Shenzhen Airport Co., Ltd.
227.	Shenzhen Development Bank Co., Ltd.
228.	Shenzhen Energy Investment Co., Ltd.
229.	Shenzhen Heungkong Holding Co., Ltd.
230.	Shenzhen Kaifa Tech Co., Ltd.
231.	Shenzhen Overseas Chinese Town Holding Co., Ltd.
232.	Shenzhen Seg Samsung Glass Co., Ltd.
233.	Shenzhen Yan Tian Port Holdings Co., Ltd.
234.	Shenzhen Zhongjin Lingnan Nonfemet Co., Ltd.
235.	Sichuan Changhong Electric Co., Ltd.
236.	Sichuan Hongda Co., Ltd.

(Continued)

	Company
237.	Sichuan Jinlu Group Co., Ltd.
238.	Sichuan Lutianhua Co., Ltd.
239.	Sichuan Swellfun Co., Ltd.
240.	Sinochem International Corp
241.	Sinoma International Engineering Co., Ltd.
242.	Sinopec Shandong Taishan Petroleum Co., Ltd.
243.	Sinotrans Air Transportation Development Co., Ltd.
244.	Suning Appliance Co., Ltd.
245.	SVA Electron Co., Ltd.
246.	SVA Information Industry Co., Ltd.
247.	Tangshan Iron and Steel Co., Ltd.
248.	Tangshan Jidong Cement Co., Ltd.
249.	TBEA Co., Ltd.
250.	TDG Holding Co., Ltd.
251.	Telling Telecommunication Holding Co., Ltd.
252.	Tianjin Jinbin Development Co., Ltd.
253.	Tianjin Port Co., Ltd.
254.	Tianjin Tasly Pharmaceutical Co., Ltd.
255.	Tianjin TEDA Co., Ltd.
256.	Tongling Nonferrous Metals Group Co., Ltd.
257.	Top Energy Co., Ltd. Shanxi
258.	Tsinghua Tongfang Co., Ltd.
259.	Tsingtao Brewery Co., Ltd.
260.	UFIDA Software Co., Ltd.
261.	Wanxiang Qianchao Co., Ltd.
262.	Weichai Power Co., Ltd.
263.	Weifu High-Technology Co., Ltd.
264.	Western Mining Co., Ltd.
265.	Wuhan Iron and Steel Co., Ltd.
266.	Wuhan Kaidi Electric Power Co., Ltd.
267.	Wuhan Zhongbai Group Co., Ltd.
268.	Wujiang Silk Co., Ltd.
269.	Wuliangye Yibin Co., Ltd.
270.	Xiamen C&D Inc.
271.	Xiamen International Trade Group Corp Ltd.
272.	Xiamen Tungsten Co., Ltd.
273.	Xi'an Aircraft International Corp
274.	Xiandai Investment Co., Ltd.
275.	Xinjiang Guanghui Industry Co., Ltd.
276.	Xinxing Ductile Iron Pipes Co., Ltd.

	Company
277.	XJ Electric Co., Ltd.
278.	Xuzhou Construction Machinery Science & Technology Co., Ltd.
279.	Yantai Changyu Pioneer Wine Co., Ltd.
280.	Yantai Dongfang Electronics Information Industry Co., Ltd.
281.	Yantai Wanhua Polyurethane Co., Ltd.
282.	Yantai Xinchao Industry Co., Ltd.
283.	Yanzhou Coal Mining Co., Ltd.
284.	Youngor Group Co., Ltd.
285.	Yunnan Aluminium Co., Ltd.
286.	Yunnan Baiyao Grp Co., Ltd.
287.	Yunnan Chihong Zinc & Germanium Co., Ltd.
288.	Yunnan Copper Co., Ltd.
289.	Yunnan Tin Co., Ltd.
290.	Yunnan Yuntianhua Co., Ltd.
291.	Zhe Jiang Xinan Chemical Industrial Group Co., Ltd.
292.	Zhejiang China Commodities City Group Co., Ltd.
293.	Zhejiang China Light & Textile Industrial City Group Co., Ltd.
294.	Zhejiang Huahai Pharmaceutical Co., Ltd.
295.	Zhejiang Longsheng Group Co., Ltd.
296.	Zhengzhou Coal Industry & Electric Power Co., Ltd.
297.	Zhengzhou Yutong Bus Co., Ltd.
298.	Zhongjin Gold Co., Ltd.
299.	Zhuhai Zhongfu Enterprise Co., Ltd.
300.	ZTE Corp

INDEX